ECONOMIC POLICY FOR THE EUROPEAN COMMUNITY

The Way Forward

Sir ALEC CAIRNCROSS, HERBERT GIERSCH,
ALEXANDRE LAMFALUSSY, GIUSEPPE PETRILLI
and PIERRE URI

for the
Institut für Weltwirtschaft
an der Universität Kiel

First published 1974 by
THE MACMILLAN PRESS LTD
London and Basingstoke
Associated companies in New York
Dublin Melbourne Johannesburg and Madras

SBN 333 17419 4

Typeset by
COLD COMPOSITION LTD
Southborough, Tunbridge Wells

Printed in Great Britain by
LEWIS REPRINTS LTD
MEMBER OF BROWN KNIGHT & TRUSCOTT
(HOLDINGS) LTD
group of companies, London and Tonbridge

Contents

Chapter 3

Chapter 4

Chapter 5

Chapter 6

List of Tables and Illustrations

Preface

In the summer of 1970 a former German cabinet minister wrote a newspaper article in which he expressed his hope that European integration might receive a new impulse if independent persons sufficiently well-known in their countries could be brought together to prepare a report on the economic future of the European Community. The idea was taken up by the Institut für Weltwirtschaft, at the University of Kiel, and developed in several discussions. Funds were made available through the Deutsche Gesellschaft für Auswärtige Politik so that a start could be made on the project.

First contacts on an international level were made with Giuseppe Petrilli in Rome and with Alexandre Lamfalussy in Brussels. These led to a preliminary meeting in Rome, where it was decided to approach Pierre Uri in Paris and — with Britain's imminent entry into the Community — Sir Alec Cairncross in Oxford. None of us had to be asked twice to take part.

Over the ensuing two years many weekends were spent in discussions. Thanks to Professor Petrilli the group was able to meet in Rome where the European Community's founding treaty was signed, and thus we provisionally called ourselves the Group of Rome, not yet aware that this name might be confused with that of a club studying some problems of less moderate dimensions. We soon found that there was sufficient agreement among us to warrant a report containing more than commonplace proposals, a report which would stimulate political discussion by showing what a genuine European union would involve in terms of advantages and burdens.

Manfred Streit, of the University of Mannheim, acting as

rapporteur, prepared preliminary drafts on the basis of what we thought we had meant in our 'brain-storming' sessions. If Professor Streit had had his way the report would have been backed much more explicitly by economic analysis. We are grateful to him for the zeal and diligence he invested in our enterprise and for the competence with which he challenged us on many issues.

Thanks are due to Hugh Corbet, of Trade Policy Research Centre in London, who gave the report its final shape having, with others, contributed to our deliberations. Without him our reasoning would have been much more involved and less likely to appeal to the reader.

The others from whom we also benefited in our discussions were Veniero Ajmone Marsan, Carlo Meriano and Roland Vaubel.

But the sole responsibility for the report rests with the five signatories. Their views though should not be attributed to the organizations with which they are associated.

The report is being published in English, French, German and Italian.

HERBERT GIERSCH
Director
Institut für Weltwirtschaft

Kiel, July 1974

Foreword

In public discussion of European integration economists have played only a limited role. This should be surprising. For the gains from economic integration were held out as among the major reasons for the formation and development of the European Community. The authors of this report, all from different member countries, are specialists in economic affairs. They have come together to consider the future of the Community and the nature of the economic problems which it must face in future. Their hope has been that by so doing they may give a fresh and constructive impulse to public discussion and policy formation. Indeed, they believe it crucial for economists to have their say, particularly at this critical juncture in the evolution of the European Community.

What is the peculiar contribution that economists can make? This is not altogether an idle question. The most important problems facing the community may well be political; certainly they are not exclusively economic, although in peace-time economics is powerful politics. We do not pretend that it is only the economic gains from integration that matter. Nor do we accept the familiar notion that economic integration has to be relied on to provide an effective basis for political unification. On the contrary, we consider that there is a need for closer political cooperation, the development of a European consensus, as a preliminary to those forms of economic integration that are likely to prove sustainable.

The contribution of economists, then, is in part negative and in part positive. On the negative side they can give a warning of the dangers involved in the courses advocated by politicians. The experience of the European Community has illustrated how easy it is to embark on policies that prove to be unrealistic and generate disappointment and disillusion as they collapse or gradually fail. Take for example the debate on monetary integration or, more particularly, the discussion on 'the snake' — the narrowed margin within which it was agreed the exchange rates of European currencies should be allowed to fluctuate. Economists are more alive than others to the fact that if governments achieve monetary integration they put out of their power the independent use of monetary policy and adjustments in exchange rates to safeguard their national economy from wide fluctuations in employment and output. The fact that from the outset two members of the European Community were unable to abide by the arrangement governing exchange rates initiated in April 1972 was not as unexpected or disappointing to economists as it was to the lay public.

The point is that on economic policy issues there are technical questions on which technical expertise is required for a policy to function effectively. An understanding of economic forces is necessary in the running of an economy just as an understanding of engineering forces is necessary in the running of an automobile engine — however much politicians and drivers may think otherwise when things are going smoothly. With neither an economy nor an engine can fundamental problems be overcome by a resounding declaration, a verbose directive or an inspired opinion unless it is technically informed. In the formula⁺ion of economic policies in the European Community there has been too much of the juridical approach and not enough economic analysis.

On the positive side economists should be able to give substance to the idea of integration. For example, insofar as gains from economic integration have their roots in economies of scale, economists who are familiar with the way in which these economies operate are in a good position to point to directions which it is important for integration to take. The existence of economies of scale in manufacturing lies to a considerable extent behind the success of the European Community in raising living standards through the achievement of tariff-free trade among its member countries. But the Common Market in manufactures should not be the only application of economies of scale. There are gains to be had in transport and in the supply of energy if the efforts of the different member governments can be coordinated.

Similarly, wherever the actions of individual governments affect the interests of other countries, common action is the only way possible to deal effectively with the problems of policy involved. Defence and pollution are obvious areas for coordinated measures. The importance of achieving agreement between members of the Community in these areas is plainly very great.

This, however, illustrates the greater obstacles that now have to be faced in the further integration of the economies of the member countries. They are all managed economies in which extensive powers of control and coordination rest with the central government. And the public sector in each of them is a large fragment of the total economy. It is bound to prove more difficult to merge progressively economies nowadays than it would be under nineteenth century conditions (or eighteenth century conditions of the United States after the American Revolution). For governments are more willing to allow market forces to play on the private sector than on the matters under their immediate control. This means that it will be necessary as time goes on to move towards a distribution of powers within the European Community which limits the authority of national governments except in the domestic sphere and reserving matters of common interest for discussion and decision by the Community as a whole. But for some considerable time the Community is likely to figure chiefly as a rule-setting agency for its individual members and will be obliged to leave most issues of economic policy that do not have important external implications to the discretion of member governments.

We make these points because we fear that not enough thought is being given to the final distribution of authority in economic matters that should be sought if political unification really is the larger objective. Too much attention may be given to moving forward (and to the *method* of integration) instead of where the move should be leading (and the *prerequisites* of integration). The effect of this in the past has been a rather unnecessary desperation in a search for complete and irreversible forms of integration instead of seeking to work out what powers national governments would be bound to wish to retain and what the European Community as a whole would wish to keep under its own strict supervision or review.

If we are right, the development of consistent policies will achieve more than ambitions for comprehensive integration in all areas of policy, which is more than even the most established federations seek.

ALEC CAIRNCROSS

HERBERT GIERSCH

ALEXANDRE LAMFALUSSY

GIUSEPPI PETRILLI

PIERRE URI

Rome, July 1974

Biographical Notes

MEMBERS OF THE GROUP

Sir ALEC CAIRNCROSS, Head of the British Government Economic Service from 1964 to 1968, is Master of St Peter's College at the University of Oxford. He is also Chancellor of the University of Glasgow where he was Professor of Applied Economics from 1951 to 1961. Sir Alec was previously Economic Adviser to the Organization for European Economic Cooperation having been Economic Adviser to the British Board of Trade in 1946-49.

In 1951-52, Sir Alec was chairman of the Committee of Enquiry on Local Development, in the United Kingdom. Then in 1955 he became Director of the Economic Development Institute in Washington. Back in Britain, he was a member of the Radcliffe Committee on Banking, from 1957-59. In 1961 he was appointed Economic Adviser to the Government.

The most recent of Sir Alec's extensive publications have been *Essays in Economic Management* (1971) and *Control over Long-term International Capital Movements* (1973); and he edited *Britain's Economic Prospects Reconsidered* (1971).

HERBERT GIERSCH has been, since 1969, Professor of Economics and Director of the Institut für Weltwirtschaft at the University of Kiel. From 1964 to 1970 he was a member of the Sachverständigenrat which annually reports to the Bundestag in the Federal Republic of Germany on the state of the country's economy.

In 1950-51 and 1953-54 Professor Giersch served in the Secretariat of the Organization for European Economic Cooperation in Paris. After that, until his present appointment, he was Professor of Economics at the University of Saarbrücken. In 1962-63 he was a Visiting Professor at Yale University.

Professor Giersch has served on numerous committees appointed to prepare policy recommendations for governments. Recently, he was a member of the Study Group on European Economic and Monetary Union, established by the Commission of the European Community.

Among Professor Giersch's major publications have been *Allgemeine Wirtschaftspolitik: Grundlagen* (1960), *Growth, Cycles and Exchange Rates: the Experience of West Germany* (1970), and *Kontroverse Fragen der Wirtschaftspolitik* (1971).

ALEXANDRE LAMFALUSSY has been Chairman of the Board of Managing Directors, and Chief Executive, of the Banque de Bruxelles since 1971. He is also a lecturer in economics at the University of Louvain. In 1963-65, Dr. Lamfalussy was a member of the Segré Committee, appointed by the Commission of the European Community to enquire into capital movements.

Born in Hungary, Dr. Lamfalussy studied at the University of Louvain, then at the University of Oxford. In 1961-62, he was a Visiting Professor of Economics at Yale University. By then he had become Manager of the Research Department at the Banque de Bruxelles, having joined the department in 1955, and he became a Director in 1964 and a Managing Director four years later.

His major publications have been *Investment and Growth in Mature Economies: the Case of Belgium* (1961), *The UK and the Six: an Essay on Growth in Western Europe* (1964) and *Les Marchés financiers en Europe* (1968). Dr. Lamfalussy has written extensively on international monetary problems.

GIUSEPPE PETRILLI, President of the Istituto per la Ricostruzione Industriale (IRI) since 1960, was a member of the Commission of the European Community during its first years, being responsible for social affairs. Professor Petrilli is a member of the Consiglio Nazionale dell'Economia e del Lavoro in Italy. Since 1964 he has been President of the Italian Council of the European Movement.

After graduating from the University of Rome, he held a research post at the Istituto Superiore di Matematica. He then became a lecturer in social security, and later Professor of Economics and Insurance, at the University of Rome. In 1949 he was named President of the Ente Nazionale di Previdenza per i Dipendente degli Enti di Diritto Publico and then Professor Petrilli was, for eight years, President of the Istituto Nazionale per l'Assicurazione delle Malattie.

Professor Petrilli is the author of many works on economics, social security and insurance. He was for a time President of the Ordione degli Attuari.

PIERRE URI, Counsellor for Studies at the Institut Atlantique des Affaires Internationales in Paris since 1962, has also been Professor of Economics at the University of Paris IX since 1969. He was recently a member of the Group of Eminent Persons on Multinational Corporations that was appointed by the United Nations.

While Economic Director of the European Coal and Steel Community, from 1952 to 1959, Professor Uri was rapporteur of the Spaak Committee, which in 1955-56 prepared proposals for the formation of the European Economic Community and Euratom. For the last two years of his ECSC appointment he was also Economic Adviser to the EEC Commission and he chaired the committee which produced a report on the economic situation in the Community. In 1960-64, Professor Uri was chairman of the Commission's Expert Group on Long-term Development and then, in 1968-70, he headed the Expert Group on Competitive Capacity.

Professor Uri is the author of, *inter alia, From Commonwealth to Common Market* (1968), *Un Avenir pour l'Europe Agricole* (1971) and *l'Europe se Gaspille* (1974).

RAPPORTEURS

HUGH CORBET has been Director of the Trade Policy Research Centre, London, since 1968. He was earlier a specialist writer on *The Times*. Mr. Corbet is co-author of *Trade Strategy and the Asian-Pacific Region* (1971).

MANFRED STREIT is Professor of Economics at the University of Mannheim, having previously been a lecturer at the University of Reading. Before that he was on the research staff of the German Council of Economic Experts.

Abbreviations

Benelux	Economic alliance between Belgium, the Netherlands and Luxembourg
BTN	Brussels Tariff Nomenclature
CAP	Common Agricultural Policy of the European Community
CET	Common External Tariff of the European Community
c.i.f.	prices including cost, insurance and freight
ECSC	European Coal and Steel Community
EDC	European Defence Community (proposed)
EEC	European (Economic) Community
EFTA	European Free Trade Association
ELDO	European Vehicle Launcher Development Organization
ESRO	European Space Research Organization
Euratom	European Atomic Energy Commission
f.o.b.	free-on-board prices
GATT	General Agreement on Tariffs and Trade
IBRD	International Bank for Reconstruction and Development (the World Bank)
IMF	International Monetary Fund
MFN	most-favoured-nation clause, expressing the principle of non-discrimination; also relates to non-discriminatory rates of duty
NATO	North Atlantic Treaty Organization
OECD	Organization for Economic Cooperation and Development
OEEC	Organization for European Economic Cooperation (replaced by the OECD)
SDRs	Special drawing rights on the IMF
VAT	value-added tax

1 European Integration in a Global Perspective

The formation in 1958 of the European Community represented an historically unique endeavour. Never before had a group of nation states sought, with any serious political intent, to unite by exploiting the forces of economic integration.[1] Ten years later, the basis for a substantial degree of economic integration was laid, following the completion of the customs union. But since then little or no progress has been made towards political union. Instead there are spreading doubts as to whether anything is left of the original ambition.

From the outset, France resisted the surrender of national sovereignty to the European Community, even to the point of boycotting the Council of Ministers.[2] There was a tendency, especially in media of public opinion, to attribute the uncertain outlook for European unity to Charles de Gaulle. It may be that strong French leadership in favour of European union could have sustained the impetus of the Community's early years. But the Gaullist expression of French nationalism was not the only factor in reducing the Common Market to the state of permanent crisis, and near stagnation, that appeared to exist at the time of President de Gaulle's resignation. It merely served to obscure other factors which were more fundamental.

No sooner had the General retired from the European political scene than Willy Brandt, as Chancellor of West Germany, was quietly asserting that in future European unity would be pursued more through inter-governmental measures than by supra-national means.[3] Then, during the negotiations on the enlargement of the European Community, Georges Pompidou, as President of France, and Edward Heath, as Prime Minister of the United Kingdom, agreed that European unity could not be pursued on a supra-national plane.[4]

The idea of European union continues to command influential support. But its continuance derives from the momentum of the past. The old pioneering zeal of the Commission of the European Community has greatly diminished. And the Europeanist movement itself still relies mostly on elder statesmen for drive and inspiration. It is as if newer generations of European elites are seeking their futures in a different context.

DEVELOPMENTS IN EUROPEAN INTEGRATION

Before looking ahead, though, it is necessary to look back in order to understand how the present *impasse* was reached. What were the original motivations for European unity? Four important factors can be cited:

(a) The concept of a European union was stimulated after World War II by a determination to prevent a further repetition of Franco-German conflict.[5] In three successive generations France and Germany had gone to war.

(b) Secondly, there was a need to consolidate the economic recovery of Western Europe, thereby underpinning political stability. The process was assisted by Marshall aid from the United States for which purpose the Organization for European Economic Cooperation (OEEC) was established in 1948.[6]

(c) With the onset of the Cold War, after the lowering in central Europe of the Iron Curtain, another important factor was fear.[7]

(d) Finally, as the dominance of the United States and the Soviet Union became apparent with the rapid development of nuclear weapons, there was concern about the declining influence of 'Europe' in world affairs.

The primary aim of European unity was therefore overwhelmingly political. After the Hague Congress in 1948, the Council of Europe was created, but its political impotence was soon evident. In 1950, Jean Monnet, renewing the century-old appeal of Victor Hugo that France should take the lead in building a United States of Europe, urged that a start should be made on a concrete basis.

On the initiative of Robert Schuman, then France's Foreign Minister, the European Coal and Steel Community (ECSC) was accordingly established in 1953. Belgium, France, Luxembourg, Italy, the Netherlands and West Germany were the six which joined. But the unwillingness of the United Kingdom to become a full member was regarded — although not universally — as a serious setback.[8] In spite of the success of the ECSC, in integrating the markets of two strategically important industries, the strategy of concentrating on political integration achieved no further advance. The final blow to the strategy was the rejection in 1954 by the French National Assembly of the proposal to establish a European Defence Community (EDC) which again Britain had made clear she would not be joining.

Thereafter the emphasis shifted from the exploitation of political forces to the exploitation of economic forces. In negotiations on the liberalization of international trade under the General Agreement on Tariffs and Trade (GATT), concluded in 1947, the six ECSC countries had formed a common front — in company with Sweden, Norway, Denmark and Austria.[9] When the United States and Britain rejected the GATT plan advanced in 1954 for an across-the-board reduction and harmonization of tariffs, the outcome of an imaginative French initiative,[10] the only course open to the major continental countries of Western Europe under GATT rules was a regional free trade arrangement. Article 1 of the General Agreement requires non-discriminatory treatment to be accorded unconditionally to all signatory countries except where, under conditions laid down in Article 24, a customs union or free trade association is being formed.[11]

Thus in 1955 the Benelux countries (Belgium, the Netherlands and Luxembourg) suggested an extension of the supra-national ECSC approach to form a customs union and an organization for the non-military development of nuclear energy.[12] In the report on the proposal that was submitted to the Six in April 1956 by Paul-Henri Spaak, then Belgium's Foreign Minister, the idea was put forward that the customs union might be accompanied by free trade association agreements with certain other countries.[13]

On the basis of the Spaak Report, negotiations were sub-

sequently conducted to form the European Economic
Community (EEC) and the European Atomic Energy Commission (Euratom). The first provided

(a) for the consolidation of the tariff schedules of the
Six into a single system applicable to imports from third
countries,

(b) for the progressive reduction and removal of all
fiscal and physical restrictions on the free movement of
goods, capital and labour between member countries
and

(c) for the harmonization of their economic policies.

Because of their objective of political union, the Six were
unable to carry with them the Scandinavian countries,
Austria and the United Kingdom.[14] A decade after the end of
World War II, with the OEEC proceeding apace with the
economic reconstruction of Western Europe, the prospective
formation of the EEC posed a new set of problems and fears.

First, there was alarm that the Six would split
Western Europe, not only economically but also politically. Other OEEC countries had misgivings over the
trade diversion effects of the proposed customs union.

Second, Britain reacted against the terms of the
treaties being negotiated, as she had against the ECSC
and the EDC idea, (i) because of her global affinities
including long-standing political ties and preferential
tariff arrangements with other Commonwealth
countries, (ii) because of her agricultural support
measures which were very different from Continental
policies and (iii) because of the importance she attached
to the Anglo-American relationship.

Third, for the three neutral countries in the OEEC —
Austria, Sweden and Switzerland — the problem was to
find a solution that would preserve their international
status.[15]

Confronted, then, with the prospect of being discriminated
against in major export markets, Britain underwent a rapid
conversion to the cause of free trade, at least in a European
context. In July 1956 the OEEC, at the instigation of the
British Government, took up the free trade area suggestion

made in the Spaak Report. A working party was established to 'study the possible forms and methods of association, on a multi-lateral basis, between the proposed customs union and member countries [of the OEEC] not taking part therein'.[16] The experts reported that it was technically feasible to operate a free trade area in Western Europe which included the customs and economic union of the Six. Negotiations were accordingly begun and, in the view of some observers, came very near to success. But in November 1958, after twenty months, they were broken off when the French Government, with varying degrees of support from the other members of the EEC (which had meanwhile come into being), found it impossible to compromise.

Immediately afterwards the OEEC countries on the periphery of the EEC, who had found the Treaty of Rome too rigid and politically restrictive, set about the formation of the European Free Trade Association (EFTA). The Stockholm Convention was signed by Austria, Denmark, Norway, Portugal, Sweden, Switzerland and the United Kingdom and came into force in 1960. The Seven had two purposes. First, they envisaged working towards a single European market, ultimately embracing all the OEEC countries.[17] And secondly, they looked to the creation, in the meantime, of a free trade area among themselves in industrial products. (In 1961, Finland became a *de facto* member, although she remained an associate *de jure,* and Iceland became a full member in 1970.)

In pursuit of the first objective, the United Kingdom, Denmark and Norway applied to join the EEC in 1961, while the other EFTA countries sought associate membership. The negotiations broke down late in 1962 over the difficulty of reaching agreement on the transition of Britain's agricultural-support system, based on 'deficiency payments' and a liberal import policy, to the EEC's common agricultural policy that was being formulated on the basis of high farm-support prices sustained by variable import levies.[18] It was left, though, to President de Gaulle to administer the *coup de grace,* which he did in January 1963.

EFTA persisted with its efforts to bring together the two trading blocks of Western Europe. But the EEC plainly was not interested. The schedule of tariff reductions in both blocks was accelerated, with EFTA achieving tariff-free trade at the beginning of 1967, the EEC doing so a year and a half later.[19] The completion of the customs union was the last enduring achievement of the EEC's initial political impetus.

FAVOURABLE CONDITIONS FOR EARLY INTEGRATION

In assessing the achievement, it should be recognized that conditions in the late 1950s and early 1960s favoured the gradual reduction and elimination of tariffs within the EEC — and within EFTA as well.

1. For a start, the promotion of European integration began at government level when, following the Great Depression and World War II, the governments of the major market-economy countries throughout the world were well on the way towards restoring orderly conditions in international trade and payments. What this entailed *inter alia* was the reform of the autarkic and discriminatory policies that resulted from the protectionist excesses of the 1930s. These goals were being sought through the liberalization of international commerce under the aegis of the GATT which together with the International Monetary Fund (IMF) and the World Bank formed the basis of the new world economic order. In short, by the middle 1950s the governments of Western Europe were already in the habit of negotiating on the lowering of barriers to trade, albeit on a multilateral or world-wide basis.[20]

2. Moreover, under the Marshall aid programme for the post-war reconstruction of Western Europe, the United States was encouraging European economic integration through the OEEC, reinforcing the European Payments Union (EPU). Thus by 1958, the thirteen OEEC countries had eliminated among themselves not only exchange controls, but also bilateral commercial arrangements and quantitative import restrictions. The progressive reduction and elimination of tariffs was the next logical move.

3. In the first decade or so after World War II, as normal economic activity was resumed and gathered momentum, the political climate for trade liberalization in Western Europe was highly favourable. An abundant supply of labour, access

to the vast American capital market, investment in new plant and equipment, opportunities to imitate technological advances and, in some countries, under-valued currencies which stimulated export-led growth were some of the factors which helped to foster economic reconstruction and development. The post-war boom, reflected in spectacular rates of growth and glowing prospects, provided the material basis for governments to embark on a more ambitious stage in the process of economic integration.

4. Most of the countries of Western Europe were regarded as industrially developed although there were between them significant differences in economic maturity. In all, however, considerable resources and innovational opportunities remained to be fully exploited. Only limited shifts in production were therefore expected to result from the greater degree of specialization, and more efficient use of resources, that it is the purpose of trade liberalization to achieve. The probability of serious problems of adjustment, in the event of further economic integration, was accordingly rated very low — in spite of fears expressed in certain industries and for certain regions such as the Mezzogiorno.[21]

5. Because of their low degree of interdependence, and the absence of full convertibility between their currencies, the Six could exercise considerable freedom of national action, even with rigidly-fixed exchange rates. Apart from France, until her devaluation in 1958, no balance-of-payments difficulties imposed external constraints on internal policies. There was thus little pressure to coordinate short-term economic policies.

Since the European Community began contemplating a monetary union, the question of coordinating short-term economic policies has had to be addressed, as it is in Chapter 2 below. But the Community does not have any of the instruments of policy that are necessary for such a role to be effective. What a monetary union requires is a reconciliation of national economic objectives, the coordination of large bureaucratic machines and the imposition on economic management at the national level of economic management at a supra-national level.

The ostensible surrender of power by national governments to a supra-national authority that is entailed in the formation of a monetary union is of an entirely different order from that entailed in the formation of a customs union. Perhaps this is beginning to be better understood in European policy-making circles. We believe the time has anyway come to reconsider the ways and means of pursuing European integration.

PRAGMATIC APPROACH TO INTEGRATION

The attempt to exploit economic forces to promote political unification was bound to encounter serious problems. For the institutions of the European Community, never mind other factors, have provided only limited scope for such a grand conception. But those institutions reflect the extent to which member countries have so far been prepared to surrender national sovereignty.

A glance at the institutional structure of the European Community is enough to demonstrate the constraints on progress in the political field. The major and final decisions are taken by the Council of Ministers which is collectively responsible to nobody. Its decision-making process is hampered by the requirement of unanimity that was reinforced in 1965 on French insistence.[22] The Commission, as the executive of the Community, has the right to make policy proposals. In preparing them, though, it is drawn into a process of inter-governmental bargaining, because it is required to consult with the permanent representatives in Brussels of the member countries. The Commission is responsible to the European Parliament which to date has not exerted control of any significance. Besides its right to dismiss all the Commissioners, the Parliament, made up of delegations from national legislatures, has no influence yet either in budgetary matters or of course on policies adopted by the Council.

In short, the Council has been transformed into an inter-governmental conference, the Commission is treated as a technocratic organization and the Parliament reduced to a consultative body, with inter-governmental control of the Commission substituted for parliamentary control. This does not mean, though, that the situation is hopeless. At all levels, from the opinion-forming to the policy-making plane, a more conscious effort could be made to develop a European consensus on vital issues, by which is not meant a centrally-imposed view determined on doctrinaire grounds.

At the opinion-forming level, there is much that could be done through the European Parliament, given that its most important if not its sole power at present is to dismiss the entire membership of the Commission. If a serious interest was shown in exercising this right, the Parliament could render the Commission more accountable to public opinion, carrying a stage further the introduction of 'question time' by requiring Commissioners and other officials to testify in person and submit written reports on specific avenues of enquiry. For this purpose, the Parliament could develop its committees, have them professionally staffed and initiate studies and hold public hearings, not only in Strasbourg and Luxembourg but also in other major cities. Furthermore, the Parliament could appoint a committee of economic advisers, comprised of economists of high professional standing, to prepare independent reports and provide guidance on technical questions relating to the conduct of economic policies. The role of the European Parliament could thus be greatly strengthened even before considering the complex question of direct elections.

In order to counter the tendency of the political process to become farther and farther removed from the 'grassroots' of public opinion, consideration should be given to the establishment of a chamber of regions, on a basis similar to that of the Senate in the United States. As argued in the chapter on regional policy, such an institution could also, indeed primarily would, help to bring about a better political balance between the prosperous and densely populated areas and the rest of the Community.

At the policy-making level, consultations and negotiations in the Community probably have to continue to be conducted, for the time being, on an inter-governmental basis until the habit of thinking in European terms is more widespread. Looking further ahead, a number of questions might be posed. Should the European Community — which is today not much more than a customs union — be developed into an effective economic union? If so, what is the political motivation behind the drive towards European integration, however it may be defined? And last but not least, does economic integration pre-suppose supra-national institutions, or can it be carried out by inter-governmental coordination of policies?

There has been much debate on these questions and it is evident that European public opinion — both broadly and in individual countries — is divided on the issues. Some are 'integrationists' on general political grounds; others, for technical reasons. Still others would be content to let economic integration take its course through the static and dynamic effects of trade liberalization. Supra-national institutions are sometimes suggested for political reasons, sometimes for their technical efficiency, whether supposed or proven. The inter-governmental approach is favoured by others because it appears the most practical in current circumstances.[23]

As a group, we have not escaped these divisions of public opinion. But we have thought that open confrontations of our political preferences on these questions would lead to little more than a reassertion of our individual positions, however respectable they may be, and would be unlikely to produce new ideas on which a consensus could be sought. We accordingly decided to adopt another approach. This consists of looking at the European Community as it is today, in today's international environment, and bearing in mind some simple economic and social objectives that are generally accepted in our respective countries. Among these objectives can be numbered growth and price stability, full employment, more equal income distribution among people and between regions, greater social mobility and the European Community's responsibilities in the world.

This approach leads us in the succeeding chapters to propose new lines of action in monetary affairs, taxation and public expenditure, regional policy, agricultural support, industrial organization and competition, social policy and international economic relations. Most of our proposals imply 'common' policies, either at Community level or on a basis of coordination among member countries, not because we believe that policy harmonization *per se* is a good idea in itself, but because economic analysis and pragmatic reasoning suggests that in the absence of such measures the more limited goals of the European Community may not be attained. What is left of the Community may disintegrate if it is not able to resume its former momentum.

CHANGES SINCE THE 1950s

Since the EDC was rejected there have been major changes in the nature and substance of international relationships. The circumstances of the 1970s are therefore not as propitious perhaps as were those of the 1950s to embark on a supra-national initiative. In addition, the European Community — together with the United States, Japan and other countries — is faced with a number of momentous problems that cannot be resolved in isolation from the rest of the world.

When the immediate post-war motives for European unity are recalled, the consolidation of the *rapprochement* between France and Germany, however uncertain it may sometimes appear superficially, has been achieved. Indeed, it was the first, if best forgotten, achievement of the European Community. Whether old Franco-German rivalries would be revived in the event of the Community coming to grief is a moot point. Differences between the two countries would be overshadowed by wider considerations.

Since the 1940s the peace of the world has been determined by a global balance of power in which the technological advances of the super-powers in the business of nuclear armaments have become a persuasive factor.[24] No longer is Europe the centre of world power or a source of tensions that could erupt with world-wide consequences. What is more, there is between the United States and the Soviet Union a nuclear stalemate, which means that on Europe, the principal area of direct Russo-American confrontation, a certain immobility has descended. Threats to Europe's security and welfare, to the world's stability and prosperity, no longer derive from fear of Soviet aggression, much less from the quarrels of France, Germany and Britain. Instead, they are by-products of pressures in the Middle East or Southern Africa or South-east Asia where the super-powers are not facing each other in entrenched positions. They are bound up with Russo-American relations, where Europeans have urged *détente,* and with world-wide economic problems to do with the management of the international trade and monetary systems and with the interests of developing countries.[25]

The increasing integration, and growing interdependence, of the world economy now exerts a much more powerful influence on inter-governmental relations than was the case in the 1950s.[26] Intense competition, large-scale capital flows, technological advances in industry and agriculture, still greater economies of scale and the development of rapid transport and communications, and of new and expanding markets, are all factors that are having profound and continuing effects on international trade and production patterns. In addition, six rounds of multilateral tariff-cutting negotiations have helped to promote a doubling of world trade over the last decade; indeed, world trade has been expanding twice as fast as world income.

In fact, the restoration of prosperity, self-confidence and security to the countries of Western Europe owes much to the restoration of some semblance of order in the world economy, which has facilitated the enormous expansion of international trade, capital movements and transfers of technology in the 1960s. After the disorders of the 1930s and 1940s, the continuance of order in the world economy should not be taken for granted, particularly when there are two groups of countries beginning to expect more, not less, from the international trading system. Both groups have begun to entertain hopes that a coordinated approach to their problems might at last be possible.[27]

First, there are the exporters of temperate-zone agricultural products, some of which have been parties to the GATT from the outset, but have not benefited greatly to date from its principles and rules. Then there are, secondly, the developing countries, which are not in a position to negotiate on a reciprocal basis with industrially advanced countries, but are looking to them for markets for their products.[28] In an international trading system dominated by industrially advanced economies which, over two hundred years, have generally come to accept the basic philosophy of free trade, the two groups would seem entitled to benefit from the laws of comparative advantage and the international division of labour.

As suppliers of primary products, many of the countries in the two groups, both developed and developing, are likely in future to have a larger 'voice' in international discussions. But there have in any case been big changes in the composition of councils responsible for the international scheme of things. In the 1950s 'the developed world' and 'the North Atlantic region' were virtually synonymous terms. In Western Europe and North America were concentrated the nations whose wealth and power gave them special responsibility for world order and prosperity.[29]

But during the 1960s the geo-political boundaries of the 1950s began to blur as new powers began to make an impact on international relations. No longer was it appropriate for international institutions to be confined to Atlantic countries. Japan joined the Group of Ten (since superceded in importance by the executive committee of the IMF) and also the Organization for Economic Cooperation and Development (OECD) where Australia and New Zealand are now members. In addition, greater account now has to be taken of Mexico, Brazil and South Africa, while the oil crisis (discussed below) has given a strong impetus to the role of developing countries – especially the Arab oil producers.

With their post-war recovery and further economic expansion the countries of the European Community have ceased to depend on the United States for the perpetuation of their prosperity. In an integrating world economy they are affected by American developments. But this relationship differs profoundly from the former dependence on Marshall aid and on the willingness of the United States to refrain from advancing its interests at the expense of the Community's.[30] On the American side there has also been a profound change in attitude. For it has been noticed that as the Soviet threat to Western Europe has receded, and as the countries of the region have recovered their prosperity and self-confidence, there has been a decline of governmental interest in a supra-national European union. West Europeans are free to unite themselves as tightly as they wish, but they show no signs of actually doing so, even for the proclaimed purpose of matching the United States in power and influence. Doubts are therefore expressed about the wisdom of planning in the expectation that the European Community will unite in a full political sense.[31] No longer is the United States prepared to overlook its interests in order to provide greater latitude for the European Community.

Not that the United States has turned against the European idea. It is evident though that American spokesmen are becoming more critical of European policies. In due course this shift in attitude can be expected to affect other countries' attitudes towards the European Community. In the pursuit of European interests the Community therefore has to pay greater heed to the interests of others lest external tensions develop that might hamper international policies.

This has been made all the more necessary by the enlargement of the European Community in 1973 to include the United Kingdom, Denmark and the Irish Republic. Britain's global affinities — her long-standing economic, political and cultural relationships with other Commonwealth countries and with the United States — have reinforced the need for the Community to consider the international implications of its actions, if only because British public opinion is likely to remain sensitive to them for the foreseeable future.[32] Similarly, Denmark's interest in maintaining close economic, political and cultural ties with other Scandinavian countries is bound to affect Danish attitudes towards policy developments in the European Community. And it has to be remembered that in politico-strategic matters the Irish Republic is a neutral.

So much for the changed circumstances that must affect the way in which European economic integration is pursued. Two further considerations have an important bearing on the matter. The first is the universal tendency to chronic inflation while the second is the energy crisis precipitated by the dramatic increase in crude oil prices at the end of 1973.

INFLATION AND ECONOMIC INTEGRATION

Although universal, inflation proceeds at a different pace in different countries, making it impossible to achieve stable relationships between prices of all kinds. It generates instability in commodity markets, in sectors of activity, in currencies and exchange rates and, indeed, throughout the entire world economy. The disintegrating effects of inflation stand out as perhaps the most important single obstacle to the monetary union of the European Community. It is hardly to be wondered that so little progress has been made towards monetary union in a world increasingly dominated by inflation.

It is perhaps not altogether accidental that inflation gathered speed just as the debate began in the European Community on closer monetary integration. The monetary disturbances of the late 1960s threw into relief the importance of international cooperation on currency problems and the need for the Community to come to terms with a world in which the American dollar no longer functioned as a stable international currency. Until well into the 1960s the United States had provided a convenient point of reference to which other countries could adjust. Prices in the American market were sufficiently stable to operate as a brake on prices elsewhere. But once domestic inflation in the United States accelerated with the Vietnam war this source of international stability was lost. The Community set out to find a new anchor for itself by seeking to tie European currencies more closely together. But it did so with no real prospect of success until inflation could be brought under control.

It would take the discussion too far afield to analyse in any detail what this would involve. Here we must limit ourselves to a broad indication of the forces underlying the sharp acceleration in price increases over the past few years and the implications for the European Community of this acceleration and of the anti-inflationary policies that are called for.[33]

First of all, the acceleration reflects an unusually sustained upswing in demand that happened to coincide in the main industrial countries to a greater extent than in earlier postwar booms. This upswing was intensified in the commodity markets by speculation that was itself a product of inflation and the fear of inflation. But underneath the speculative pressure there was evidence of unusual pressure on the limited sources of some of the major primary products. This pressure was most vividly apparent in the changes at work in the United States which made her either less self-sufficient (for example, in petroleum) or a less abundant reservoir for exports (of grain, for instance). Cyclical expansion, in other words, encountered an unusually inelastic supply.

This element in the situation was superimposed on a state of affairs in the labour market that was bound to produce inflationary wage settlements. Full employment — underwritten by governments, not employers — conferred on workers a bargaining power of which they were increasingly aware, whether on the shop-floor or in wage negotiations between their representatives and those of employers. Workers' expectations grew with affluence and they took for granted a steady improvement from year to year in real earnings without regard to the state of trade or the terms on which imports were procured. At the same time, as the pre-war generation of workers died out, wage claims were urged more forcibly, particularly after the dramatic events of May 1968. To greater bargaining power and greater militancy was added greater uncertainty: workers sought to protect themselves against an unpredictable fall in the value of money by claiming wages high enough to match their worst fears.

A double-headed cost inflation, stemming simultaneously from wage-push and a shortage of primary products, was thus interacting with demand inflation of the traditional kind just when the Arab oil producers set off an unprecedented explosion in the price of petroleum. It remains to be seen whether this will do what previous increases in commodity prices have failed to do: operate as a demand deflator because money incomes are prevented from keeping pace with the rise in costs.

That money incomes *have* kept pace is attributable to one more element in the situation: the growth in the money supply. The monetary component in contemporary inflation can be variously explained. But the essence of the matter is that governments have put full employment before monetary stability and have sought rather ineffectively to combat the resulting inflation by various types of incomes policy. We do not suggest that there is a simple trade-off between the degree of labour shortage and the rate of price increase, or that a mere tightening of the money supply would produce a determinate and graduated response in the behaviour of prices. The point is rather that governments have acquiesced in inflation as a social mollifier and the form that their acquiescence has taken has been a willingness to expand the money supply at whatever rate was dictated by the need to preserve full employment.

If the members of the European Community are to master inflation they will have to find ways of dealing with all the elements giving rise to it.

(a) They will have to prevent — by monetary and fiscal policies — excessive pressure of demand: all the more if there is a convergence of cyclical peaks and troughs throughout the member countries.

(b) They will have to be prepared to leave higher import prices for staple commodities uncompensated by higher money earnings: foreign borrowing — except in the special case of mitigating the balance-of-payments effects of the oil crisis — is rarely the appropriate way of financing a swing in the terms of trade except for relatively short periods.

(c) They will have to work out ways of facing workers' organizations with the need to keep wage settlements within bounds if the level of employment is to be safeguarded.

(d) And they will have to allow commodity prices to fall, ensuring that the benefits go to consumers, and find different ways of protecting the interests of producers.

None of these things will be easy; but unless they are done, inflation may yet destroy the European Community.

IMPLICATIONS OF THE OIL CRISIS

Turning to the energy crisis, the war of *Yom Kippur* in October 1973 provided the occasion for a major change in the conditions under which oil would in future be supplied, but it was not itself the cause. The festering of the Arab-Israeli problem, and the responses to it of Western governments, had influenced the attitudes of the oil-producing countries towards the Western powers. But there were two more important factors which influenced the situation:

(a) First was the determination of the oil-producing countries to obtain control over the extraction and disposition of their major natural resource rather than delegate that power to others.

(b) Then there was the shift in the balance between supply and demand, largely as a result of the spectacular increase in demand in the United States for imported oil which, by the early 1970s, had created a sellers' market.

The events of the autumn of 1973 were in fact the culmination of a process which began with the creation of the Organization of Petroleum Exporting Countries (OPEC) in 1960. In the mid-1960s the oil-producing countries unilaterally changed the terms of their agreement with the oil companies. During the 1960s, however, the posted price of crude oil remained stable and in real terms it actually fell. The market price, on the other hand, declined and in real terms fell significantly. It was not until 1970 that the oil-producing countries began to exploit their stronger position which was strengthened by the economic growth being enjoyed by the major industrial countries and by the temporary interruption of pipe supplies of Arabian crude oil to the ports of the Eastern Mediterranean.

Under the Teheran Agreement of 1971 the 'take' levels of the producer governments were to rise steadily until 1975. This was followed by the Geneva Agreement of 1972 which was intended to compensate the oil-producing countries for exchange-rate adjustment — but it has since been shelved. These events marked the point when the oil-producing countries were able towards the end of 1973 to demand substantial price increases.[34]

There has thus begun a major transfer of economic power from the oil-importing countries to the oil-producing countries. This shift in power will continue until such time as the more fortunate oil-importing countries can bring into production additional sources of energy to meet domestic requirements. Many of these countries are not likely to have much room for manoeuvre. But for all of them there will be a period when the oil-producing countries will hold most of the trump cards and will be able to exercise considerable control over both the supply of oil and the price at which it is sold.

Even so, the greatly increased prices for crude oil can be 'lived with' by the industrialized countries, although the consequences are far reaching. When considered as a proportion of the total income of oil-importing countries, the cost in terms of real income transferred to the oil-producing countries, even with revenue at round $11 per barrel, is of an order of magnitude that can be managed. The order of magnitude still amounts to many billion of dollars. Thus, the institutions and management of the international system of trade and payments cannot fail to be affected, however much the oil-producing countries see their own economic interests dependent on the orderly development of the world economy as a whole.[35]

All aspects of economic life will be affected by developments in the international oil market: the direction of social and economic policies, the rate of inflation, conditions in capital markets, exchange-rate relationships, the movement in the European Community towards economic and monetary union, the reform of international monetary arrangements, the maintenance of the multilateral trading system and the problems of developing countries. Failure to understand the situation fully and, on a basis of international cooperation to adopt concerted policies, could pose a serious threat to the level of world economic activity. The greatest danger facing the world economy is that individual governments will try in isolation to cope with the situation from a nationalistic standpoint.[36]

RESPONSIBILITY FOR INTERNATIONAL ORDER

Somehow, then, the European Community has to reconcile the pursuit of internal objectives with the responsibilities it must bear, by virtue of its size and importance (see Table 1), in the management of the international economic order. The first has been made harder, and the second has been made greater, following the enlargement of the Community's membership. And both have been made more complicated by the enlargement, achieved and prospective, of the circle of countries linked with the Community through 'association' and other discriminatory trade arrangements.

For there is a growing prospect — heightened by the bilateral agreements arising out of the oil crisis — of the market-economy world being divided into economic spheres of influence.[37] The multiplying number of discriminatory trading arrangements that have been appearing on the world scene in recent years is at the heart of what is to be done about remaining tariffs on industrial products among developed countries.[38] The issue is not likely to be discussed at inter-governmental level in such bald terms. But that is the way it is being posed by those, not only in the United States but also elsewhere, who are calling for a reform of the GATT system of international trade — the cornerstone of which is the principle of non-discrimination.

TABLE 1

Size of the European Community compared with other major countries, 1971[a]

	EEC (Nine)	USA	USSR	Japan
Population ('000)	253,142	207,050	245,090	105,600
GNP[b] ($'000m)	693.7	1061.9	288[c]	225.6
GNP per capita ($)	2,740	5,130	1,175	2,136
Imports ($m)	129,805	45,602	12,479	19,704
" (% of world total)	35.8	12.6	3.4	5.4
Imports excluding intra-EEC (Nine)				
" ($m)	64,209	45,602	12,749	19,704
" (% of world total)[d]	21.6	15.4	4.2	6.6
Exports ($m)	128,277	44,137	13,806	24,012
" (% of world total)	36.9	12.7	4.0	6.9
Exports excluding intra-EEC (Nine)				
" ($m)	63,241	44,137	13,806	24,012
" (% of world trade)	22.4	15.6	4.9	8.5

SOURCES: *Information Statistics* and *Monthly Bulletin of General Statistics,* Statistical Office of the European Community, Luxembourg; *Monthly Bulletin of Statistics,* United Nations, New York; and *Main Economic Indicators,* OECD Secretariat.

[a]Although the European Community was not enlarged until 1973, the comparisons are based on 1971 figures.
[b]Gross national product at current prices and exchange rates.
[c]Net material product.
[d]Excluding Intra-EEC trade.

Japan and the United States have, from time to time, urged the phased elimination of substantially all tariffs as a means of overcoming the economic and political tensions being generated by the proliferation of the European Community's discriminatory tariff arrangements around the Mediterranean, in Africa and even farther away.[39] If the tariffs of the major industrial countries were to be phased out, there would be the prospect of preferential tariff arrangements being diminished over time, thereby easing tensions and restoring some credibility to the principle of non-discrimination.

But the very idea of phasing out the European Community's common external tariff fills some Europeans with foreboding. The fear, somewhat ill-defined, is that the Common Market would fall apart and, of course, that feeling is exploited by others more concerned with maintaining protection. In its 'overall' approach to the Tokyo Round of GATT negotiations, the European Community agreed that *inter alia* the customs union 'may not be called in question'.[40] If the common external tariff, however, is really a major unifying force in the European Community today, it says little for the spirit of European unity about which so much is made. It will say even less if tariff discrimination against the rest of the world is still a major unifying force in, say, ten years time.

Part of the trouble has been psychological in that the European Community's common external tariff, its commercial agreements with 'outside' countries and also its common agricultural policy have come to be regarded as symbols of European unity. Any criticism of these policies, whether from inside or outside the Common Market, is interpreted by some as an attack on the Common Market itself. Yet the process of European integration must be pursued in harmony with the integration of the world economy as a whole if it is not to incur the hostility of countries which happen to be located elsewhere. And the more the Community is able to progress in this respect the easier it will be to discharge its international responsibilities.

This is the spirit in which the European Community should be encouraged to pursue integration in the 1970s and 1980s. Policies must adjust to circumstances which — already described — have greatly changed since the 1950s. This means that Europeans must find a more constructive approach to unity than what is tantamount, in an age of increasing interdependence, to provoking economic conflict with the rest of the world.

In recent years the European Community has been seeking a distinct political identity between the United States and the Soviet Union. Such an identity could be found and asserted through bold initiatives for the reconstruction of the international economic order which, already in growing need of repair, has been badly shaken by the energy crisis (see Chapter 7). Waiting to react to initiatives from others only invites internal dissent. For the reactions of member countries are likely to differ and thus, even before discussions begin at Community level, individual governments are 'digging themselves into positions'. The reluctance of governments to work out external initiatives therefore impedes integration and makes the search for identity more difficult.

INTER-RELATIONSHIP OF ECONOMIC POLICIES

What is to be done about restoring the momentum of economic integration in the European Community? High hopes were attached to the goal of monetary union. For the reasons given in the next chapter, the attempt to achieve monetary union was bound to fail, as it has done, given the international monetary environment. This would have been so even if a radical approach had been made towards union instead of a 'gradualistic' one.

Monetary union should nevertheless be a long-run aim of the European Community. (i) Divergencies in economic policies, and the exchange-rate changes which ensue, may lead, in a highly integrated area, to wastes and distortions in terms of intra-Community trade. (ii) Without monetary union, countries may be tempted to impose restrictions on convertibility, with implications for the functioning of the Common Market. (iii) The European Community cannot play a constructive role in international monetary reform unless it develops a unified approach.

Once a monetary union has been established, the international adjustment process, relating to balances of payments, will become an inter-regional adjustment process; that is, there will still be an adjustment process that has to be managed by governments. Our purpose, in preparing this report, has *inter alia* been to propose measures that should make the process as little painful, and therefore as acceptable politically and socially, as possible. These measures would therefore create the conditions necessary for monetary union. They comprise much more than the coordination of short-term economic policies.

They should include the longer-term measures directed towards the gradual integration of capital markets, increasing the possibility of transferring assets to finance short-term deficits (see Chapter 2). The implementation of a Community-wide fiscal system would help to redistribute incomes towards lower income groups in member countries (Chapter 2). A regional policy (Chapter 3) would perform a similar function in favour of backward areas. Reforms in agricultural-support measures should be aimed at the twin problem of low-income farmers and depressed rural communities (Chapter 4). Industrial policies need to be developed to increase the flow of direct investments (Chapter 5). Attention has to be given, too, to the gradual integration of labour markets by promoting socially acceptable migration and to securing conformity with labour productivity of wage increases and intra-Community wage differentials (Chapter 6).

NOTES AND REFERENCES

1. On the evolution of the European Community there has been built up over the years a formidable literature. An objective account, set in an historical context, is provided in W. O. Henderson, *The Genesis of the Common Market* (London: Frank Cass, 1962). Also see *International Organizations in Europe and the European System* (Geneva: Carnegie Endowment for International Peace, 1972).

For earlier critiques of the European Community, as it has worked in practice, see: Ralf Dahrendorf, *Plädoyer für ein Zweites Europa* (Munich: Piper, 1973); Hans von der Groeben and Ernst-Joachim Mestmäcker (eds.), *Ziele und Methoden der europäischen Integration* (Frankfurt: Athenäum, for the Zentrum für Interdisziplinäre Forschung der Universität Bielefeld, 1972); F. A. M. Alting von Geusau, *Beyond the European Community* (Leyden: Sijthoff, 1969); and Pierre Drouin, *L'Europe du marché commun* (Paris: Julliard, 1968).

Regarding the role of the European Free Trade Association (EFTA) in the process of European integration, an analysis, in institutional terms, is provided in Hans Krämer, *EWG und EFTA-Entwicklung: Aufbau and Tätigkeit* (Stuttgart: Kohlhammer, 1968). A full economic analysis, comparing the experience of EFTA and the European Community, can be found in Victoria Curzon, *The Essentials of Economic Integration* (London: Macmillan, for the Trade Policy Research Centre, 1974).

2. In resistance against the making of decisions in the Council of Ministers by majority voting, France adopted the policy of 'the empty chair', as it was called, until an agreement was reached in Luxembourg early in 1965 that decisions would continue to be implemented on a basis of unanimity, thereby safeguarding the use of the veto.

3. Interview on BBC radio, London, 5 March 1970.

4. *The Economist*, London, 29 May 1971, p. 15. As for the position of Harold Wilson, as Prime Minister of the United Kingdom after the 1974 general election, he reaffirmed the opposition to a federal European union that was made clear when his previous Government (1964-70) launched the negotiations on British membership of the European Community that were concluded by the Heath Government. 'Whatever the long-distance future may hold,' Mr. Wilson told the House of Commons on 22 May 1969, in the course of rejecting proposals for an Anglo-French nuclear force, 'a European federal state is not a reality. Nor is it what we are asking for.' *Parliamentary Debates* (*Hansard*), Official Report, House of Commons, London, Vol. 784, No. 121, 22 May 1969, c. 654.

As an immutable factor in the European situation, the British attitude has been neatly stated by a German observer: 'Wilson's rejection of any form of European federation is as authentic as was Churchill's, Eden's and Macmillan's and springs from the same source. Nowhere does the idea of a supra-national authority meet with such instinctive rejection as in Britain.' See Heinz Höpfl, 'Nicht nur Wilsons Nein', *Frankfurter Allgemeine Zeitung*, Frankfurt, 9 September 1969.

5. To keep the post-war vision of a 'united Europe' in historical perspective it might be recalled that there have been similar grand designs going back to the Duke of Sully's in seventeenth-century France. The fall of Rome in AD 426 left to later rulers the dream of unifying by military means the whole of Europe. Justinian, Charlemagne and Charles V all tried to emulate Caesar as did, more recently, Napoleon Bonaparte.

6. For a discussion of the evolution of the OEEC and its successor, the Organization for Economic Cooperation and Development (OECD), see Henry G. Aubrey, *Atlantic Economic Cooperation: the Case of the OECD* (New York: Praeger, for the Council on Foreign Relations, 1967).

7. In addition, there was concern over the possibility of Communist takeovers from within, especially in France and Italy.

8. A thorough account of the establishment of the ECSC can be found in William Diebold, *The Schuman Plan: a Study in Economic Cooperation* (1950-59) (London: Oxford University Press, 1959).

9. Gerard Curzon, *Multilateral Commercial Diplomacy* (London: Michael Joseph, 1965).

10. *A Proposal for the Reduction of Customs Tariffs* (Geneva: GATT Secretariat, 1954).

11. Other exceptions are provided in the General Agreement for pre-existing preferential trading arrangements and, more recently (in Part IV), for the benefit of, and among, developing countries.

12. Miriam Camps, *Britain and the European Economic Community, 1955-63* (London: Oxford University Press, for the Royal Institute of International Affairs, 1964).

13. The document, published on 21 April 1956, was simply entitled *Le Rapport des chefs délégations aux ministres des affaires étrangères,* Spaak Report (Brussels: Belgian Ministry of Foreign Affairs, 1956).

14. Commenting more than a decade later, Ludwig Erhard, the former Chancellor of Germany, wrote that 'it was an obvious mistake to try to give the European Economic Community, in its initial stages, the character of a political, as well as an economic, union. Not only did this idea generate opposition even inside the Community, but it was precisely the emphasis of this aspect which made it hard for outside countries (and, in particular, the United Kingdom) to agree in advance to an increasingly extensive sacrifice of sovereign rights and powers.' See Ludwig Erhard, 'Prospects for European Integration', *Lloyds Bank Review,* London, January 1969.

15. The position of Sweden and Switzerland is examined in Thor Støre, *Nyttan av Norden* (Stockholm: Föreningen Norden, 1968), Paul Veyrassat, *La Suisse et la création de l'AELE* (Neuchâtel: Baçonnière, 1969), and Eric Roethlisberger, *La Suisse dans l'AELE* (Neuchâtel: Baçonnière, 1970).

16. See *Negotiations for a European Free Trade Area: Documents Relating to the Negotiations from July 1956 to December 1958,* Cmnd. 641 (London: Her Majesty's Stationery Office, 1959), p.7.

17. See the preamble to the Stockholm Convention, the 'constitution' of EFTA, signed on 4 January 1960.

18. Mr. Heath, as Britain's chief negotiator, and Christopher Soames, as Minister of Agriculture, stated four points in respect of agricultural production and trade that they wanted satisfied. When the European Community was not able to meet them the talks were deadlocked and shortly afterwards pressure began developing in the House of Commons for the negotiations to be broken off.

19. Both the EEC and EFTA completed the elimination of internal tariffs well ahead of Schedule. For a tabular account of 'the EEC and EFTA tariff-cutting tournament 1959-68', see V. Curzon, *op. cit.,* table 2, p. 67.

20. Karen Kock, *International Trade Policy and the GATT 1947-67* (Stockholm: Almqvist & Wiksell, 1969), and G. Curzon, *op. cit.*

21. In respect of the Mezzogiorno, for instance, the Italian Government negotiated a special protocol to the Treaty of Rome.

22. The so-called 'Luxembourg compromise' was reached in January 1965.

23. Attitudes appear to vary according to the degree of emphasis placed on economic integration, on the one hand, and political unification, on the other. In this connection, see Hugh Corbet, 'Political and Commercial Perspectives on Trade between Developed Countries', in *A Foreign Economic Policy for the 1970s,* Hearings before the Joint

Economic Committee, Congress of the United States, Part 2 (Washington: US Government Printing Office, 1970).

The extent to which it is necessary to harmonize policies in the European Community has been strongly queried in Dahrendorf, 'Wieland Europa', *Die Zeit*, Hamburg, 9 July and 16 July 1971.

For professional analyses on this theme, see V. Curzon, *op. cit.*, especially Chapter 10, on 'Customs Union Theory Extended to Free Trade Areas'; and Harry G. Johnson, Paul Wonnacott and Hirofumi Shibata, *National Economic Policies under Free Trade* (Toronto: University of Toronto Press, for the Private Planning Association of Canada, 1968).

When the EEC and EFTA were formed 'customs union theory' was still in its infancy, as it were, the three major contributions being: Jacob Viner, *The Customs Union Issue* (New York: Carnegie Endowment for International Peace, 1950); James E. Meade, *The Theory of Customs Unions* (Amsterdam: North-Holland, 1955); and Richard G. Lipsey, 'The Theory of Customs Unions: Trade Diversion and Welfare', *Economica*, London, Vol. XXIV, 1957.

On the subject of economic integration in Western Europe, see: Tibor Scitovsky, *Economic Theory and Western European Integration* (London: Allen & Unwin, 1958); Meade, Hans Liesner and Sidney Wells, *Case Studies in European Economic Union: Mechanics of Integration* (London: Oxford University Press, 1962); Bela Belassa, *The Theory of Economic Integration* (London: Allen & Unwin, 1962); Paul Streeten, *Economic Integration: Aspects and Problems* (Leyden: Sijthoff, 1964); Jan Tinbergen, *International Economic Integration* (Amsterdam: Elsevier, 1965); and G. R. Denton (ed.), *Economic Integration in Europe* (London: Weidenfeld & Nicolson, for the Reading Graduate School of Contemporary European Studies, 1969).

24. The shift from a European balance was discussed in Lionel Gelber, 'Canada's New Stature', *Foreign Affairs*, New York, January 1946, and elaborated upon by the same writer in *Reprieve from War* (New York: Macmillan, 1950) and later in *America in Britain's Place* (London: Allen & Unwin, 1961).

With respect to the implications of nuclear weapons for international relations, see Leonard Beaton, *The Reform of Power* (London: Chatto & Windus, 1972).

25. Sir Robert Scott, 'Asian-Pacific Arena of Conflict', in Corbet *et al.*, *Trade Strategy and the Asian-Pacific Region* (London: Allen & Unwin, for the Trade Policy Research Centre, 1970), pp. 112-14.

26. Richard N. Cooper, *The Economics of Interdependence: Economic Policy in the Atlantic Community* (New York: McGraw-Hill, for the Council on Foreign Relations, 1968).

27. This point was emphasized by the Director-General of the GATT, Olivier Long, 'Reflections on Changes in International Trade', a lecture to the Institut Universitaire des Hautes Etudes Internationales, Geneva, 6 October 1970.

28. The impetus behind the drive of the developing countries for greater access to industrial markets was developed at the first United

Nations Conference on Trade and Development (UNCTAD) in Geneva in 1964. See the report of the then Secretary-General of UNCTAD, Raoul Prebisch, *Towards a New Trade Policy for Development* (New York: United Nations, 1964).

The developed countries later agreed in principle to introduce generalized tariff preferences in favour of developing countries, but where they have been introduced in practice they have been severely limited by quotas, thus defeating the purpose of preferences which is to offer an additional incentive to new exporters and new investors. These points are discussed more fully in Chapter 7 below.

In frustration, renewed attention has been devoted to 'inward-looking' policies for development, as reflected in Streeten (ed.), *Trade Strategies for Development* (London: Macmillan, for the Cambridge Overseas Studies Committee, 1973), which also covers 'outward-looking' policies.

29. Corbet *et al.*, *op. cit.*, pp. 28-39.

30. This development was anticipated in Theodore Geiger, 'End of an Era in Atlantic Policy', *The Atlantic Community Quarterly*, Washington, Spring, 1967. Also see Harold van B. Cleveland, 'The Common Market After de Gaulle', *Foreign Affairs*, July 1969. (Both Dr. Geiger and Dr. Cleveland were members of 'the Club' in the Department of State in Washington which developed in the early 1950s the policy of the United States in support of European union.)

31. See, for example, John Holmes, 'The Fearful Symmetry: Dilemmas of Consultation and Coordination in the North Atlantic Treaty Organization', *International Organization*, Boston, No. 4, 1968.

32. Opinion polls have indicated that, in spite of the generally unsympathetic press which the Commonwealth received during the 1960s, the association continues to enjoy widespread support among the British at large as does the relationship with the United States. See, for instance, the survey conducted by the Gallup Poll published in *The Sunday Telegraph*, London, 26 January 1969; and, too, the survey conducted by the Opinion Research Centre published in *The Sunday Times*, London, on the same day.

On the subject of the 'renegotiation' of British membership of the European Community this report refrains from commenting. But perhaps the clue to reconciling British public opinion to membership lies in the development of the European Community's external relationships.

For it has been widely noted that in pursuing the question of membership of the Common Market, political leaders have tended to play down Britain's relations with the rest of the Commonwealth and with the United States, a tendency further accentuated by the 'serious' British press. Opinion polls on the specific question of British accession to the Community have fluctuated widely over the last decade and a half, although during the last few years they have shown consistent majorities against membership, but it has been clear that the British electorate is interested in generally closer relations with the rest of Europe. What has also been clear though is that, in spite of the influential advocacy of the Europeanist case, the British electorate remains interested in generally closer relations with the rest of the Commonwealth and with the United States.

33. For a discussion of the factors contributing to inflation, see Herbert Giersch, 'Neglected Aspects of Inflation in the World Economy', *Public Finance*, The Hague, Vol. 28, No. 2, 1973.

34. The result has been a rise in the revenue per barrel for the producing governments, taking Arabian light crude as a representative marker, from $0.91 in 1970 to $1.27 under the Teheran Agreement to about $3.30 in October 1973 and to around $8.00 in January 1974.

35. On how the 'oil crisis' might be approached by governments, see Jan Tumlir, 'How the West Can Pay the New Arab Oil Bill', *The Sunday Times*, London, 3 February 1974. This article was later developed as 'Oil Payments and Oil Debt in the World Economy', *Lloyds Bank Review*, London, July 1974.

36. At the ministerial meeting of the OECD in May 1974 governments pledged themselves not to adopt restrictive trade measures in order to correct any balance-of-payments deficit cause by the increased cost of oil imports.

37. There have been warnings of such a development since the early 1960s. For recent analyses, see Theodore Geiger, 'Toward a World of Trade Blocks', *The Atlantic Community Quarterly*, Winter, 1971-72; Corbet, 'Division of the World into Economic Spheres of Influence', *Pacific Community*, Tokyo, January 1974; and Ernest Preeg, *World Economic Blocs and US Foreign Policy* (Washington: National Planning Association, 1974).

38. The issues posed here are discussed more fully in Chapter 7 below.

39. Japan, supported by the United States, proposed at the 1972 session of the GATT that the phased elimination of industrial tariffs on trade among developed countries should be 'a working hypothesis' of preparations for the Tokyo Round of multilateral trade negotiations.

For a European, if non-official, statement on the substantial elimination of tariffs, see Frank McFadzean *et al.*, *Towards an Open World Economy*, Report of an Advisory Group (London: Macmillan, for the Trade Policy Research Centre, 1972).

40. 'Overall Approach to the Coming Multilateral Negotiations in GATT', Document I/135 e/73 (COMMER 42), Commission of the European Community, Brussels, para. 6. The common agricultural policy and the common commercial policy were also declared by the Council of Ministers to be beyond questioning. The 'fear' earlier mentioned seemed to be expressed in Günther Harkort, 'A Concept for an Open World Economy', *Intereconomics*, Hamburg, No. 4, 1973, reviewing the McFadzean Report, *op. cit.* The former State Secretary of the Ministry of Foreign Affairs in the Bonn Government wrote: 'Nowhere [in the report] is it made clear that the EEC has been launched as a legal instrument containing important articles which for some time have to be left essentially unchanged if the existence of the EEC is not to be put at risk.'

2 Monetary and Fiscal Integration

The objective of monetary union, on which so much debate has raged, did not feature in the Treaty of Rome. It only came to the forefront of inter-governmental discussion after a series of international monetary crises in the late 1960s. Changes in exchange rates, the threat that currency fluctuations were thought to pose for the Community's common agricultural policy and a growing desire in some quarters for a monetary counter-weight to the American dollar were major factors which combined to stimulate interest in closer monetary integration.

In addition, the prospective completion at the end of 1969 of the transition period envisaged in the Treaty of Rome, the change in the presidency of France and the consequently improved prospects for the enlargement of the Common Market suggested the need for a fresh impetus to be given to the process of European integration, over which much frustration was then being experienced. The lack of success up to that date in coordinating economic and monetary policies, and hence the failure to give effect to articles 103 to 109 of the Treaty of Rome, was indication enough to Brussels officials of the direction an initiative should take. Following the Hague summit meeting of the Six in December 1969 the Council of Ministers accordingly established a committee under Pierre Werner, the Prime Minister of Luxembourg, to work out proposals.[1] The report of the committee, submitted in October 1970, formed the basis of discussion on the subject in the European Community in the succeeding year.[2]

MONETARY INTEGRATION

The Werner Report called for full economic and monetary union within a decade. By 'monetary union' was meant

(a) the total and irreversible convertibility of currencies,

(b) the elimination of margins of fluctuation in rates
of exchange,

(c) the irrevocable fixing of parities and

(d) the total liberation of movements of capital.[3]

For psychological and political reasons the best guarantee of
the irreversibility of the undertaking was thought to be the
adoption of a single currency.

These are ambitious objectives as, indeed, the report
recognized. They presuppose (i) that responsibility for key
economic decisions will be transferred from the national
plane to a supra-national level, (ii) that the necessary powers
will be surrendered to the European Community and (iii)
that the institutions to give effect to these powers will be
created. Above all, they take for granted (iv) that the
political will exists among the member countries to make
those transfers of responsibility and power, relying on the
progressive development of political cooperation that the
process would entail.

Economic and monetary union were assumed in the
Werner Report to operate 'as a leaven for the development of
political union which in the long run it will be unable to do
without'.[4] But in negotiating a plan of action, finally agreed
in March 1971, governments resisted in the Council of
Ministers any delegation — never mind surrender — of
national sovereignty.

There is no way of achieving monetary union on the
cheap. What matters is making genuine progress towards it
rather than simply insisting on the desirability of getting
there. We recognize that in the long run monetary union, in
some sense, is necessary in order to give permanence to
European integration. Without monetary union the advantages of free trade within the European Community are likely
to remain in jeopardy. There is a risk that convertibility may
be restricted — just as recent monetary disturbances have led
to the re-introduction of controls over the free flow of
capital among the member countries. Monetary union is at
once the symbol and guarantee of an irreversible integration.
If carried through in appropriate circumstances it would not

only underwrite the advantages enjoyed by the members of the Community from free access to a larger 'home' market; it would bring other conveniences in payments of all kinds made in other parts of the union.

DANGERS OF PREMATURE MONETARY UNION

It is therefore necessary to emphasize the far-reaching nature of the measures that would be required in the circumstances of the middle 1970s to achieve a unified European currency by 1980 (or, for that matter, by 1984). In the absence of such consistent action the time would appear inappropriate and the goal unrealistic. If monetary union were pushed through prematurely, and without complementary policies to reinforce it and complementary powers and common institutions to give effect to those policies, the result might well be needless unemployment and waste of resources. Since the political prerequisites for the strategy of monetary unification envisaged in the Werner Report are not acceptable to national governments, any other approach towards monetary union which presupposes a similar surrender (or delegation) of national sovereignty is bound to be self-defeating.

The danger is that instruments of policy now employed at the national level might be withdrawn, or their free use forbidden, before instruments have been devised to supercede them at the Community level.[5] The existence of separate national currencies *ipso facto* provides a powerful weapon in the form of depreciation for bringing a country's trade and payments back into balance when for any reason it runs into deficit; and when it is in chronic surplus, appreciation of the currency can be equally effective in restoring balance. No doubt there is a need for some international surveillance of the use of this weapon. For one country's depreciation is everybody else's appreciation. But to abandon exchange-rate changes completely and finally without indicating how imbalances will be dealt with in future (and not much indication is given in the Werner Report) would be to run serious risks in relation both to economic stability and to that political will without which economic union will not hold.

Contrast, for example, the consequences of inflation

before and after monetary union. Before monetary union, inflation in any one country, and the higher cost structure that goes with it, will produce a deficit in the balance of payments unless it is possible to match a fall in the domestic value of the currency by a fall in its external value (that is, in the rate of exchange). If this option does not exist, as it could not after monetary union, the external deficit will drain away purchasing power and employment until a fresh balance is restored — with costs higher than is compatible with the previous level of employment and, hence, with unemployment correspondingly increased.

This is only one side of the coin. Under a regime of fixed exchange rates and free trade, inflation in one country exerts an upward push on price levels in other parts of the European Community. To this extent the pressure on the inflating country to redress its external balance by deflation is reduced. This implies for the Community as a whole that some countries may end up with more inflation than they want and others with more unemployment than they are prepared to tolerate.

The outcome just described is not the only one possible. It is conceivable that prolonged unemployment might slow down the rise in costs and restore the competitive situation. Other countries may take over part of the burden of adjustment by allowing their price levels to rise. But it is also possible that the decline in employment might become cumulative, that new industry would be driven elsewhere and, thirdly, that high costs would become progressively higher in the absence of adequate investment in new equipment and new products. Moreover regional development becomes all the more necessary, but at the same time all the more difficult. If economic activity is depressed throughout the entire country the remedy is to expand aggregate demand and take steps to bring costs to a level consistent with external balance.

It may be asked, first, how the movement of costs could diverge within a monetary union and, second, whether in fact the very existence of such a union would not exercise a harmonizing effect, both on raw material costs and on wage rates. The answer to both questions lies ultimately in the fact of separate national labour markets, with only limited migration between them, and in the very restricted impact of wage bargains in one country on wage bargains in other countries. As long as governments have no means of determining the outcome of wage bargaining in their own labour market, and have little control over the behaviour of that element in costs which is peculiar to their economy, they are necessarily unable to control with any precision the value of their currency in relation to the value of other currencies. They can hope to maintain full employment and avoid external deficits only if they can offset the uncontrolled internal devaluation of their currency by a similar external devaluation. But unless they control prices there will be a further round of devaluation. To engage themselves in advance never to devalue, and, what is more, to put devaluation completely out of their power, would be to surrender responsibility for the maintenance of full employment. The same holds true for the less inflationary countries which are prevented from revaluing their currency in order to protect themselves against an inflationary spillover from abroad, thus surrendering their responsibility for internal price stability. This would at once invite the question: to whom has this responsibility been surrendered?

In a common market that was genuinely a single market under common management, the answer to that question would be simple. It would be part of the business of common management to assign responsibility for demand management to a Community-wide authority; and it would be one of the aims of this authority to establish a single monetary unit and pursue a single, harmonized monetary policy. Such an aim implies the subordination of the monetary authorities of each member country to decisions taken collectively or by the common monetary authority.

It is only necessary to reflect for a moment on the scope and consequences of those decisions to see that delegation of the power to make them to some newly-created international agency is a long way off. Monetary policy forms part of demand management, the creation of purchasing power on a scale dictated by the economic outlook in the light of general economic objectives. So long as the outlook (for example, employment prospects and the pressure of demand) differs throughout the European Community, no general policy laid down centrally can be adapted to the requirements of the different parts when the monetary instruments that might have been brought into play, so as to modulate the policy to local circumstances, have been abandoned. At the same time, the fiscal component of demand management, in the shape of budget surpluses or deficits, will no longer be within the unfettered discretion of national governments. If, for instance, an expansionary policy involving deficit finance appears to be appropriate, governments will not be free to issue debt to cover the deficit in ways requiring support by the central bank and an addition to the money supply. Once there is a single European money, it will not be possible to allow each national government to create, and put into circulation, additional money without approval from the monetary authority of the Community in whatever form it is established.

Monetary union, therefore, presupposes much more than the locking of exchange rates. It presupposes provision for a single monetary policy under a central monetary authority, for collective demand management to meet agreed economic objectives, for common debt management in the interests of monetary control, and, too, for regional balance and labour mobility et cetera. It therefore presupposes, conversely, a subordination of national economic management to the collective will and the decay of important instruments of national economic policy. Thus, however indispensable to full economic integration, monetary union could prove disastrous by itself if it was not accompanied by the political and other conditions inseparable from full integration and collective economic management.

In this respect economic integration under present-day conditions is quite unlike economic integration a century ago when the role of the state in economic affairs was relatively small and confined largely to tariff policy. The reconciliation of national economic objectives, the coordination of large bureaucratic machines, the supercession of economic management at the national level by economic management at a supra-national level: none of these provided a major obstacle to the formation of earlier 'common markets'. Even in the case of the European Community the creation of a customs union, involving a *diminution* in government intervention, by reaching agreement on a common external tariff, is in no way comparable with the continuing effort of coordination in changing circumstances that full economic integration implies — *management of the management* of nine separate economies.

STRATEGIES FOR MONETARY UNIFICATION

In the light of these considerations, the appropriate course would seem to be to concentrate on the broad *strategy* for monetary unification in the European Community, considering the ways in which it might be approached. A number of proposals have been made. Four are discussed below.

1. Immediate Shift to a European Currency

First of all, then, there is the apocalyptic solution which we have already rejected, namely the immediate replacement of national currencies by a single European currency without any transitional phase.

This would call for the setting up at once of a central monetary authority with wide powers and the subordination to it of each of the national central banks. The political powers of such an authority, as already mentioned, would be very far-reaching and would have to be sustained by a deep sense of community of interest.

Divergent trends within the member countries usually assert themselves both in relation to the level of costs, given the limited connection between national labour markets, and in relation to the pressure of demand, given the vagaries of demand patterns and the continued autonomy of national budgets. These divergencies, which are difficult enough to contain without monetary union, might well be exacerbated by monetary union and could cause the union to founder in a mixture of frustration, bewilderment and resentment.

2. Exchange-rate Unification

A second approach — endorsed by the Werner Report — concentrates on exchange rates and envisages a gradual narrowing of margins for fluctuations in rates and of the

scope for changes in parities. This process would lead ultimately to a locking of exchange rates and can be thought of
as 'exchange-rate unification'.

The first step in the process, which was supposed to be
completed by the end of 1973, has not been reassuring. Ever
since the Werner Report was prepared rates of exchange have
become progressively *less* stable. There have been repeated
crises affecting all currencies at intervals throughout the
ensuing three years whatever the agreements in force as to
exchange-rate fluctuations; and the crises have been no less
frequent in the latter part of the period, following the
decision to limit from 1 July 1972 the swings between any
two member currencies to 2.25 per cent on either side of the
rate implied by existing parities. By mid-1974, the currencies
of four of the member countries were floating independently
of the others, while one other member was operating a dual
exchange-rate system with the 'free' exchange rate outside
the provisions of the scheme to narrow the band. All member
countries had resorted to exchange controls. And by then all
had declared new par values for their currency in relation to
the others on at least one occasion and some twice or even
thrice.

The net result, as far as narrowing the margins of fluctuation is concerned, is that where the swing in intra-
Community margins could not exceed 1.5 per cent each side
of parity up to 1971, and the original purpose would have
involved moving to 1.2 per cent, the limit finally accepted
and still in force among the five countries still adhering to the
scheme is 2.25 per cent. From this point of view, there has in
fact been a widening, not a progressive narrowing, of margins.

In our view the strategy of approaching monetary union
through a progressive narrowing of margins is misguided. It
is in effect an attempt to repeat in relation to monetary
policy the same technique of stage-by-stage approximation to
a declared objective on a fixed time-table that proved so
successful in the approach to a customs union. But there is
no real parallel between the two. Indeed, there is a strong
case for the view expressed to the Werner Committee by the
experts of one central bank that 'the outright suppression of
the intra-Community margins, once the harmonization of the
economic policies of the member states has made sufficient

progress, would have important advantages over a gradual elimination beginning at the first stage'.[6]

The scale on which parity changes have taken place between European currencies since 1967 has not only been very large by past standards. It far exceeds what might reasonably be attributed to different rates of inflation or productivity growth within the Common Market during the period. Even before the French franc was allowed to float downwards in January 1974, for example, it had fallen against the German mark by a further 22 per cent after a fall as recently as 1969 of 17 per cent. Changes of this magnitude, however they are to be explained, are symptomatic of the forces operating against fixity in exchange rates and of the distortions that would follow any attempt to contain these forces merely by declining to make provision for variations in exchange rates.

During those years national economies in the European Community have been submitted to very different stresses in their domestic markets; they have been unevenly vulnerable, for instance, to 'outside shocks'. They have had to face different pressures in their balances of payments, which have revealed structural factors associated with differences in the pattern of their imports and exports. And looking ahead, member countries are expected to be affected to very differing degrees, as pointed out in Chapter 1, by the dramatic increase in oil prices.

But the forces making against stability in exchange rates have not sprung exclusively from the different circumstances and policies of the member countries — important as those differences are. The destabilizing forces have been reinforced by changes taking place outside the European Community altogether. The currency flows set up by distrust in the dollar, for example, have of themselves been sufficient to create exchange crises within the Community and force major changes in rates of exchange between the currencies of the member countries. There is no good reason why such flows should cease of their own accord. And, as we emphasize below, it will be necessary, long before monetary unification can take place, to find some means of preventing or mitigating the undesirable repercussions of such flows on exchange relationships.

Thus in a period of monetary turmoil the second approach to monetary union has also proved completely unrealistic. The financial facilities granted by the member countries to each other were inadequate for handling anything more than day-to-day fluctuations. At the same time, the speculative pressure on exchange rates usually originated outside the Community and obliged individual member countries to change their parities, often with a minimum of consultation with other members. Whatever success this approach might have in more stable conditions, or with the national self-discipline to give it substance, it ignores the complex conditions that are necessary for the maintenance of monetary equilibrium between the member countries.

3. Coordination of Monetary Policies

A third possibility would be to try to meet these conditions directly and aim at a progressive coordination of monetary policies throughout the European Community as a pre-condition for fixing exchange rates. The approach recognizes the danger that a premature fixing of exchange rates may serve only to bring about a suspension of convertibility and put an end to the free flow of goods and services as well as of capital and labour. If the common political will is strong enough against divergent national trends, coordination of monetary policy will lead eventually to constant rates of exchange; but if it is not, the outcome will not be to forfeit convertibility.

This approach acknowledges that each member country will seek to retain its own currency, its own monetary and financial system and its own monetary authority and monetary policy. If there is agreement though on the need for closer monetary cooperation with a view to eventual union, it would express itself in arrangements for a closer tie between credit conditions in any one member country and those in other parts of the Community and, too, for an integrated capital market.

These arrangements would be intended to lead in the course of time to a second stage, the creation of a central monetary authority which would take over responsibility for the framing of a unified monetary policy, not just for the coordination of the independently-conceived policies of the member countries. Once such an authority existed, and had been entrusted with this responsibility, the way would be clear for a locking of exchange rates and the introduction of a common currency.

We do not doubt the desirability of greater coordination of monetary policies. But to rely exclusively on this is to invite the objection that it was precisely because of disillusionment with efforts to secure coordinated monetary policies that this approach was abandoned in favour of exchange-rate unification. It was believed that the latter would *impose* a need for coordination that in the past had been evaded. In spite of consultations in the Monetary Committee of the European Community, member countries had been left largely to fend for themselves in coping with financial instability, domestic or external. In these circumstances they had sought to preserve the scope for independent initiative in monetary policy that comes from uncertainty about future rates of exchange. The proposals of the Werner Committee sought to close this escape route by removing that uncertainty. With fixed rates of exchange and no margin of fluctuation around parity, interest rates would come together automatically, in the money market at least.

The above objection does therefore have substance. But if there were genuine difficulties in coordinating monetary policies it would seem better to face these difficulties than suppress them unexamined. The reason why countries seek to maintain independence in their monetary policies is essentially that they expect their own economic circumstances to differ from those in other parts of the Community or they expect to have different priorities in their policy objectives. The problems involved in harmonizing monetary policies arise mainly out of differences in the conjunctural situation in different countries and differences of view about the treatment of the conjuncture that are often associated with different political conditions and election cycles.

It is common ground that the increasing inter-penetration, or interdependence, of the economies of member countries makes for a synchronization in short-term fluctuations in economic activity and usually intensifies them. To this extent the policies appropriate to each country are likely to diverge less and less. But member countries remain sensitive to the risk that they may be tying their hands in the use of an important instrument of policy once they allow monetary policy to take shape elsewhere. If they have no assurance that the Community will devise adequate instruments of demand management, they will hesitate to submit to a central monetary authority or give up the freedom in monetary policy which they can enjoy (or believe they enjoy) so long as future rates of exchange are uncertain and capital flows are subject to control.

Need to Remove Capital Controls

There thus seems to be little doubt about the direction in which the European Community should move. The fixed rates of exchange contemplated in the Werner Report would be far more destructive of independence in monetary policy than coordination through a central authority. To the extent that exchange rates are flexible, there can be divergencies in interest rates in the various member countries and national governments are free to follow divergent monetary policies; in particular, the greater risks implicit in flexible exchange rates tend to operate as a brake on flows of 'hot money'. These divergencies can then be used to bring monetary policy more closely into harmony in each country with the national employment situation and the national strength of inflationary pressure. On the other hand, capital controls, as argued later, are a very uncertain instrument and do not go very happily with the idea of economic integration. It is only by a curious logic that a country can seek full economic and monetary union through the fixing of exchange rates, see no need for a central monetary authority and simultaneously cling to exchange controls.

The European Community is not equipped to coordinate short-term economic policy. The actual instruments of policy remain exclusively national. Only when the Community has developed the necessary instruments to supplement, and ultimately displace, national monetary policies can it hope to influence the conjuncture directly within each country. Among these instruments, and by far the most important potentially, is the power of the Community to tax and spend.

These powers and the place of fiscal policy in economic integration are dealt with towards the end of the present chapter.

Accepting the need for enlarged powers — fiscal as well as monetary — in the hands of the European Community, in what kind of exchange-rate regime should they be exercised? We assume that rates of exchange between European currencies are unlikely to remain fixed in relation to one another or to third currencies while the indispensable pre-conditions for exchange stability (and of course for a common currency) are not met. We assume, in addition, that the stability of European exchange rates will depend as much on extra-European as on intra-European forces operating on trade and payments.

We accept the need to curtail exchange-rate fluctuations and to pursue domestic policies which contribute to that end. Once the force of world inflation has subsided, it may again become possible to aim at stability in the rates of exchange between the currencies of the European Community: or at least at a degree of stability that would not preclude parity changes from time to time of particular currencies. The Community for its part could contribute to exchange-rate stability if it encouraged and assisted financially the kind of structural change for which parity changes are frequently no more than a poor alternative. But for the present, with the French franc, the Italian lire and the British pound floating independently of one another, joint action along these lines is obviously impossible. All that survives from the famous 'snake' that uncoiled from the Werner Report is 'a mark bloc' in which the exchange rates of a number of smaller countries — some of which are not even members of the Community — are pegged against the German mark.

If the European Community wishes to achieve a measure of exchange stability, it may be tempted to resort for this purpose to the use of controls over capital movements, particularly if the threat to stability comes from flows to or from third countries in North America or the Near East. Such controls already exist and they are not incompatible with the existing code of good international behaviour. But since they apply just as much to capital flows within the European Community as to capital flows to and from third countries they are difficult to reconcile with the aim of economic integration and certainly do not promote that free flow of capital to the points of greater scarcity which the Community wishes to encourage. Yet, just as exchange rates have become less stable the more talk there has been of monetary integration, so capital controls have multiplied the nearer the community has come to the date set for their removal.

It is possible to make a case in principle for efforts to limit, rather than encourage, certain types of capital flow. The dynamics of industrial growth and decline, for example, may make for cumulative movements of capital out of areas or countries badly in need of additional investment. Moreover, capital controls — especially those directed towards short-term capital movements — do not necessarily have much to do with the productivity of real assets or with the continuing need for credit of capital importing countries. Hence it could be argued that although the removal of capital controls forms part of full economic integration it is not particularly urgent and might even be counter-productive if other pre-conditions of economic and monetary integration are not fulfilled.

We should not wish to be interpreted, however, as recommending capital controls as an appropriate remedy for industrial decline. To the extent that industrial decline reflects excessive wage settlements, the remedy lies in an incomes policy conducive to economic development; and since it is associated with a shortage of capital, it should be taken care of by regional subsidies or by infrastructure investment.

More important is the question whether it would be advisable to aim at abolishing controls within the European Community and still continue to exercise them over movements to or from third countries. Those in favour of this proposal are impressed by the danger of large-scale transfers between European currencies and the dollar and would like to see these transfers submitted to control, even if this meant instituting a system of exchange control where none exists at present, and retaining it indefinitely as part of the apparatus of European monetary union.

In the absence of control at the American end, recent experience has demonstrated the vulnerability of European exchange relationships to transfer out of (or into) dollars.

The potential flow of short-term funds from one country to another was already enormous when the dollar was a currency of unquestioned stability. When the dollar fell from favour the volatile funds previously held in dollars were no longer firmly attached to one currency or financial centre; and the changes in exchange rates that have since occurred have added to the volatility of these funds and increased the scale that transfers may reach. European countries faced with inflows of unwanted funds may reasonably ask themselves why they should allow what may prove to be temporary movements in the capital balance to push up the rate of exchange and depress the balance on current account over a much longer period.

Although we see the force of this argument we are doubtful whether capital controls are a satisfactory answer. Experience does not encourage whole-hearted reliance on them as a method of checking capital flows and stabilizing exchange rates. The authorities may be misled into holding exchange rates too long; and the controls themselves, even when apparently effective, may simply divert capital movements into other channels where control is difficult or impossible. This would apply particularly to any efforts to make control directional and allow capital to move freely within the Community but not between the Community and third countries. The example of the sterling area suggests that discrimination of this kind is possible only when there is a common system of exchange control under rules laid down by some accepted authority and applied willingly by all administrative agencies throughout the area. Such a system is not feasible for the Community.

An Exchange-Equalization Account

We have therefore looked at alternative ways of dealing with the problem. We suggest that it would be much better to make use of a thoroughly adequate exchange-equalization account as a means of coping with capital flows than to seek to tighten controls. An exchange-equalization account would absorb foreign currencies when money flowed in and would sell foreign currencies when people sought to make withdrawals. The account would hold a portfolio of currencies, including the currencies of member countries (possibly in the form of the *europas* proposed below). According to whether it was faced with an inflow or outflow, it would switch its portfolio so as to make available the currencies in demand at a fairly steady price, at the same time taking up into its portfolio the currencies on offer.

The purpose of such an account would be to steady exchange rates without fixing them or preventing adjustments called for by changes in competitiveness reflected in the current account. So far as capital movements took place within the Community, and were ostensibly reversible, no insuperable problems would arise. So far as they represented a movement of capital into the Community from outside, affecting member countries unequally, the proposed account would be a means of broadening the impact, just as would happen if the flow were subsequently outwards. But for this purpose it would have to be very much larger than anything hitherto created.

The management of the exchange-equalization account would presumably be in the hands of the central monetary authority, whatever form that took. If intervention were to be effective, however, the authority would presumably have to enjoy considerable discretion, on the understanding that it would act in conformity with agreed rules and, too, that its operations would in due course be made public and submitted to scrutiny by outside experts, such as a committee of economic advisers that it is proposed in Chapter 1 should be associated with the European Parliament.

Although the proposed account would be in a sense a substitute for capital controls, not all countries could be expected to give up the use of capital controls as soon as it came into operation. This would apply particularly to control over outflows, since countries may feel reluctant to abandon a means of limiting their indebtedness to the account. Control over inflows would be easier to abandon. For a country doing so would merely add to its credit balance in the account.

We would hope that in the course of time, if the exchange-equalization account allowed reasonable latitude and was aimed specifically at the capital rather than the current account, governments might allow capital controls to wither.

The capital movements giving rise to interventions by the exchange-equalization account would be largely out of, or into, dollars or Euro-dollars. This might well be so even when the source of the capital was Japan, the Middle East or South America. Until recently the main source of disturbance was distrust of the dollar and this gave rise to the much-debated problem of the 'dollar overhang'; that is, dollars in the hands of reluctant holders who would have preferred some other international asset, such as gold. The dollar component of foreign-exchange reserves in the hands of central banks (or other monetary authorities) rose from under $20,000m in mid-1970 to over $70,000m in mid-1973. But with the recovery of confidence in the dollar this total has been falling and is now seen in a very different perspective.

The main reason for the change is the impact on balances of payments, current and prospective of the very big increase in petroleum prices. At the prices established in December 1973 in international markets there is little doubt that for some time to come, exporters of crude oil — particularly in Arab countries — would add to their export earnings on a scale well in excess of any likely addition to their current imports. If, as is possible, this excess persisted until, say, 1980 it might mean a cumulative total of the order of $400,000m or even a much larger total by that date. This cumulative deficit on oil account would involve the rest of the world in borrowing from the oil exporters to cover the deficit; and it would result, therefore, in a vast accumulation of debt to the oil countries, most of it perhaps in the form of liquid balances. At the same time there would be a serious danger that each industrial country, alarmed at the increase in its external debt and the indefinite continuance of a large deficit on current account, would take steps to reduce the burden by measures that could only transfer it to others among the oil importing countries. The world might then be faced with a general deflation of formidable proportions as countries struggled to keep their external trade deficits within reason.

This aspect of the energy problem is discussed elsewhere. From the more limited aspects of international liquidity, the existence of enormous holdings of liquid assets in the hands of the oil exporters would greatly complicate the tasks of an exchange-equalization account. It would be highly desirable for the account, acting on behalf of all member countries, to come to some understanding with the oil countries both as to the way in which the deficits of individual countries should be financed and the form the resulting debt should take. Without some such understanding, the transfers between currencies could reach enormous proportions and make the rate of exchange of any one currency subject to arbitrary and unforeseeable decisions by the major oil suppliers.

It will be apparent from what has been said that the problem of monetary integration is very much wrapped up in the wider problems of international monetary reform. The kind of exchange stability that the European Community needs for integration is more difficult to attain if there are no agreed rules of the game to which any country may be expected to conform: rules limiting the freedom of individual countries to steal a march on their neighbours by holding down the exchange value of their currency; rules as to the creation of new international money by the International Monetary Fund; rules or conventions as to what is legitimate when a country is in heavy deficit; and so on. As long as each country has its own currency, the Community, too, will have to work out rules for its members. But if its rules are to be consistent with those adopted for the international system, it has to ensure that the latter take due account of the Community's views and circumstances.

4.   Means of Settlement of Accounts: the Europa

The approaches so far discussed leave open the question of settlement of accounts between the European Community's member countries. They might settle in either dollars, SDRs, gold or the currency of a member country. Or they might settle in some unit created specially for the purpose. Such a unit might serve both as a means of settlement and as an international unit of account within the Community. But it could also serve a wider purpose and contribute towards eventual monetary union.

There have been a number of proposals for the creation of such a unit as a complement to, rather than as a substitute for, existing European currencies.[7] A new currency, the 'europa', might be issued to circulate side by side with the currencies of member countries and gradually replace them as it came to be seen as a more convenient unit of account and store of value. It would be possible to bring such a currency into existence as part of the arrangements for a joint float.

Provision could be made for settlements between the monetary authorities of the Nine either in a European national currency, or in an amalgam of the currencies used by members of the Community (or a unit representing such an amalgam), without resort to dollars, gold or SDRs. It is unlikely that there would be agreements on any single currency and in any event none of the member countries is anxious to promote the use of reserve currencies issued by a national government. On the other hand, the alternative of defining the new currency in terms of a bundle of European currencies in some agreed ratio to one another seems to us to have many advantages. Not only might it pave the way to eventual monetary unification. It would also bring into existence a currency unit which could simultaneously provide an acceptable reserve asset for central banks and serve as an intervention currency with a value tied to that of the package of national currencies of which it was composed.

There is room for argument as to the precise way in which the europa might be constituted: on what basis it should unite different national currencies, what interest it should carry and what guarantees, if any, might be offered against changes in exchange rates.[8] We do not think it necessary to suggest in advance what answers to these questions are likely to prove most workable since they would inevitably involve negotiation between member governments. Nor do we see any reason why it should prove impossible to arrive at satisfactory answers.

By way of illustration it would be possible to issue to each member country a quantity' of europas in proportion to its GNP (or its external trade, including invisibles) while each country delivered in return a quantity of its own currency to the same value. As far as the backing is concerned, the value of the europa would then be equal to the sum of the national currencies supplied divided by the number of units issued. It might also be agreed that there should in no circumstances be an appreciation of any national currency against the europa and that, whenever any change took place in exchange rates between the currencies of member countries, those currencies that were depreciated would be the subject of supplementary payments to bring the value of the total holding of each devalued national currency into the previous relationship with the holdings of currencies that were not devalued. The europa would then be at least as attractive an asset as the strongest national currency at any point in time.

This formulation implies nothing about the character of the issuing authority. It could take the form of an account, with no banking operations involved. Alternatively it could be a central monetary authority with power to issue additional units, to intervene in exchange markets, to extend credit to member countries, to hold balances for member governments in their individual or collective capacity and to exercise regulatory functions over the financial institutions operating on a Community-wide basis. Our own preference, as will become apparent, is for the latter.

In order to prevent a net increase in the foreign exchange reserves of member countries, the latter could be required to surrender some proportion of their reserves in exchange for the allocation of europas that they receive. The reserves could have to be surrendered either instead of or in addition to the amount of national currency which member countries may be obliged to transfer to the Community's monetary authority.

A composite currency, such as we suggest, could also form the basis of international banking operations. This could occur in one of two ways. If europas were traded in commercial operations, as is implied in their suggested use as an intervention currency, they would have a function akin to that of the Euro-dollar and would provide both a credit instrument and a liquid asset for external as well as domestic operators. But they would, if extensively held, open up the possibility of speculative pressure on individual currencies in much the same way as if these currencies became reserve currencies in their own right. The europa would have to be convertible at sight into the component currencies since its use as an intervention currency in itself requires unlimited convertibility between the europa and national currencies. For this reason there might be some unwillingness to allow the europa to be used in commercial operations and as an intervention currency. If so, this would be tantamount to a decision to leave international banking to countries that are prepared to face the risks implicit in international banking operations, including the risks that reserve currencies cannot avoid in the form of quick external liabilities.

The second way in which international banking operations might be encouraged would be through the use of the europa as a unit of account. In the capital markets of the European Community it would be possible to denominate loans, particularly those issued by public authorities, in terms of the europa along the lines of issues already made by European banking consortia. This would not automatically extend the European capital market except insofar as this made subsequently for easier trading in the loan obligations across national frontiers. But it would familiarize the financial community with a unit of account that promised greater stability than any single national currency and might displace these currencies from an increasing range of financial operations.

The europa would be little more than a token of eventual monetary integration unless reinforced by other measures: the working out of these measures, especially fiscal measures, may be said to constitute another approach to economic and monetary union, which some of us believe to be the most promising one. To fiscal integration we now turn.

FISCAL INTEGRATION

Fiscal policy is of central importance in the management of a modern economy. The reasons for its importance lie in the sheer volume of government expenditure, the intrusion of tax considerations into nearly all spending decisions, and the influence on the level of employment and activity of any variations in the flow of expenditure or in rates of tax. Direct expenditure by governments, central and local taken together, represents around 20 to 25 per cent of the gross national products of most industrialized countries. If subsidies and income transfers — either through the budget or through social security funds — are included, it is found that the proportion rises to 40 to 45 per cent.

The central role of fiscal policy implies a corresponding need for coordination and harmonization in order to establish consistency of policy within the European Community. This is not something that can be done at a stroke. It requires a prolonged and continuous effort in the course of which national differences have to be defined, examined and, where possible, resolved.

Such an effort, designed to strengthen the political cohesion of the Community, would still leave the major responsibility for fiscal policy with national governments, but would permit a steady enlargement of the tasks falling on the Community and financed out of a common budget. This enlargement of the Common Market's responsibilities would represent a transfer from the national level but need not necessarily involve any net additional burden on taxpayers. At the same time, harmonization could not be pushed to the point at which national differences in tax structure, in public expenditure and in the ways in which expenditure was financed were completely abolished.

Some of the most difficult problems in harmonization are on the side of public expenditure. For even if social and economic priorities were the same throughout the Community — as they obviously are not — the levels of expenditure for which member countries could provide from their own resources must inevitably differ. And uniformity of provision would be possible only if large transfers took place between members through the medium of a common budget. While large transfers do occur already as a result of the operation of the European Community's common agricultural policy it would require a much firmer acceptance of the need for closer union, political as well as economic, before member countries would be prepared to formulate common policies without regard to the inter-country financial transfers implied in the proposals.

. Some of the same difficulties attach to tax policy. Again there are divergencies in social and economic priorities that cause the pattern of taxation to differ from country to country; and again, even in the absence of these divergencies, countries might decide on different levels of taxation because of differences in tax yield at a given level. Differences in administrative systems, in business habits, in compliance by taxpayers, and so on, further complicate the problem of tax harmonization.

A third set of problems is short-term in character and relates to the use of fiscal policy as one component in demand management. If the European Community wishes to regulate economic activity in order to maintain an even pressure of demand it cannot rely simply on monetary policy. It must try to ensure that fiscal policy is working in the same direction.

The need to link fiscal and monetary integration was stressed in the Werner Report which argued that an effort to coordinate the budgets of member governments was one of the first steps to be taken on the way to monetary union. But the report contented itself with suggesting a thrice-yearly comparison of budgets and argued that any common budget would be much too small to play a decisive part even after full integration. Both the concept of coordination set out in the report and the outright abandonment of a large common budget seem open to question.[9]

Coordination, as envisaged in the Werner Report, would be limited to considering (i) the total amount of budgetary expenditure in each member state, (ii) its relationship to national income, (iii) the size of the surplus or deficit and (iv) the method of financing the deficit or utilizing the surplus. There might also be some general consideration of capital, as opposed to current, expenditure on the basis of ordinary accounting definitions of capital expenditure so that, for example, military aircraft might be included and expenditure on higher education excluded.[10]

This seems a rather inadequate approach since it concentrates on the total amount of expenditure and its excess over revenue. It neglects the varying relationship between financial outlays and absorption of real resources and proceeds as if the composition and direction of expenditure did not have profound effects on costs, competitive conditions, the distribution of income, regional imbalances et cetera and hence on inflationary pressures. It is too unsophisticated in its equation of one expenditure with another from the point of view of employment, and too narrow in its view of the variety of ways in which fiscal policy can contribute to economic management.

If progress is to be made towards fiscal integration, the composition and direction of public spending needs to be analysed in the terms suggested — distortions of competition, the contribution to growth and social equality, the regional allocation of resources and the relief of inflationary pressures.[11] Otherwise the tendencies which have manifested themselves within the Community from the outset will continue to prevail. Governments will continue to compete with each other in granting fiscal concessions in order to attract investment in industrial development. They will continue to sacrifice public investment which generally contributes more to social amenities and the quality of life than does industrial competitiveness. An analysis under the headings listed should be the starting-point for harmonization in the proper sense; that is, concerted action to forestall the unwanted consequences of competition left to itself.

Harmonization of this kind between national budgets does not by itself constitute fiscal integration. We have also to consider the role of a common budget. It is sometimes argued that in a true economic union two conditions should apply. One is that industries in the various parts of the market should enjoy similar standards of public services. The second requirement would be that rates of taxation should be in line from one part of the Community to another. The two conditions are obviously incompatible if the bulk of budgetary revenue and expenditure in the Community remains national. As long as incomes per head differ from state to state, comparable standards of public services can only be obtained if the poorer areas tax themselves more heavily. The effect of this would be to make it more difficult to catch up with the richer areas and so perpetuate, or even intensify, the initial differences in levels of income. Common standards throughout the Community in such fields as transport, communications, education and health services are in the interest not only of fairness in inter-regional competition but of achieving similar living conditions in different parts. They require continuous concerted action which could be implemented through a common budget, or an agreed system of transfers between member countries, and equal access to a common capital market.

This is necessary to hold together the various regions of a

single country. Even in federal countries the central budget tends to assume a growing proportion of total public expenditure. A key feature of central budgets in such situations is that a proportionately higher share of the revenue is derived from the more prosperous states whereas expenditure is distributed across the whole territory thus favouring the less prosperous states. This is true even when the major share of revenue comes from indirect taxation. But it is still more so when revenue relies more broadly on a progressive income tax.

Of course there may be misguided provisions which provoke some transfers in reverse: for instance, when the central budget subsidizes the national capital far beyond the extra burdens which a city shoulders for serving as a capital. An effective regional policy should begin by eliminating those artificial inducements to geographical concentration. But one of the main purposes of a central budget is to achieve automatic net transfers from rich to poor areas in order to make productive investment more attractive in localities requiring development or conversion.

Thus a sizeable central budget is an essential prerequisite of monetary union which must exclude not only divergencies between member countries in the movement of prices, which would be untenable, but also growing regional disequilibria, which would be intolerable. Movement towards a central budget could be begun straight away. The Community could start by eliminating the inconsistencies that have developed between the various funds it administers. For each fund is run according to special rules without regard to any overall balance or cohesion.

At present more than 90 per cent of the sums administered by the European Community go to agriculture — a share comparable to the space occupied in the *Journal Officiel* by decisions under the common agricultural policy. The rules of the Agricultural Guidance and Guarantee Fund are such that a major share of the burden falls on the member countries which depend more heavily than others on meeting their agricultural needs out of imports. Most of the benefits, on the other hand, go to the countries with the highest production. This distribution obviously bears no relation to the wealth of each member or to its food consumption from all sources.

The Social Fund aimed at retraining and securing employment for unemployed workers, may have to make transfers to a member country which is pursuing a deflationary policy that gives rise to domestic unemployment. This may occur at a time when the country is in external surplus so that the transfer merely adds to reserves of foreign exchange. Similarly the European Investment Bank, which exists to finance projects in the least developed areas of the Community, may provide funds at a time when there is no shortage of domestic capital and ample foreign exchange.

The way out of this distorting, and confusing, situation would be to consolidate in the Community budget all the various funds, including the Fund for Regional Development. To these should be added the investments by the European Investment Bank that are considered as part of the capital budget. It probably would not be possible to revise immediately the terms governing the allocations of monies from the funds. But it could be agreed that the amounts should stand to the credit of countries with undesirable surpluses until such time as they are running down their reserves at which time the transfers could take place.

As new activities are undertaken by the European Community, the financing of them would fall, naturally, into the common budget. Projects are pending, for example, in the field of advanced technology. Experience has shown that, despite the efforts of one country or another to invest in new techniques, their capacity for development and production has been limited and costs, too, have been unduly high. The cases in which cooperation has been initiated on a supranational basis — as in Euratom — or on an inter-governmental basis — as with the European Space Research Organization (ESRO) and the European Vehicle Launcher Development Organization (ELDO) — were doomed to failure because of the insistence of each country on getting back for its industry the equivalent of its financial contribution. This practice of *juste retour* has been contrary to any reasonable division of labour. It is only on a much broader basis that each country stands a chance of benefiting from a common endeavour.

Furthermore, some common infrastructures to link the main centres of activity in the countries of the European Community, either by super highways or by entirely new railroad lines, can be envisaged. The fight against pollution in some industries, as well as for the rivers or the seashore, will require a substantial effort. And eventually, if the Community ever becomes a real political entity, in the fullest sense, the Common budget would contain a very large expenditure for a joint defence effort.

HARMONIZATION OF TAX MEASURES

So much for the expenditure side of a common budget. Turning to the revenue side, the Werner Committee urged a minimum degree of harmonization between the taxation measures of member countries. In the first place, the general adoption of value-added tax is not enough as long as exemptions and rate reductions for specific products and services vary from country to country. For in this case controls cannot be eliminated at internal borders even though tariffs and quotas have disappeared. If the value-added tax becomes a truly general tax, however, there is no need to compensate at the borders for the differences in these rates, for international differences in rates of general taxes are offset by exchange-rate adjustments. From an allocational point of view, what has to be harmonized is the pattern of taxation.

As for direct taxes, the Werner Report emphasized their effect on movements of capital, rather than on immediate conditions of competition. For this reason its proposals were limited to taxes on interest and dividends and also, to a certain extent, on company profits. What is meant by this is that rates of taxation, rules of assessment and exemptions are made more clearly similar, so that as between member countries net incomes after tax stay in the same proportion as gross incomes before tax. Such an attempt to avoid distorted movements of capital will become more necessary the more an effort is made to develop an integrated capital market.

Disparity in Tax Collection

Nominal rates of taxation and rules of assessment are not the only aspects that would matter on the revenue side of a common budget. For there is in the European Community a fantastic disparity in the efficiency with which taxes are actually raised. This disparity should not be ignored. The absence of control on investment income in Belgium and Luxembourg, the extensive reporting of purely notional profits for taxation purposes that exists in others, the widespread evasion of taxation on non-wage income which plagues some countries more than others have a significant inflationary impact. Not only do they reduce in large proportions the revenue which governments should obtain. They also force a more extensive recourse to indirect taxes which, by increasing the cost of living, add to the pressure for higher wage demands.

DEVELOPMENT OF A COMMON BUDGET

The emphasis of the Werner Committee's proposals is too heavily on uniformity of national rates of tax, particularly in view of the arguments against this developed above, and too little on the development of a common budget that would make such uniformity tolerable. If a common budget is to be developed in the European Community, the pooling of customs duties, the present contribution by member countries of up to 1 per cent of their gross national product, plus whatever is yielded by variable import levies on agricultural imports when such imports are reduced still further, will be much too small to cover expenditure and shape the economic environment that is conducive to monetary union. It will become necessary to develop a Community system of taxation which can yield the revenues required to cope with responsibilities to be handed over by national governments, together with any obligations supplementary to national ones, such as a common regional policy. For example, we propose a tax on land values or increases in land values to raise revenue and redistribute income from centres of congestion, where land values are high and rising, to the less developed regions.

Any Community system of taxation should be designed to provide a strong inducement to savings and thus provide a weapon against inflation. And it should introduce a self-checking mechanism which would help to counter tax evasion. To meet these objectives a number of suggestions might be considered.

1. Instead of differentiating between earned and unearned income — wages and salaries, on the one hand, and investment income, on the other — by the earned income allowance (that is, counting wages and salaries for less than their total amount, thereby reducing the level of taxation) which is common to the British, French and Italian systems, the differentiation might be accomplished through a yearly wealth tax as in the German and Dutch systems. This wealth tax need not be progressive as wealth is usually a progressive function of income. At a proportional rate around 1 per cent, it would be more advantageous than the present taxation on the most productive investments, while discouraging the least productive ones. It would make it possible to reduce the rate of tax on interest and dividends to the level on wages and salaries.

2. The inducement to save should come from reduced taxation, not — as is often the case now — on income from saving, but on the share of income which is saved at the time it is saved. This would avoid the consequences of some of the present systems where dividends and interests are taxed at a lower rate than income from work. To that effect a tax credit would represent a fraction of the income which is used for an addition to the patrimony of the tax-payer as declared for the assessment of the wealth tax. In order to obtain the tax credit on income saved, it would be necessary to make a return on wealth, which in turn would render it very difficult to cheat on income at a later date.

3. The additions to wealth through savings must, however, be distinguished from additions through capital gains. These are taxed in all Community countries save two. This taxation has to be generalized so that the main source of enrichment does not escape its share of the tax burden.

As this description of the fiscal component of monetary union suggests, it does not necessarily follow that full political union has to be achieved before monetary union can be embarked upon, unless far-reaching common action is immediately implemented. An increase in common expenditure, a reform of taxation and, even more, the establishment of a joint tax system launch a debate which is highly political in character. Budget expenditure involves decisions to grant money to some and refuse it to others; and taxation involves decisions to take money from some and to exempt others. Both involve conflicts of conception as well as conflicts of interest. Gradually the debate could be lifted from the national to the Community level — as has been happening in the case of agricultural policy. In other words, if monetary union is taken seriously, it could gradually 'politicize' the European Community. Rather than any blueprints or pre-fabricated schemes, it is this organic process which could make the Community gradually ripe for political union proper, manifested by a common foreign and defence policy.

CONCLUSIONS AND RECOMMENDATIONS

That said, the problems of starting the European Community firmly on a course towards economic and monetary union are formidable, as the below review of our conclusions and recommendations tends to show.

1. First, it is quite unrealistic to aim at a unified European currency by 1980, or for that matter by 1984, unless far-reaching common action is immediately embarked upon.

2. Monetary union, as envisaged in the Werner Report, pre-supposes not only a locking of exchange rates among the national currencies of the European Community, but also provision for a single monetary policy under a central monetary authority, for collective demand management to meet agreed economic objectives and, too, for common debt management in the interests of monetary control. It pre-supposes, indeed, a subordination of national economic management to the collective will of the Community and the decay of important instruments of national economic policy.

3. Once a monetary union has been established, as remarked in Chapter 1, the international adjustment process, relating to balances of payments, will become an inter-regional adjustment process. In preparing conditions for monetary union, policies need to be developed for making internal adjustment as little painful, and therefore as acceptable politically and socially, as possible. These policies would therefore need to focus on the integration of capital markets, regional balance, mobility of labour and so forth.

4. If monetary union were pushed through prematurely, without being reinforced by complementary policies and without complementary powers and common institutions to give effect to those policies, the result might well be needless unemployment and waste of resources.

5. The strategy of approaching monetary union through a progressive narrowing of margins and fixing of parities is misguided. Strong destabilizing forces, both within and outside the European Community, make it unrealistic to aim at a system of locked exchange rates in the foreseeable future.

6. Experience does not encourage whole-hearted reliance on capital controls as a method of checking capital flows and stabilizing exchange rates.

7. We suggest that it would be preferable to make use of a thoroughly adequate exchange-equalization account as a means of coping with destabilizing capital flows. The purpose of such an account would be to steady exchange rates without fixing them or preventing adjustments called for by changes in international competitiveness.

8. The operations of the exchange-equalization account should be in conformity with agreed rules and open to scrutiny by outside experts (such as the committee of economic advisers to the European Parliament that is proposed in Chapter 1).

9. The existence of large holdings of liquid assets in the hands of oil exporters would greatly complicate the tasks of an exchange-equalization account, but at the same time it would reinforce the case for introducing such an arrangement. It would be highly desirable for the managers of the account, acting on behalf of all member countries, to come to some understanding with the oil countries both as to the way in which the deficits of the individual countries should be financed and as to the form the resulting debt should take.

10. The kind of exchange stability that the European Community needs for integration requires international agreement on rules of the game to which each country may be expected to conform: rules for limiting the freedom of individual countries to steal a march on their neighbours by holding down the exchange value of their currency; rules to regulate the creation of new international money by the IMF;

rules or conventions on what action is legitimate when a country is in heavy deficit; and so on.

11. We recommend the issue of a new European currency, the europa, to circulate side by side with the currencies of member countries and gradually replace them. The europa could be defined in terms of a bundle of European currencies in some agreed ratio and would always have a value as great as the strongest national currency.

12. Initially the europa would provide an acceptable reserve asset for central banks; and subsequently it could be used as an intervention currency used by a central monetary authority constituted by the member countries.

13. The europa could also form the basis of international banking operations.

14. The europa would, however, be little more than a token of eventual monetary integration unless it was reinforced by other measures. The working out of these measures, especially fiscal measures, constitutes another approach to economic and monetary union which some of us believe to be the most promising one.

15. The central importance of fiscal policy in the management of a modern economy implies a corresponding need for national economic policies in the European Community to be coordinated and harmonized in order to establish consistency. But this requires a prolonged and continuous effort in the course of which national differences have to be defined, examined and, where possible, resolved.

16. If progress is to be made towards fiscal integration, the composition and direction of public spending needs to be analysed in terms of their effects on costs, competitive conditions, the distribution of income, regional imbalances and, as a result of these elements, on inflationary pressures. Otherwise governments will continue to compete with each other in granting fiscal concessions in order to attract investment in industrial development. And they will continue to sacrifice public investment which generally contributes more to social amenities and the quality of life than does industrial competitiveness.

17. It can be questioned whether it is necessary for public services and social security benefits to be comparable, and for rates of taxation to be in line, throughout a common market.

In the European Community the two conditions are clearly incompatible if the bulk of budgetary revenue and expenditure remains national.

18. Thus a sizeable central budget is an essential prerequisite of monetary union which must exclude not only divergencies between member countries in the movement of prices but also growing regional disequilibria.

19. In our view too much emphasis tends to be placed, in much discussion of fiscal integration, on uniformity of national rates of taxation. Not enough attention is focused on the development of a common budget.

20. Nobody should be under any illusions about how easily a common budget could be developed. But a start could be made by eliminating the inconsistencies that have become apparent in the various funds the European Community administers.

21. In order to facilitate this objective, we recommend that all funds administered by the European Community should be consolidated into the common budget, to which should be added the investments by the European Investment Bank that are considered part of the capital budget. And the financing of all new activities of the Community should be from the common budget.

22. Until the rules governing the allocation of monies from the funds can be revised, amounts due to countries with adequate reserves could be credited to their account, to be transferred when their reserves are running down.

23. The revenue yielded from the contributions of member governments, from customs duties and variable import levies on agricultural products is not enough to match the expenditure required to shape the economic environment for a monetary union.

24. It will become necessary in due course to develop a Community system of taxation. That system should embrace a self-checking mechanism in order to counter tax evasion and should favour investment and saving while reducing inequalities. Instead of differentiating between earned and unearned income, we recommend a yearly wealth tax of a moderate and proportional rate and, as an inducement to save, an income tax credit on savings declared as additions to wealth. The taxation of capital gains should be generalized.

25. The European Community should introduce a tax on land values and increases in land values as a source of revenue and to redistribute income from the advanced to the less developed regions.

NOTES AND REFERENCES

1. The Werner committee had before it four plans put forward by Belgium, Luxembourg, Germany and the Commission.
2. For a professional clarification of the economic issues involved in the proposal for monetary union, see W. M. Corden, *Monetary Integration*, Essay No. 93 in International Finance (Princeton: Princeton University Press, 1972). Also see the report of the Study Group on Economic and Monetary Union, *European Economic Integration and Monetary Unification*, Document II/520/1/73-E (Brussels: Commission of the European Community, 1973), which contains several background papers by specialists.
3. *Report to the Council and Commission on the Realization by Stages of Economic and Monetary Union in the European Community*, Werner Report (Brussels: Commission of the European Community, 1970), hereafter cited as the Werner Report.
4. *Ibid.*
5. For a wide-ranging discussion of problems of demand management, see Sir Alec Cairncross, *Essays in Economic Management* (London: Allen & Unwin, 1971).
6. Supplement to Werner Report, *op. cit.*, p. 44.
7. See *inter alia*: C. C. von Weizsäcker, 'Ein Vorschlag zur Währungsunion', in Hubertus Müller-Groeling, *Beiträge und Stellungnamen zu Problemen der Währungspolitik*, Kieler Diskussionsbeiträge 10 (Kiel: Institut für Weltwirtschaft, 1971); Leon Lambert, 'Une monnaie européenne tout de suit', *Le Monde*, Paris, 19 December 1971; Norbert Walter, 'Europäische Währungsintegration: Kartellösung versus Eurowährung', *Die Weltwirtschaft*, Kiel, No. 1, 1972; Giovanni Magnifico and John Williamson, *European Monetary Integration* (London: Federal Trust for Education and Research, 1972); F. Boyer de la Giroday, *Intégration Monétaire Régionale*, Série 10B (Strasbourg: Société Universitaire Européenne de Recherches Financières, 1972); François Elsassr, 'Pour une union monétaire européenne des 1973', *Chroniques d'Actualitiés*, Paris, February 1972; Robert A. Mundell, 'A Plan for a European Currency', in Harry G. Johnson and Alexander Swoboda (eds.), *The Economics of Common Currencies* (London: Allen & Unwin, 1972); Bela Balassa, 'Monetary Integration in the European Common Market', in Swoboda (ed.), *Europe and the Evolution of International Monetary System* (Leyden: Sijthoff, 1973); Study Group on Economic and Monetary Union, *European Economic Integration and Monetary Unification*, Document II/520/1/73-E (Brussels: Commission of the European Community, 1973); and Dieter Biehl, Fritz Franzmeyer and Hans-Eckart Scharrer, *Gutachten zur Übergangs-*

phase der Wirtschafts- und Währungsunion (Bonn: Bildungswerk Europäische Politik, 1973).

8. In the proposals by Mundell, *op. cit.*, by Richard N. Cooper, 'Monetary Unification in Europe: When and How', *Morgan Guaranty Survey*, New York, May 1972, by Magnifico and Williamson, *op. cit.*, and by Elsasser, *op. cit.*, the europa is seen as a European pivotal currency. In order to limit fluctuations between the member currencies, national central banks would have to intervene *vis-à-vis* the europa only, while the Europa Bank could steer the exchange rate of the europa *vis-à-vis* non-member currencies, notably the dollar.

In the papers by James E. Meade in *European Economic Integration and Monetary Unification, op. cit.*, a solution is favoured whereby the europa would be defined as the equivalent of a sum of fixed amounts (a bag) of the national currencies of the European Community.

Weizsäcker, *op. cit.*, and others want to provide the europa with a purchasing power guarantee.

9. Werner Report, *op. cit.*

10. *Ibid.*

11. The issues in fiscal integration are surveyed in the papers by Douglas Dosser in *European Economic Integration and Monetary Unification, op. cit.*, pp. 57-106. Also see Richard A. Musgrave, 'Approaches to a Fiscal Theory of Political Federation', in National Bureau of Economic Research, *Public Finance: Needs, Sources and Utilization* (Princeton: Princeton University Press, 1961).

3 Community Role in Regional Policy

Wide regional differences in economic opportunities and performance have long existed between different parts of Western Europe. They exist also within the individual countries of the European Community and have persisted over many years in spite of strenuous efforts to assist the more backward regions and depressed areas.

Overcoming regional imbalances is crucial in creating conditions in the European Community that are conducive to progress towards eventual monetary union. For in a monetary union there will be inter-regional adjustment problems to resolve. Much can be done before monetary union to minimize those problems and thus smooth the process of economic integration.

The magnitude of regional disparities — in economic terms — can be expressed in various ways. Such differences can be conceived in terms of income per head or in terms of levels of productivity or rates of growth in productivity. Or they may focus on industrial agglomeration or on the growing concentration of population in particular areas. Or the contrast may be in employment opportunities or regional unemployment. Finally, emphasis may be put on the physical apparatus and infrastructure, such as the transport system, educational arrangements, housing, et cetera. While the various measures of regional backwardness are inter-related, they have a somewhat different significance from the point of view of policy implications.[1]

REASONS FOR REGIONAL POLICIES

An approximate measure of regional disparity is income per head. This brings out the extent of regional differences within the European Community.[2] In 1970, for example, the *per capita* income of the most affluent regions of what is now the enlarged Community was about five times as great as average income in the poorest regions. Indeed, income per head in the poorest regions was little, if at all, higher than in some of the less developed countries of Latin America.

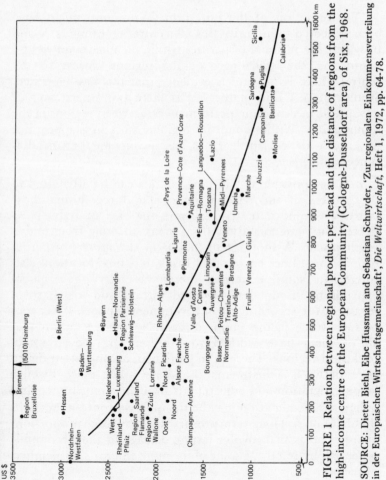

FIGURE 1 Relation between regional product per head and the distance of regions from the high-income centre of the European Community (Cologne-Dusseldorf area) of Six, 1968.

SOURCE: Dieter Biehl, Eibe Hussman and Sebastian Schnyder, 'Zur regionalen Einkommensverteilung in der Europäischen Wirtschaftsgemeinschaft', *Die Weltwirtschaft*, Heft 1, 1972, pp. 64-78.

Income per head appears to fall steadily the further away a region is from the European Community's industrial centre in the lower Rhine valley,[3] as is shown in Figure 1. There is also evidence of a kind of curved development axis running down from a high point near the mouth of the Rhine in one direction to London and Coventry and in the other along the valley of the Rhine and over the Alps to Milan. The area lying along this axis covers about one-quarter of the surface area of the Community and contributes almost one-half to its total product. (The economic ranking of the regions of the enlarged Community is shown in Table 2.)

The formation of the European Community might have been expected to intensify this concentration of industry and to widen the regional disparities within member countries by reinforcing the advantages of the regions closest to the centre. There is not much evidence that this has happened. Studies suggest that in the 1960s there was a narrowing of the spread in economic performances between regions in the Community.[4] Within countries regional variations appear not to have widened, at least as far as income per head is concerned.

It is not possible to say how far this can be attributed to the success of the regional policies in force during those years. To some extent, notably in the case of Italy, it reflected outward migration from areas suffering from underemployment. A shortage of labour in the more prosperous regions sometimes encouraged firms to choose locations elsewhere. In some countries there was heavy government expenditure in the less favoured regions and a variety of measures for according them government support. We cannot be sure which factors counted most. Nor can we be sure that all of them have worked to the long-term advantage of backward regions. There is, in particular, an important difference between adjustments that have taken place through labour migration and adjustments brought about by regional policy. While migration may be the only way out for locations that have no real long-term prospects, it may reach proportions in other areas that involve lasting damage to their economic potential, by removing some of the more enterprising members of society.

TABLE 2
An economic ranking of the regions of the European Community of Nine[a]

Regions	Rating	Regions	Rating
1 Region Parisienne (F) . .	26	43 Utrecht (N)	198
2 East Midlands (UK) . .	51	44 Oberfranken (G)	203
3 Nord-Württemberg (G) .	59	45 Unterfranken (G)	203
4 Darmstadt-Wiesbaden (G) .	72	46 Zuid-Holland (N)	206
5 Nord Baden (G)	72	47 Bourgogne (F)	207
6 Bremen (G)	88	48 Midi-Pyrénées (F)	207
7 Brabant (B)	89	49 Champagne-Ardenne (F) . .	208
8 Berlin (West) (G) . . .	89	50 Lorraine (F)	210
9 Rhône-Alpes (F) . . .	89	51 Auvergne (F)	210
10 Sjaelland and other islands to the east of the Grande Belt (D)	96	52 Braunschweig (G)	210
		53 Nord (F)	211
11 Hamburg (G)	96	54 Yorkshire-Humberside (UK) .	212
12 Düsseldorf (G)	102	55 Koblenz-Montabaur (G) . .	214
13 Mittelfranken (G) . . .	104	56 Liguria (I)	216
14 Luxembourg (L) . . .	105	57 Valle d'Aosta (I)	217
15 Köln (G)	110	58 Flandre Occ./West Vlaand. (B)	220
16 Oberbayern (G) . . .	117	
17 Süd-Wurttenberg (G) . .	120	59 Saarland (G)	221
18 Provence-Côte d'Azur-Corse (F)	128	60 Flandre Or./Oost Vlaand. (B)	225
		61 Noord-Brabant (N) . . .	227
19 Lombardia (I)	130	62 Pays de la Loire (F) . . .	231
20 Haute Normandie (F) . .	130	63 Fyn (D)	231
21 Hannover (G)	132	64 Languedoc-Roussillon (F) .	232
22 Süd-Baden (G)	134	65 South West (UK)	236
23 Detmold (G)	136	66 Oldenburg (G)	242
24 Schwaben (G)	143	67 Gelderland (N)	243
25 Rheinhessen-Pfalz (G) . .	147	68 Münster (G)	245
26 Alsace (F)	150	69 Emilia (I)	251
27 West Midlands (UK) . .	152	70 Limbourg/Limburg (B) . .	252
28 Picardie (F)	155	71 Oberpfalz (G)	253
29 Anvers/Antwerpen (B) .	161	72 Limousin (F)	254
30 Lüneburg (G)	166	73 North (UK)	256
31 Franche-Comté (F) .	171	74 Basse Normandie (F) . .	256
32 Aquitaine (F)	171	75 Namur/Namen (B) . . .	257
33 Aachen (G)	172	76 Hildesheim (G)	262
34 South East-East Anglia (UK)	172	77 Scotland (UK)	263
35 Piemonte (I)	173	78 Jylland (D)	265
36 Noord-Holland (N) . . .	175	79 Toscana (I)	267
37 Centre (F)	177	80 Hainaut-Henegouwen (B) .	267
38 Arnsberg (G)	180	81 Lazio (I)	269
39 Liège/Luik (B)	183	82 East (IR)	271
40 Schleswig-Holstein (G) . .	188	83 Osnabruck (G)	275
41 Kassel (G)	189	84 Wales (UK)	283
42 North West (UK) . . .	197	85 Limburg (N)	286
		86 Poitou-Charentes (F) . .	289

Continued

Regions	Rating	Regions	Rating
87 Bretagne (F)	295	103 Umbria (I)	376
88 Drenthe (N)	298	104 North East (IR) . . .	387
89 Overijssel (N) . . .	298	105 South West (IR) . . .	394
90 Luxembourg/Luxemburg		106 Molise (I)	405
(L)	302	107 North West (IR) . . .	418
91 Stade (G)	303	108 Mid West (IR)	420
92 Niederbayern (G) . .	307	109 West (IR)	424
93 Zeeland (N)	309	110 Midland (IR)	431
94 Friuli-V. Giulia (I) . .	312	111 Donegal (IR)	431
95 Groningen (N) . . .	320	112 Campania (I)	431
96 Aurich (G)	326	113 Sardegna (I)	433
97 Marche (I)	343	114 South East (IR) . . .	437
98 Veneto (I)	350	115 Abruzzi (I)	438
99 Trier (G)	356	116 Sicilia (I)	438
100 Northern Ireland (UK) .	369	117 Puglia (I)	442
101 Trentino - A. Adige (I) .	370	118 Basilicata (I)	459
102 Friesland (N)	374	119 Calabria (I)	463

SOURCE: Guglielmo Tagliacarne, 'Le regioni forti e le regioni deboli della Comunita allargata: indicatori socio-economica per la politica regionale della Comunita', *Note Economiche*, Siena, No. 4, 1973.

[a]The ratings represent the sum of the rank orderings of the 119 regions of the enlarged European Community (as defined by the Commission) according to the following four separate indicators: (i) GNP per head in 1970; (ii) ratio of agricultural to total employment; (iii) ratio of employed to total population; and (iv) ratio of net migration to total population over the period 1966-69.

B	=	Belgium	I =	Italy
D	=	Denmark	L =	Luxemburg
F	=	France	N =	Netherlands
G	=	Germany	UK =	United Kingdom
IR	=	Ireland		

Equal rates of growth between regions are quite consistent with a widening gulf in income levels and living standards in absolute terms. In the post-war period the more prosperous areas have tended to use their greater affluence to expand the proportion of their resources devoted to services. They have also tended to run down the proportion of their working population engaged in agriculture — with advantage to the rate of income per head. These sectoral shifts have been accompanied by expansion in manufacturing employment and output and a greater concentration of economic activity in the more advanced regions. The growth in productivity and the sectoral shifts accompanying it were combined with a third element in the situation, namely migration of labour from the periphery to the centre.

Migration, which is at least as significant a feature of the regional problem as differences in income per head, has been on a vast scale. In Italy, for example, the loss to other countries in the 1960s of over half a million emigrants, mostly of working age, is only part of the story; during the same period migration from the agricultural south of the country to the industrial north was three times as large. In Britain, France and parts of Belgium an internal drain towards expanding industrial centres has been in progress — clearly far less important, both in absolute and relative terms, when compared with what happened in Italy. To some extent this drain was out of rural areas, but to a considerable extent it was out of older industrial areas. On the other hand, the expanding industrial centre of Western Europe, especially but by no means only in Germany, has sucked in an enormous number of migrants from other regions and other countries.

Migration of labour is a normal feature of rapid development and was on an even greater scale in the second half of the nineteenth century. But movements in the labour force pose acute social problems in both the areas losing and the areas gaining population. Economists have long insisted on the cumulative and self-reinforcing effects of heavy outward migration on the long-term prospects of a region and the difficulty of restoring balance or resuming growth under such conditions. They are now increasingly aware of the social costs and environmental damage that go with a further concentration of economic activity and population in the central regions of Western Europe. On both grounds it is highly desirable to keep the volume of migration within limits and this should be one of the principal purposes of regional policy.

Unemployment is a further reason for embarking on policies to improve regional balance. Even when differences in living standards are relatively small and the scale of migration is tolerable, employment opportunities vary from region to region, and this is reflected in unemployment figures. It has been shown that these differences increase in the sixty-one regions of the original member countries of the Community the greater their distance from the Rhine-Ruhr area.[5] Similarly in Britain unemployment since World War II has been higher the greater the distance from Birmingham and London. The percentages in each region have maintained a fairly stable pattern throughout: unemployment in Scotland, for example, has remained about twice as high as unemployment in the rest of the United Kingdom with some oscillation around this ratio.[6] The flow of migration reflects these differences in employment levels and prospects quite as much as differences in earnings.

The uneven pressure of demand from region to region, reflecting weaknesses in the economic structure of which the unemployment figures are a symptom, can be an important constraint on short-term economic management. Governments may be moved by the high level of unemployment in a few regions to persist in expansionary policies that overheat the rest of the economy. The fresh bout of inflation which results can then bring only temporary relief to the regions where unemployment is relatively high. In other words, demand management is no substitute for a regional policy that comes to grips with the causes of backwardness, namely the conditions of regional supply. On the other hand, a successful regional policy would bring into play the under-utilized potential of backward regions, enlarging employment and output in these regions without the risk of over-heating.

There are thus strong arguments, based on economic benefit to the country as a whole, in favour of measures aimed at narrowing regional differences in economic activity and achieving a better regional balance. Without such measures there may be a waste of man-power through unemployment or under-employment with all the human problems and social unrest that go with them. There may be migration on a scale which is not desirable from the point of view either of the region from which movement takes place or of the regions to which it is directed. In addition the less prosperous regions may stand in need of assistance because they are often less capable of adjusting to a new economic situation even when changed economic circumstances bring fresh opportunities as well as fresh burdens.

These considerations underlie national regional policies and should also underlie regional policy at the Community level. It is, however, more difficult to devise effective measures than to explain the need for them. For the past. generation countries have been experimenting with a wide variety of measures, but experience with some of the more hopeful of them has not been very fully studied so that it is not possible to know with any confidence which of them has been most effective and successful. What is clear though is that, on the one hand, there is no simple and inexpensive cure for regional problems and, on the other, there are ways in which government action can have a quite perceptible influence on the regional pattern of economic activity.

EFFECTIVENESS OF REGIONAL MEASURES

Some countries have made use of negative measures aimed at preventing firms from settling or expanding in advanced regions. Most countries have preferred to rely exclusively on positive measures aimed at attracting firms to backward regions. The principal positive instruments of policy have been various forms of public assistance to private enterprise — grants, loans and preferential tax treatment — and the provision of public finance for the development of the regional infra-structure — the construction of roads, schools, houses, power stations and so on.

Regional policy would be a simple affair if it was easy to divert economic activity from one region to another by subsidies, grants or other facilities.[7] But in practice financial incentives operate slowly and relatively feebly. Industry tends to expand *in situ* and only contemplates a change of location with great reluctance. Changes are easier to bring about if expansion takes the form of branch factories that may be relatively foot-loose and can take advantage of government offers of assistance. New branch factories, how-ever, do not form a high proportion, in terms of the employ-ment they offer, of current economic activity. To rely on influencing their location is inevitably to operate incrementally on the distribution of industry and to effect changes of any size in the existing pattern only over a period of decades, rather than years. True enough, manufacturing employment in industrialized countries is normally well under half of the total; and other forms of activity are more difficult to influence directly, since they tend as service occupations to be tied more firmly to the location of existing industry.

Post-war experience, however, does bear out the common-sense conclusion that in the long run governments can exert a considerable influence over industrial location and that there is also scope for government action on the location of various non-industrial employments, such as office work, research activities, higher education, tourism, et cetera. To achieve results it is necessary to show perseverance over a long period with policies that are bound to be costly and may be slow to show results. The most common mistakes are to underestimate the size of the problems and to look for swift solutions. Too often the policies adopted — in the United Kingdom for example — are changed at short intervals, abandoned and then re-introduced. Lacking the necessary comprehensiveness and consistency, they are consequently distrusted by the business community whose response it is hoped to influence. This is not to deny that regional policies must be adjusted in relation to the progress or lack of progress achieved and to changing conditions in the rest of the country and in the wider international context.

There can, of course, be no question of promoting development in every laggard area and stifling development wherever it is obviously being directed by market forces. That would be absurd. But it is possible to detect the more promising centres of development in the backward regions, help to remedy their deficiencies and, in addition, reinforce what success they enjoy in attracting new industry or in generating additional activity from their own resources.[8] It is not as if some natural law assured the more advanced regions of a lasting locational advantage and no area that was late in starting ever caught up with the leaders and left them behind. This is not the lesson of history if we may judge from the experience of countries like Britain which fell behind on the one hand and Japan which rose fast on the other.

COMMUNITY STATE OF PLAY

What, then, is the present state of play within the European Community with respect to overcoming regional imbalances?

Ministers have been concentrating on the size of the common regional fund and the incidence of payments into and out of it without much discussion of the principles put forward by the Commission for the shaping of regional policy. Some of them seem to wish to compound the errors of agricultural policy by compensating errors of regional policy provided the effect is to offset payments for one purpose by payments in the reverse direction for the other. But there is no obvious reason why countries that are net importers of food should coincide with those suffering most severely from regional problems; or, for that matter, why the principle of *juste retour* should govern the financial arrangements of the Community.

In our view, however, it shows a right instinct on the part of Ministers that they associate regional policy with agricultural policy.[9] The Agricultural Guidance and Guarantee Fund should be merged with the Social Fund and the Fund for Regional Development. For aid to agriculture is essentially a matter of regional and social policy and it would be a great advance if agricultural policy came to be regarded as a form of regional policy. Agricultural communities in backward areas are the typical case in terms of which regional policy is usually conceived; and there seems no good reason for letting assistance to such communities take the form of price-support policies that are not very effective as instruments of regional policy.

The Commission's proposals for regional policy seem unduly negative. They envisage three tasks: the coordination of national policy measures; the development of criteria for the allocation of aid; and the prevention of escalations of aid for individual regions where this would distort competition. The first of these presupposes some view of regional development over the Community as a whole, at least in broad outline; and this is true also of the second. But the Commission, in elaborating the various criteria governing aid, lays emphasis exclusively on what are primarily symptoms such as

unemployment, outward migration and income per head
rather than on the long-term prospects and development
potential of the regions. What the Community requires are
acceptable guide-lines for deciding which areas can hope to
expand on the basis of aid and which should be given support
only as a means of meeting the social cost of adjustment to a
limited development ceiling. In the absence of these guide-
lines the Community's regional policy is in danger of becoming an exercise in chronic subsidization without bringing
about much sustainable growth. There is also a danger, as the
European Parliament's regional policy and transport committee has rightly emphasized, that aid will be dispersed on
small projects throughout the Community instead of being
concentrated on particular areas that would repay assistance.

The Commission's proposals for the use of regional aid
recognize the key role of investment in infrastructure but
give little clue to the basis on which major projects are to be
assessed. They rely heavily on the use of capital subsidies.
But for areas suffering from unemployment or under-employment this seems a rather inefficient policy. Such subsidies, as
experience in Italy and Britain has shown, tend to attract
capital-intensive industries without developing the more
labour-intensive activities appropriate to the circumstances
and more capable of using linkages with basic industries.
There is also a risk that regional aid from the Commission
might be used to support industrial activities that were out of
keeping with comparative advantage. This would create a
serious non-tariff distortion particularly harmful to the
interests of less developed countries.

The proposal to raise contributions to the fund by taxing
congested areas has been silently withdrawn because of
opposition from countries like Germany that have most need
to limit congestion. Instead, a characteristically European
minimum proposal has been adopted to begin work on the
harmonization of existing measures for the discouragement
of investment in areas of congestion. Similarly it would seem
illusory for member countries to renew the proposal to create
industrial employment in agricultural priority areas through
the use of part of the Agricultural Guidance and Guarantee
Fund when the Guarantee Section was in deficit in 1973.

Until the regional policy of the European Community

takes final shape it would be premature to pass judgment on it. But the outlook is not very bright:

(a) There is no intention to make serious efforts to examine the economic policies and institutional arrangements of the member countries as well as those of the Community in order to find out whether they contain avoidable or reducible obstacles to regional balance

(b) There is no intention to take measures in common to discourage tendencies to agglomeration that result from a divergence between private and social costs and benefits

(c) And there is no clear view of the principles that should govern the spatial development of economic activity within the Community or of the forms of aid that are in the common interest.

Accordingly, it needs to be asked: what should be the role of the European Community in regional development? And what is the appropriate division of labour between the Community and member governments?[10]

FUNCTION OF THE COMMUNITY

From many points of view the major responsibility for regional development is bound to remain with national and provincial governments. They have the strongest motives for using their own resources as fully as possible and for assisting the areas that have fallen behind the rest of the country. But the responsibility cannot be exclusively national and provincial.

The need for Community action arises in part because the formation of the Community, and the adoption of policies aimed at promoting economic integration, was bound to have unequal effects on different regions.[11] Some regions gain substantially from improved market opportunities through trade liberalization. On the other hand, other regions may gain little or even lose because of the opening of local markets to more intense competition. Regions cannot count on the kind of reciprocal advantage from free trade that national economies enjoy thanks to their ability to adjust, if necessary, the exchange rate of their currency. A common policy is necessary in order to deal with the regional impact of economic integration and to help individual regions to make the structural adjustments which it induces or accelerates. Solidarity in sharing the burdens of integration which, like the benefits, are unequally distributed is a condition for the survival of the Community. This must include a continuous scrutiny of the regional policies adopted in member countries in order to assess their impact on the progress of backward regions in other member countries — particularly on those which have to overcome the greatest obstacles to catch up with the rest of the Community.

A further reason applies to the less prosperous members of the European Community who lack the necessary resources to deal adequately with their regional problems. The backward regions in these countries are often strongholds of separatist movements; and it is in the common interest of the Community as a whole to discourage the forces of disintegration by offering additional help for the development of such regions.

But there is in fact no need to look beyond the commandments of justice in making a case for Community assistance to backward regions. Such assistance can provide them with the means to achieve a level of economic performance more in keeping with that of the rest of the Community by bringing into use resources hitherto under-utilized. At the same time, it can help to preserve the cultural life of the Community, by putting the economy of backward regions on a more secure footing. Community assistance can also restrain an exodus of population that could mean a loss of cultural identity on the one hand and an undesirable congestion in major agglomerations on the other. If successful, it can act, too, as a brake on inflation because it can provide the increase in productivity in backward areas that is necessary to match claims for money incomes which are largely based on the productivity of the more prosperous regions. There are ample grounds, therefore, for looking to the European Community for assistance to regions faced with awkward problems of adjustment or with loss of economic potential because of economic integration.

STRATEGIES FOR REGIONAL DEVELOPMENT

The aim of regional policy is to bring about more even economic development within the European Community and within each member country. The policy has to be powerful enough to achieve this purpose. But it should not be carried too far. In a fully employed economy, resources put at the disposal of backward regions are at the expense of other parts of the country. Although they may be glad of some brake on their expansion — since it involves a continuous inflow of manpower and population from other regions — it is important that the economic momentum and potential of the advanced regions should not suffer. Fundamentally what is required is that a higher proportion of available man-power should find employment in the backward regions in jobs that are competitive and continuing. Aids to regional development, whether by national governments or by the Community, should be directed towards creating and maintaining such jobs in the most laggard areas.

In order to bring this about, there are three complementary courses of policy that can be pursued. National governments acting independently or with the active support of the Community may:

(a) keep under review their policies with a view to changing any arrangements that might have undesirable effects on regional balances;[12]

(b) try to make market forces operate more strongly in favour of desired locations; and

(c) take powers to intervene directly by controlling industrial location and reinforce the effects by large-scale public or government-directed investments in particular areas.

Let us consider each of these courses in turn.

Reducing Obstacles to Regional Balance

In some member countries (in Germany for instance) the fiscal system operates in favour of the more prosperous areas by attributing tax revenues to the home-base of the tax-payer rather than to the geographical source of the taxable receipts.

Insofar as public funds are then spent where the taxes are collected, a bias is introduced in favour of the richer areas which act as financial centres. These last become still more attractive in consequence of this expenditure unless steps are taken to channel public revenues from rich to poor areas.

Central funds are not necessarily allocated for public investment on the basis of needs for regional development. There may, for example, be administrative limitations which, for lack of the necessary expertise, prevent the more backward regions from submitting carefully prepared plans. At the political level, concentrations of electors in the industrial areas have been able to draw the special attention of governments to their problems, among them bottlenecks in transport and social infrastructure which make heavy demands on public investment and are forever arising as urban development proceeds. The same kind of distortion in favour of existing urban centres may result from the financing of their deficits on transport services out of the budget of a higher fiscal authority. This, too, means that the larger industrial centres are being subsidized by the rest of the country. The less densely populated areas and medium-sized urban centres — unless they happen to include 'marginal' constituencies — tend to be the losers in the contest for public funds and are thus deprived of the means to improve their own attractions as industrial locations. Even if marginal constituencies manage to secure funds, this does not necessarily make things any better, for their demands may not be justified by their development potential. Furthermore, the political power of such regions can be easily misused to support existing but declining industries, thereby delaying necessary structural changes.

Considerations of this kind, and the consequent need to aim at improving efficiency in the regional allocation of public funds, suggest the need for continuous parliamentary scrutiny. But such a scrutiny promises to be efficient only if all regions can compete for the funds on an equal footing within the legislature. We accordingly propose, at community level, the establishment of a separate house in the European Parliament to represent regional interests. Such a Chamber of Regions might be instituted on a basis similar to the Senate in the United States.

Incentives to Decentralize

There is no easy way of charging to produce the full economic cost to the community of expansion in an already congested area. Nor is there even any way of assessing what that cost should be. Similarly there is no easy way of assessing the gain derived by the community from location in an area which is still in process of development and lacking the complementary economic and social activities that would make it attractive without further inducements. All that can be done is to impose financial penalties or offer financial incentives on a rough-and-ready calculation of costs and benefits.

More powerful incentives could be provided through differential investment grants or allowances that gave preferential tax treatment to productive investment in laggard regions. This could be done through tax credits or actual subsidies. Depreciation provisions could be relaxed so as to allow businesses in the favoured regions larger or more elastic allowances against tax liabilities: for example, businesses in these regions might be allowed to enjoy free depreciation — that is, the right to depreciate their assets for tax purposes at whatever rate they chose.

Experience suggests that provisions of this kind tend to attract the more capital-intensive investments which stand to gain most from investment incentives. These may — as with aluminium smelters, petro-chemical plants and so on — create comparatively few jobs in the area where the investment is made and so may contribute disappointingly little to the utilization of surplus man-power. It may therefore be helpful, in addition to financial incentives, for the fiscal system to be brought to bear in another way, by taxing employment more heavily in some areas and less heavily in others.[13] The regional employment premium in the United Kingdom operates on this principle as a subsidy on employment in some parts of the country financed by payments levied on employment in other regions.

Yet another way of affecting the regional employment pattern is by making grants to meet the costs and risks of location in a new area: grants towards the training of labour or to cover losses over the first year or two of operation

while workers and management settle in and master the
initial teething troubles. For small businesses without access
to the capital market, loans may also be important in enabling them to shoulder the risks of expansion. Once it is
accepted that financial incentives and disincentives are
necessary there is a wide range of measures that governments
can draw upon.

The revenue needed to encourage decentralized economic
growth may, for example, be raised through the tax on land
values or increases in land values which has already been
mentioned.[14] It would be possible later to convert the tax to
a Community tax in order to siphon off some of the advantages accruing to the beneficiaries of integration for the
benefit of parts of the Community not sharing in those
advantages.

Direct Intervention

In the past, governments have not limited themselves to
incentives to regional development, but have also made use of
administrative measures and compulsions. They have sought,
for example, to control location in particular areas, except
under licence. Sometimes this control has been exercised
through the issue of industrial development certificates;
sometimes it has meant directing foreign investment to
specific locations or locations selected within stated limitations. More commonly, governments have sought to influence
major investment decisions by advance planning of industrial
facilities: by providing and financing industrial estates; by
investment in public transport systems, docks, housing and
other forms of infrastructure; by contributing to the finance
of major projects that might bring in their train ancillary
investments by suppliers of components or materials or by
users of the finished product.

In a mixed economy, development is governed by the
interaction of public and private investment decisions, not by
either alone. And even within the private sector, investment
decisions are often complementary in the sense that the
value, private or social, of any given investment is dependent
on the creation or pre-existence of an entire industrial environment through simultaneous or prior investment in other

directions. Hence the active participation of central, regional and local governments may be indispensable to successful regional development.

INTER-RELATIONSHIP WITH OTHER POLICIES

One of the main tasks at Community level is to ensure that regional policies are consistent with other policies and vice versa. In respect of competition policy within the Common Market the aim should be to make sure that regional measures at national level take a form that does not conflict with the objective of free trade with other Community members.

Difficult as it may be to determine in practice, a distinction should be drawn between

    (a) measures which discriminate in favour of *specific* economic activities in a backward region as compared with the rest of the Community and

    (b) measures which are directed at raising competitiveness at large in a backward region and thus do not distort competition.

Granting a production subsidy to one manufacturer as opposed to another would be an example of the first kind of measure. On the other hand, exemplifying the second kind, general assistance to a region in the form, say, of infrastructure investment would not afford special advantages to any specific industries.

The creation of free trade conditions in the European Community may in itself serve to accentuate regional problems of imbalance. As argued earlier, backward regions are often less able to adjust to a new economic situation, thus rendering all the more important the task of ensuring that regional policy measures do not frustrate the objectives of trade liberalization.[15]

Similar arguments have to be born in mind in considering international economic policy and the European Community's place in an integrating world economy. For many instruments of regional policy fall within the definition of non-tariff distortions of international competition which have become a focal point of multilateral discussions on the further liberalization of international trade. But there is another aspect of regional policy which has a bearing on international trade. Most backward regions are often in direct competition with imports from outside the Community — sometimes from less developed countries. A liberal commercial policy, however much in the general interest, may then run counter to the immediate interests of the least prosperous regions, unless it is accompanied by appropriate adjustment assistance.

To take another example of the inter-relationship of regional policy with other policies,[16] the integration of capital markets may cause funds to flow towards the major centres in the European Community, thus denuding some of the less advanced regions of funds that would otherwise contribute to their own development. Under those conditions the European Investment Bank, or other agencies of the Community, could assist regions where development is held back by insufficient finance.

The European Community has a further involvement in regional policy through the use of the European Social Fund. It is, or should be, part of the purpose of the fund not merely to retrain workers in areas in the course of industrial change, but also to train workers living in regions where there is a deficiency of employment opportunities. Such training, financed by Community funds, might be provided by new firms entering a backward area which are unable to find an adequate number of workers with the necessary industrial experience.

Social policies need to be extended to agricultural regions to address more directly the social problems associated with low incomes at present indirectly addressed through measures to support farm prices.[17] The work of economists has shown that the distribution of income is related fundamentally to the distribution of income-producing assets and skills. Until governments provide greater educational opportunities for farming communities, to equip them for occupations outside agriculture, the problems of rural poverty will persist irrespective of government interventions in the market place.[18]

The European Community would have still wider responsibilities for regional development if, as the common budget developed, it accepted as one of its functions a narrowing of

differences in income levels. While differences from country
to country in social security and other benefits would continue, and would reflect the corresponding differences in
average earnings, some effort to set minimum standards for
the Community as a whole would give rise to substantial
transfers to the poorest regions.

A more immediate task is the mobilization of finance by
way of loans or grants for projects in areas judged to be
capable of more rapid development. Such finance could not
displace but would supplement national efforts with the same
purpose. It would inevitably be selective and the criteria of
selection would not be easy to establish.

In the process of deciding what projects to back, the
European Community would soon find itself trying to do
what has so far largely defeated national governments: working out a comprehensive locational strategy based on a view of
the future economic development of the community as a
whole. It would seem to us more productive to start from
national policy measures, without taking for granted that
they were well-conceived, and see what elements in these
measures merited support and what should be actively dis-
couraged. The idea would be for governments to submit their
regional policies for review at regular intervals, explaining the
principles on which they were based, and indicating the
elements in their plans to which they attached particular
importance. Community aid might then be given either towards the implementation of national or provincial plans as a
whole or towards the financing of specific projects drawn
from them.

In order to evaluate national and provincial development
plans it is necessary to assess the development prospects of
the regions in question. If attention is confined to their
present difficulties, the distribution of funds is liable to be
settled exclusively by political haggling. First, it is necessary
to identify, according to a consistent set of criteria, the major
problem areas. The criteria might include measurements of
regional disparity (such as income per head), unemployment
and migration; and these are the criteria suggested by the
Commission. But additional longer-term criteria have to be
developed which reflect the regional development potential
and enter into national and regional development plans. Only

a combination of both types of criteria will prevent funds from being distributed between regions solely for short-run satisfaction and not to secure a lasting prosperity. Moreover, it is important that regions be so defined as to be of a comparable size, otherwise the criteria for assessing regions on a comparable basis will lose their significance. In addition, reasonable threshold values for each indicator are needed, in order to prevent excessive transfer burdens on those regions providing aid.

The procedure we suggest would have the advantage that regional policies would be looked at alongside one another. Inconsistencies between them would be brought to the surface and so would the use of policy measures under the guise of regional policy that were at variance with the obligations assumed towards one another or towards third countries by the members of the European Community. So long as member countries respected these obligations, however, there would be no need for the Community to lay down in detail what form regional policy should take.

NEED FOR DECENTRALIZATION

Yet the European Community, in its approach to national policy measures, could hardly expect to exert a fruitful influence on the efforts of member countries without a clear conception of the broad aims of regional policy. In our view the overriding need is greater decentralization: a more even spread of economic activity between regions on social as well as economic grounds. In order to achieve this decentralization and stem the flow of population to the major industrial centres, we believe that it is necessary to set to work deliberately to create new centres of attraction in carefully chosen locations.

The creation of the Common Market gave a powerful impulse to industrial growth in existing centres of industry. By assuring freer play to the market mechanism it encouraged individual producers to build on facilities that were already in existence in the form either of social capital in established urban centres or of complementary industrial capital in the hands of potential suppliers and purchasers. There is always a strong incentive to site new production where the links with other industries are ready made and the need does not exist to set about creating a whole new network of social facilities from transport and training to houses and hospitals. The private industrialist, responding only to market forces, feels this incentive most powerfully because he can escape most or all of the social costs that are occasioned by his decision to expand. So long as he can attract the extra man-power he needs, he has little reason to incur heavier capital costs by moving to a new location where he may have to go it alone.

The experience of the European Community has been that the necessary labour force usually *can* be attracted. Migrant workers inside and outside the Community have shown themselves willing in enormous numbers to make the sacrifices required to earn the higher incomes they could never earn in their home regions. But in the process there have come into existence the *bidonvilles* in and around the great industrial cities of Western Europe where a defenceless and vulnerable new proletariat finds a temporary home.

The resulting social problems are such that a great effort must be made to avoid them, not least by an adequate regional policy that fosters decentralization. How is it to be done?

It is clear that, apart from some of the older industrial centres in course of structural change, regional disequilibria are more acute when the network of urban centres is under-developed. A prime requirement, therefore, is an infrastructure of public amenities, schools, hospitals, shopping facilities et cetera. A second requirement — but not sufficient unless the first is met — is adequate transport facilities: full use must be made of the new ways of reducing the drawbacks of distance by creating a Community-wide network of the different modes of transport and communication. Equally important, but also insufficient by itself, is the requirement that the new industries introduced should be complementary so as to make possible the economies that result from the linking of industrial processes.

The building up of new centres as 'growth points' from which expansionary impulses radiate to the surrounding area is an attractive but politically explosive idea. It implies a concentration of regional measures in favour of the centres showing most promise of achieving self-sustained growth. Conversely, it means refusing aid to other areas that lack such promise or confining support for those areas to grants towards moving or commuting to more favoured areas. We do not overlook the fact that the larger backward regions of the Community include more than a few urban centres of cultural and social importance. Any proper regional policy must aim at revitalizing such towns and cities by bringing modern industry to them and preventing their decay through intra-regional migration which is as unacceptable as emigration to other regions. With this proviso, we think that, in spite of the deliberate discrimination between areas and the political opposition likely to result, a strategy of growth points should be intensively pursued by the Community.

Some of the backward areas of the European Community could be selected as regions on which to concentrate efforts to decentralize industrial expansion. Such regions might include, for example, border regions that have been neglected in the past because of the division of Western Europe into nation states as well as the regions which now find themselves even more at the periphery because of European integration. There would be advantages also in inducing European research institutes or other research organizations to locate themselves in one of these regions.

If the experiment were successful it could be extended to other areas of policy. In agriculture, for example, a choice might be made of the areas likely to have long-term development prospects in order to see how they could be fitted into a common framework of policy. The same might be done for tourism, nature reserves and parks, recreation and so on.

In this way a basis could be laid for the coordination of national and Community policy. It is increasingly difficult to undertake regional development in one country in isolation from regional development in others because regions are interdependent even when separated by national boundaries. There is both a danger of competitive offers of aid without compensating advantages and of wasteful duplication of costly fixed investment in infrastructure in competing regions.

The conclusions and recommendations of the group have been summarized in the section below.

CONCLUSIONS AND RECOMMENDATIONS

1. Large regional differences in economic opportunities and performance have persisted for many years, but at least when measured in terms of income per head they would not appear to have widened since the formation of the Community.

2. One important reason for this is the large-scale migration that has been taking place from the less favoured to the richer regions.

3. It is undesirable to rely so heavily on migration as the likely improvement in the statistical measure of income per head may conceal a progressive weakening of the economic structure of the backward regions.

4. For these and other reasons there are strong arguments in favour of measures aimed at achieving a better regional balance within member countries.

5. The prime responsibility for devising regional policies must rest with national governments.

6. While no common regional policy can be an effective substitute for action by national governments, the European Community also has an interest in ensuring that national governments take action to bring about a better regional balance.

7. Aid to regional development by the European Community should in principle be directed to creating and maintaining competitive jobs in the most laggard regions.

8. In order to redress the political balance between advanced and backward regions in the European Community, and to strengthen the political cohesion of the Community, a Chamber of Regions should be established as part of the European institutions.

9. The Community should be required to submit to the proposed Chamber of Regions, or at any rate to the European Parliament, a regular review of national regional policies. The review should be specifically required to comment on the consistency of these policies, both one with another and with respect to policies in other fields, including their compatibility with international obligations (which should not contradict the objectives of regional development).

10. The review should also aim to facilitate exchange of views and experiences and to provide a guide to the Com-

munity in extending regional aid to particular member countries.

11. The Commission should be asked to report, on the basis of its review, on any of the policies of member countries that increase the incentive to centralize economic activities and run counter to efforts to achieve a better regional balance.

12. Assistance to regions by member governments should not discriminate in favour of specific economic activities.

13. The members of the Community should be invited to introduce a tax on land values or increases in land values with a view to providing the Community with the revenues accruing. This would be intended to provide the Community automatically with funds supplied principally by the richer regions where land values are high and rising fast and hence to reduce the amount of national contributions to the Community budget that are the product of bargaining.

14. In order to allow the social problems of the agricultural regions to be tackled more directly than through price support for farm produce, governments should provide greater educational opportunities for farming communities so as to fit them for other employment.

15. Agricultural policy and regional policy should not be dealt with in isolation from one another. Agricultural policy should be partly a matter of social policy and partly of regional policy rather than something peculiar to agriculture, and the Agricultural Guidance and Guarantee Fund should therefore be merged with Social Fund and the Fund for Regional Development.

16. The European Investment Bank and the European Social Fund should increasingly provide funds for selective projects and measures in the framework of national and regional development plans.

17. The European Community should be allowed to take the initiative in developing a selected number of regions in co-operation with national governments. This would involve support for new areas chosen for their promise as future centres of economic activity.

NOTES AND REFERENCES

1. For a general discussion of the economics of regional policies, see: Bela Balassa, 'Regional Policies and the Environment in the European Common Market', *Weltwirtschaftliches Archiv*, Kiel, Band 109, Heft 3, 1973; A. J. Brown, *The Framework of Regional Economics in the United Kingdom* (Cambridge: Cambridge University Press, for the National Institute of Economic and Social Research, 1972); and Herbert Giersch, 'The Economics of Regional Policy', *The German Economic Review*, Stuttgart, No. 3, 1969, pp. 13-24. Also see Pasquale Saraceno, 'Development Policy in an Over-populated Area: Italy's Experience', in E. A. G. Robinson (ed.), *Backward Areas in Advanced Countries* (London: Macmillan, for the International Economic Association, 1969).

2. See, *inter alia, Report on Regional Problems in the Enlarged Community* (Brussels: Commission of the European Community, 1973).

3. Dieter Biehl, Eibe Hussmann and Sebastian Schnyder, 'Zur regionalen Einkommensverteilung in der Europäischen Wirtschaftsgemeinschaft', *Die Weltwirtschaft*, Kiel, Heft 1, 1972, pp. 64-78.

4. *Ibid.*

5. *Ibid.*

6. The subject is discussed in Thomas Wilson, 'Finance for Regional Development', *Three Banks Review*, Manchester, September 1967.

7. P. Saraceno, 'Obiettivi attuali di una per il Mezzogiorno', in *La Programmazione negli anni '70* (Milan: Etas Kompass, 1970).

8. See, for example, François Perroux, 'Note sur la Notion de "Pole de Croissance" ', *Economie Appliquée*, Paris, No. 3, 1955; *Regional Policy in EFTA: an Examination of the Growth Centre Idea* (Edinburgh: Oliver & Boyd, for the EFTA Secretariat, 1969); and Manfred E. Streit, 'Regionalpolitische Aspekte des Wachstumpolkonzepts', *Jahrbuch für Sozialwissenschaft*, Gottingen, No. 2, Vol. 22, 1971.

9. See the three contributions — German, French and Dutch — to Hermann Priebe *et al., Fields of Conflict in European Farm Policy*, Agricultural Trade Paper No. 3 (London: Trade Policy Research Centre, 1972).

10. The need for the European Community to develop a role in regional development has long been recognized. See Robert Marjolin, 'Rapport Introductif', in *Documents de la Conférence sur les Economies Régionales* (Brussels: EEC Commission, 1961).

For further discussions of the issues, see: Heinz-Michael Stahl, *Regionalpolitische Implikationen einer europäischen Währungsunion* (Tübingen: J. C. B. Mohr, for the Institut für Weltwirtschaft an der Universität Kiel, 1974); Gavin McCrone, 'Regional Policies in the European Communities', in Geoffrey Denton (ed.), *Economic Integration in Europe* (London: Weidenfeld & Nicolson, for the Reading Graduate School of Contemporary European Studies, 1969); and R. M. Bird, 'Regional Policies in the Common Market', in Carl S. Shoup (ed.), *Fiscal Harmonization in Common Markets*, Vol I (New York and London: Columbia University Press, 1967). Also see Pierre Uri,

L'Europe se gaspille (Paris: Hachette Litterature, 1973), pp. 135-45.

In 1965 the Commission prepared a memorandum published as *Regional Policy in the European Community*, Community Topics Document 4 (Brussels EEC Commission, 1965). But the document was not so much a common policy as a survey of the situation. It was based on, among other papers, *Rapport du Groupe d'experts sur la politique régionale dans la CEE* (Brussels: EEC Commission, 1964).

11. See *Memorandum on Regional Policy in the Community* (Brussels: Commission of the European Community, 1969), reprinted in Supplement to the *Bulletin of the European Communities*, Brussels, No. 12, 1969, p. 49 *et. seq.*

12. On this point, see Saraceno, 'Risultati e nuovi obiettivi dell' intervento straordinario', *Informazioni SVIMEZ*, Rome, September 1973.

13. Saraceno, 'Sui criteri di incentivazione degli investimenti industriali nel Mezzogiorno', *Mondo Economico*, Milan, November 1973.

14. Giersch, *op. cit.*

15. Hans Liesner, 'Harmonization Issues under Free Trade', in Harry G. Johnson (ed.), *Trade Strategy for Rich and Poor Nations* (London: Allen & Unwin, for the Trade Policy Research Centre, 1971), pp. 152-55.

16. For the thinking of the Commission of the European Community on the inter-relationship of regional policy and general economic policy, see *First Medium-term Economic Policy Programme: 1966-70* (Brussels: EEC Commission, 1966), Annex III.

17. In 1971 the Commission of the European Community prepared proposals for joint regional policy measures in 'priority agricultural regions'. See *European Community*, Brussels, October 1971.

18. The need to accelerate the extension of full educational and social services of all kinds in rural areas was strongly emphasized by the group of European agricultural economists which produced the Wageningen Memorandum: *Reform of the European Community's Common Agricultural Policy* (London and Wageningen: Trade Policy Research Centre and the Agricultural University of Wageningen, 1973), p. 8.

4 Reform of the Common Agricultural Policy

Agriculture is probably the best example of a sector affected by the problems of 'growing maturity'. An unfavourable income elasticity of demand for many farm commodities has meant over the years a deterioration in agriculture's terms of trade as compared with manufacturing industry's terms of trade.[1]

ADJUSTMENT PROBLEMS IN EUROPEAN AGRICULTURE

Pressure on employment in the agriculture of the European Community would be relieved if incomes earned in the sector could keep pace with those earned in other sectors. If agriculture is not to remain a permanent burden on tax-payers and on consumers at large, a substantial decline of employment in the sector, perhaps by more than one third, is the price that has to be paid for achieving levels of income on a par with incomes in the industrial sector. Only a reduction in employment of such proportions is likely to bring about the necessary increase in value-added per person working on the land. That agriculture has a solid chance of catching up with other sectors if — in view of a rather inelastic demand for its products — the employment problem is resolved, is indicated by its past growth in physical productivity which has out-paced almost everywhere in the European Community the growth of physical productivity in industry.

Besides the need to adjust to an unfavourable long-term trend in demand, agricultural production has to cope with short-run instabilities in the market. These last arise from unforeseeable changes in the conditions of production, particularly the weather and disease, and from the gestation periods of production which can range from several months for the usual crops to a number of years for livestock products. Long gestation periods mean that adjustments to changes in absolute and relative prices take a while to be put into effect — creating, in some cases, sharp swings between shortage and glut. Although some industrial products have longer gestation periods, many of the products of agriculture are perishable and/or comparatively expensive to store. As a consequence, short-run variations in prices are difficult to reduce by regulating supply, particularly in view of the large number of producers involved.

Adjustment to the long-run conditions of demand and to the short-run problems of supply cannot be quickly achieved. Three points might be highlighted:

(a) First of all, there needs to be, as mentioned in the previous chapter, a great improvement in educational and training facilities in rural areas, so that members of farming families can be fitted for employment in non-farm activities. While young people can take advantage of alternative employment opportunities outside agriculture, they leave behind the aged and less adaptable, the opportunity cost of whose continued employment on the land is very low.[2]

(b) Turning to the physical problems of adjustment, the concentration of production in large commercial farms is difficult to achieve in the continental part of the European Community because agricultural land is, in many regions, divided into small units belonging to different owners. Moreover, it is difficult to use machinery suitable for large acreages, even where the total acreage of farms is large, because they are as often as not divided into small plots. It is, indeed, difficult to expand farms to a more economic size.

(c) What also needs to be stressed is that the agriculture of continental Western Europe has had a long history of extreme protection and heavy state intervention.[3] As a result continental farmers have hardly had to face competition, let alone competition from abroad, and thus they have been alienated from normal market forces.

The adjustment process in agriculture has been complicated because rural poverty is regionally concentrated. But even where regions of rural poverty are close to centres of industrial production, adjustment may take the unwelcome form of an out-migration of the younger part of the population into the cities, thus depriving rural areas of any long-term economic viability. In other regions of rural poverty it is only a matter of time before heavy under-employment will lead to an exodus. There is thus a strong inter-relationship between regional and agricultural policies.[4]

But there are some promising considerations which should not be overlooked. Certain agricultural areas which cannot hope to become competitive could still experience a revival by providing a service to the urban population which is longing for open space, fresh air and clean water for recreation. This environmental need could provide new opportunities for marginal farmers. And as demonstrated by hill farming, farmers can fulfil a role in protecting the environment of mankind which, without subsidies, would have to be taken over by the state.

In view of the difficulties facing European agriculture, there is a need for a policy which assists long-run development by raising the incomes of low-income farmers, while contributing to the short-run stability of farm prices and incomes. But the measures taken should not exempt farmers from changing the structure of production according to changes in the structure of demand.[5]

Such was the intention of the European Community's common agricultural policy if the Treaty of Rome is taken seriously. The common policy was designed to

(a) remove the distortions of production, as between member countries, which resulted from national farm-support policies,

(b) allow farmers to compete in a common market unhampered by restrictions on trade,

(c) provide common solutions to common problems, and

(d) constitute financial solidarity between the member countries because of the large differences in the burden of adjustment.

The political compromise which was reached on the instruments of the common agricultural policy, and the way in which it has been managed, was completely inappropriate for achieving the above objectives.[6] Basically, the failure of the common agricultural policy results from the attempt to stabilize and improve incomes in agriculture by fixing minimum prices for many of the sector's products at common levels, providing at the same time an unlimited sales guarantee to producers.

COMMON AGRICULTURAL POLICY

It would be as well to outline the salient features of common agricultural policy. Protection of the Community market for agricultural commodities is based on three sets of prices that are fixed by the Council of Ministers: 'target prices', 'intervention prices' and 'threshold prices'.[7]

(a) Target prices are theoretical prices fixed with the purported aim of ensuring reasonable prices to consumers and reasonable incomes to producers, as well as fostering the harmonious development of international trade. For some commodities, such as beef, 'guide prices' are fixed instead of target prices, but these are similar in intent.

(b) Intervention prices are guaranteed prices at which government agencies will undertake support buying of some commodities if necessary. They range from 40 per cent of the target price for some of the fruits and vegetables to 95 per cent for sugar and some grains. Producer organizations may undertake support buying of some other commodities. The intervention price represents a floor to the market, although producers pay for the cost of transportation of their produce to the intervention centres.

(c) Threshold prices are minimum prices at which imports can enter the Community market. If trade prices on the world market are below threshold prices, a (variable) levy is imposed to the extent of the difference. Imports entering at the threshold price should sell at around the target price on internal markets because the two prices are linked by the notional cost of transportation.

Farmers in the European Community are thus encouraged to produce, to the limit of their technical capabilities, commodities for which intervention prices are in force or support buying is conducted by their organizations. Sugar is the only commodity subject to production controls — actually an escalating price inhibition.

About half the agricultural imports of the European Community are subject to 'variable import levies', the main commodities affected being grains, poultry, eggs, milk and sugar. Each variable levy is equal to the difference between the threshold price and the most favourable c.i.f. import price (including cost, insurance and freight) for the particular commodity. Other commodities are subject to fixed tariffs except for a few which are in deficit supply. In the case of beef, fruit and vegetables, fixed tariffs may be supplemented by variable levies equal to the difference between duty-paid import prices and threshold prices. Frozen beef is also subject to import quotas. (Restrictions on beef imports were temporarily lifted in 1973 in the face of world-wide shortages.) Levies on grain-fed products, such as pork, poultry and eggs, take account of differences between grain prices in the Community and in world markets; levies on processed products, such as milled rice contain an element for the protection of processors in the Common Market.

The European Community's protectionist machinery is completed by its provision for export subsidies or 'restitutions'. In principle the subsidy per unit of export may not exceed the import levy currently applying to the particular commodity. The common agricultural policy also has a safeguard clause for some commodities, allowing appropriate measures to be taken if imports cause, or threaten to cause, grave disturbances in members' markets which might interfere with the basic objectives of the policy. Moreover, when world prices for some commodities exceeded Community prices, export levies were introduced to ensure domestic supplies.

Criticism of the System

The mistakes and abuses of the common agricultural policy have received widespread coverage by the press, in official publications and in academic research.[8] It can be safely said that, apart from reducing the multitude of national interventions by establishing a common system, not much more has been achieved by the policy, unless it is a degree of short-run stabilization of prices. This last was only possible though by isolating agriculture from the rest of the economy of the European Community and by suppressing market forces with an ever increasing number of *dirigiste* manoeuvres.

Until the series of currency crises which began in 1969, it could at least be said that a common agricultural market had been established in which most goods moved freely. But the free movement of goods only serves a useful economic purpose if it is allowed to induce a reallocation of productive resources in the direction of greater overall efficiency. But in practice the management of the common agricultural policy prevented this from happening.

For in effect the common agricultural market was supplied by a state-sponsored multinational and multi-product cartel. The members of the cartel in the various countries were allowed to produce what was most profitable at prices which were the result of inter-governmental bargaining and not the result of market forces. The prices were supported against pressure from outside the cartel by variable levies on imports which had to be much greater than would have been required for the purpose of removing the destabilizing effects of short-run variations in world market prices. What is more, the risks of over-production were borne by the urban population, either as taxpayers or as consumers. In part directly, by paying the import levies through higher prices, and indirectly through the budget, consumers have provided the funds which have been necessary to take surplus production out of the market by having it stored, denatured or dumped (with the aid of export subsidies) on the 'world' markets of traditional agricultural-exporting countries.

In pursuit of the income objective through price-support measures a series of deleterious effects were accepted.

(a) Prices were supported far above what an open market would have supported. Since the production of every member country required support, political compromises — in the bargaining process — produced relative prices for different products that did not reflect relative scarcities.[9] Consequently, prices could not be used to direct production, making additional subsidies necessary. Indeed, being fixed so high, they rather delayed the necessary reduction in agricultural employment.

(b) Price-support was used as an instrument of social policy in order to raise the level of income of low-income farmers. But high prices have largely benefited farmers already on high incomes, increasing income inequalities and contributing, thereby, to greater dissatisfaction in the farming community.[10]

(c) High supported prices, the extension of the common agricultural policy to cover some 300 products and the distortion of relative prices combined with technological advances to stimulate increased production. Given the unlimited guarantee by the Agricultural Guidance and Guarantee Fund to purchase a farmer's entire production, and the continuous increase in the number of commodities supported, the cost of intervention increased dramatically to $2,783m in 1969/70. The average burden of expenditure for agriculture in the budgets of the six member countries during that period was almost trebled, amounting in 1969 to 1.5 per cent of the European Community's total GNP, compared with 0.6 per cent both in the United States and in the United Kingdom.

(d) The steep rise in the cost of market interventions prevented the Community from devoting sufficient resources to the long-run problems of structural adjustment. The proportion of the Agricultural Guidance and Guarantee Fund devoted to 'guidance' declined from one-sixth to one-twelfth. The solution to the structural problem in European agriculture was left to national governments. This produced striking distortions in national farm-support programmes. But hardly any serious effort was made to reduce the farm population.

What reduction there was would have taken place anyway. Furthermore, since excess employment in agriculture tends to be concentrated in regions with no alternative employment opportunities, politicians were tempted — in the absence of sufficient structural means — to put still greater emphasis on price-support means as the means of improving farm incomes.

As for 'financial solidarity', by which the burden of agricultural adjustment would be shared by all member countries, some really absurd consequences have been recorded. Solidarity implies transfers from the economically strong to the economically weak. Italy, however, with the lowest income *per capita* and the highest proportion of employment in agriculture and of 'marginal' land in production was — even when wine was included under the common agricultural policy in 1970 — a major and in some years the largest net contributor to the Agricultural Fund. Again the explanation is found in an inappropriate use of prices.

First, the volume of guaranteed purchases required to stabilize farmers' revenue varies conversely with the response of demand to changes in price. And Italy is a major producer of products like fruit where small changes in price have a considerable impact on demand. Thus, comparatively small guaranteed purchases, ultimately paid out of the Agricultural Fund, have been enough to stabilize the income of Italian producers. The north of the European Community, though, produces products like cereals for which demand is not very responsive to changes in price and there intervention to stabilize agricultural incomes is necessarily more expensive. On the other side of the equation, all revenues from import levies go to the Agricultural Fund. For these reasons Italy pays on balance more into the fund than she receives — as just explained — in terms of reimbursements.[12]

The other major contributor to the Agricultural Fund is Germany who frequently complains about the burden she carries. Her representatives at the negotiating table behave as if they do not realize that Germany's contributions are high because she has pleaded successfully for high prices to protect her farmers against more competitive farmers in other parts of the Community and elsewhere — cereals being a case in point. It can well be argued that in paying for surpluses induced by high prices, Germany is paying for the protection of her own farmers; and, by contrast to the intention of the common agricultural policy, she is conserving an inefficient structure of production instead of encouraging an efficient reallocation of resources.

COLLAPSE OF THE COMMON POLICY

In retrospect, the collapse of the European Community's common agricultural policy was only a matter of time, because it was becoming increasingly difficult to isolate a whole sector from the rest of the economy by defending arbitrarily-decided common prices in terms of a third currency, namely a unit of account equivalent to the American dollar defined in terms of gold. Similar to the plans for monetary integration, hopes were set on the 'green dollar' forcing member countries to act according to a common line, not only in agricultural policy but also in other fields.

The development of prices outside the agricultural sector, however, varied from country to country in the European Community, reflecting different national economic policy problems and priorities. Through various inputs, agriculture has many price links with other sectors, competing with them for factors of production. Different national trends for these input prices combined with uniformly fixed prices for agricultural output were bound to become increasingly incompatible and a source of tension. As far as this amounted to a negative impact on agricultural incomes, it contributed to a huge increase in providing for agriculture out of national budgets.

When, with growing and differing rates of inflation, changes in exchange rates became unavoidable, member governments proved they were only prepared to accept the logic of the common agricultural policy as long as it suited what they perceived as their national interest. If they followed the dictates of economic logic, a country that devalued its currency would have allowed its domestic agricultural prices to rise, while its export capacity would have been improved and the competitiveness of imports from other member countries would have been reduced. In the case of a country that up-valued its currency the reverse should have applied.[13] But neither France when she devalued in 1969 nor Germany when she revalued in 1970 accepted this logic. France refused to accept the consequent rise in her domestic price level and to reduce the stimulus to industrial exports provided by devaluation. And Germany did not want her agriculture coming under pressure to reduce prices.

In both cases, domestic agricultural prices were initially left unchanged, backed in the case of France by export levies and import subsidies and vice versa in the case of Germany. These compensatory border payments were temporarily abandoned later on, but subsequent exchange-rate changes between nearly all member countries have made them a permanent feature of the 'common' agricultural policy. When the fixed point, the American dollar, began to move in relation to other currencies, following the Smithsonian Accord of 1971, and the European Community was split into different exchange-rate regimes, the collapse of the common agricultural policy was complete although member governments have gone on with their game of pretence. With compensatory payments at all borders, the free — though largely meaningless — movement of agricultural goods within the Common Market had come to an end.

Short-term Relief of World Prices

In view of recent developments in agricultural markets all over the world our criticisms of the common agricultural policy may seem extravagant. Poor weather conditions in the major agricultural producing areas of the world in 1972/73, the exhaustion of American stock-piles and a steadily growing demand for high-protein diets combined to produce a world-wide shortage of a few basic agricultural commodities, particularly grains.

The embarrassing surpluses of the European Community, beef excepted, have largely disappeared. And not only ministers but also officials in the Commission are inclined to say these developments have proved that the common agricultural policy has all along been right in principle. We reject this interpretation of events. There would be some truth in it if ministers and officials had anticipated world-wide shortages.

And if they did they should have no qualms now about reducing the level of protection accorded to European farmers. (There is an old political adage that the lie is half way round the world before the truth has got its boots on. It seems to be the motto of many apologists for the European Community's shortcomings, but it does not serve the cause of European unity any good, no good at all.)

Anyway, the turnabout in world agricultural markets has provided further proof, if further proof was needed, that the dumping of surpluses outside the European Community has been the worst aspect of the common agricultural policy. Not only was it uneconomic to sell storable surpluses when prices were relatively low rather than stockpile for the times when prices would be relatively high. It was also a scandal in human terms to have run down stocks which in drought and famine in other parts of the world could have contributed to the saving of lives.

As far as ministers are concerned, the reforms they envisage are largely cosmetic, aimed at improving the face of agricultural support, but really concerned with achieving self-sufficiency at almost any cost. The Commission, on the other hand, has plainly scaled down its ambitions, mainly to altering a few relative prices and to thinking aloud about producers sharing the costs of surpluses which might still arise in the future.[14] We do not share these attitudes because the optimism they reveal appears to be built on weak foundations.

First, weather remains a major factor of uncertainty which may, from time to time, help to cover up ill-conceived policies. As far as storable products are concerned, a rational policy of maintaining buffer-stocks to compensate short-term variations in production is preferable to an indiscriminate inducement, as a by-product of an inappropriate incomes policy, to surplus production.

Second, to interpret recent shortages as the first signs of an imminent world-wide food crisis is not only untenable because of the temporary nature of poor weather conditions. Perhaps more important has been the fact that the recent shortages have been partly self-inflicted. The shortage is largely limited to temperate-zone products, particularly cereals. But the 'world' markets for these products have been dumping grounds for surpluses produced in high-cost areas, mainly the European Community, whose common agricultural policy began to make an impact on international trade in 1966. World prices of cereals were depressed and low-cost producers like the United States, Canada and Australia were obliged to cut production. And by the time poor weather conditions affected many areas in 1972/73 the large stockpiles in the United States, built up in the 1950s and early 1960s, had been virtually exhausted.[15] In an economic activity as subject to government intervention as agriculture it is simply nonsense to assert or imply, as most politicians do, that world food shortages are not the fault of governments and are beyond their control to correct.

Third, in view of world-wide shortages there has been increasing concern about security of supplies, partly provoked by the imposition by the United States of export controls in 1973 on agricultural products, as a measure to combat inflation. Greater self-sufficiency at high cost is not, however, the appropriate answer to shortages of supply. Instead, the European Community should seek international agreements on security of access to supplies, on the development and management of stock-piles and on security of access to markets (trade liberalization) to stimulate production in low-cost areas of the world.[16]

Fourth, the outbreak of fresh attempts to achieve as much self-sufficiency as possible will have a serious impact on international trade in agricultural products, possibly provoking protectionist responses in other countries to international trade in industrial products.

Opportunity for Fundamental Reforms

The tightening of the agricultural markets observable in the years immediately following the 1971 harvests should influence, first of all, the broad objectives of national and Community-wide agricultural policies, while at the same time facilitating the politics of their reorientation. It is now in the interest of the whole world that the largest agricultural producing countries should allow the forces of comparative advantage to influence to an increasing degree the patterns of their production and so optimize their combined agricultural output. This can best be done by adjusting domestic agricultural price structures to the price-relatives prevailing in the world market which indicate relative scarcities *vis-à-vis* the pattern of global demand. The general inflation of agricultural prices should facilitate such an adjustment.

The opportunity presented by these developments must not be allowed to pass. The common agricultural policy, as practised recently, has been too much of a burden on the Community.

(a) It has unduly burdened both external and internal political relations. In terms of the latter, it has been of late more of an impediment to further integration than a 'cement', as it used to be regarded.

(b) It has also imposed rapidly mounting costs within the member countries. Not only have its strictly economic costs distorted production patterns. Perhaps more important in the long run, food bills have been rising and social and political costs stemming from its influence on the distribution of income within the society at large and, more particularly, within the farming community have also been increasing. As in the United States, administratively-guaranteed agricultural prices are set to give a decent income to the small farmer, who only contributes though a small fraction to internal agricultural production. Consequently, the large commercial farms, selling at the same price, make huge profits which translate themselves rapidly into rising land values and are already beginning to create something of a social scandal in several Community countries.

Is all this really worth the trouble it has imposed on those who want to make genuine progress towards European integration? The common agricultural policy absorbs 70 per cent of the time of the Council of Ministers and 90 per cent of the Community's budget. It also puts a strain on the European Community's foreign economic relations out of all proportion to agriculture's weight in the European economy. (In the United Kingdom, agriculture contributes 2.5 per cent of total economic activity, in Germany 3.5 per cent; and for the enlarged Community as a whole, agriculture's share in GNP amount to no more than 7 per cent, while its share of employment is around 12 per cent.)

ESSENTIALS OF A REFORMED SYSTEM

The discussion so far should suffice to stress that short-term developments ought not be used to delay an urgent reform of the common agricultural policy.[17] The Commission should resume the work it started in 1968 when it submitted the Mansholt Plan. The plan pointed to the most important failure of the policy, namely its handling of the long-term adjustment problem. But the plan left the problem of absolute and relative prices for agricultural products almost untouched. Hence we would like to see a reform which goes further than that. On the basic points, not necessarily in the specific arrangements where more than one solution may be acceptable, we find ourselves in agreement with proposals advanced by a study group of the Institut Atlantique des Affaires Internationales in Paris.[18] Any reform of the common agricultural policy has to provide answers to the following questions: What should the future common policy look like in outline? How should the unavoidable transition problems be solved? How should the new policy be administered? What are the likely costs of a new policy and how should they be financed?

Turning to the first question, there is widespread agreement, and not only among economists, that price policy should no longer be used as an instrument of an agricultural incomes policy. Only if it is accepted that absolute or relative prices should be allowed to fulfil their appropriate functions, namely to guide the volume and structure of production, will it be possible to stop the scandalous waste of resources in agriculture, to reduce protection and to bring about an adjustment according to the sector's long-term development prospects. Such a change in policy implies, first, that the level of producer prices for agricultural products should be lowered where necessary in order to indicate more advantageous production possibilities elsewhere and to indicate also the true position of agricultural products in the demand pattern of the consumers. Second, relative prices for some agricultural products would have to be changed to remove and prevent extreme surpluses and shortages in production; and to enlarge scope for international trade.

Income support could be justified on the grounds[19] (i) that a change-over to a new policy creates problems of transition and that the present farmers can hardly be asked to pay for moving away from the deficient policy of the past, (ii) that adjustment to structural change which would become more pressing with the new price policy cannot be expected from all farmers without creating social harm, and (iii) that the European Community, like most countries in the world, may be prepared to keep production and employment of this sector at a volume which would be somewhat larger than the one corresponding to long-term sectoral prospects and comparative advantage. In all these cases support should be provided by direct subsidies. This would not interfere with the price mechanism and would also be a more transparent procedure than a system of guaranteed prices because the public would have a better idea of how expensive the new common policy would be.

Besides the problem of adjusting to structural change, the new policy would also have to contribute to short-run stabilization. In order to allow this the Community ought to develop a system of common buffer stocks in basic and storable products. But in order to be able to reduce protection without exposing the common agricultural market to disturbances through competitive dumping — which, in the past, was not solely practised by the Community — efforts would have to be made to organize corresponding international stabilization schemes and to set up and secure an international code of conduct for this market (including sanctions against those countries who violate the rules).

The transition problem implies that producers would have to be compensated for a loss in their incomes which resulted from a change from the present to another system at a lower level of producer prices. Any compensation scheme would have to take care that

(a) it prevents an undesired expansion of production, which is what would immediately happen if compensation was paid according to the actual level of production,

(b) it does not discourage any reduction and reorientation of production, in particular by preventing a consolidation of the acreage, and

(c) it is socially acceptable in that it helps the poorest farmers more than those who are better equipped to adjust to the long-term objectives.

From this it follows that (i) compensation should be paid only for the area under cultivation, or the number of livestock, at the beginning of the policy change, (ii) compensation would have to be confined to the present generation of farmers, granting them the discounted value of their recipts if they surrendered land in cases where areas would be consolidated, and (iii) a basis for computing the amount of compensation would have to be calculated which would automatically help the poor farmers (by assuming, for example, that in the initial year all farmers had achieved the same average productivity, and by letting compensation decrease beyond a certain farm size).

The administration would involve the change-over to, as well as the execution of, the new policy. In considering a shift towards a system of support based on direct income payments, a preoccupation in the past has been the need to narrow the gap between world market prices and Community prices, which was usually envisaged in a number of stages. For a sudden change would be disruptive and would overstrain financial resources. It was realised, moreover, that the change itself would affect world market prices; and hence they could only act as a guide, not as fix points.

Following the change in the balance of supply and demand in 1972-73, differences between Community prices and world market prices have not been so much a matter of *level* as of *structure*. How long this situation will continue remains to be seen.

In any event, after a period of transition, agricultural markets would not be completely surrendered to market forces. The management of buffer stocks would be a first administrative problem. Secondly, structural change would probably still require a helping hand from the Community, and from member governments. Thirdly, some separation from world markets would need to be maintained, for the purpose of maintaining stabilization policies (but not for protectionist purposes).

Turning to the budgetary implications of a reform of the common agricultural policy along the lines indicated, an estimate is very difficult. The maximum budgetary costs of direct income payments could not exceed the total reduction in the various prices multiplied by the corresponding level of production at the beginning of the reform. For the intention would be for the compensation scheme to be degressive. As long as Community and world market prices remain close to one another the budgetary costs would not be as great as they would have been once upon a time. In any case, the budgetary costs, whether great or small, would not be incurred at once, but according to the stages at which the reform was carried out. The cost of price stabilization would also be reduced since the extreme export subsidies and import levies would no longer be necessary and the denaturation and indiscriminate storing of agricultural products would give way to a rational system of buffer stocks.

If additional finance was necessary, a Community surcharge on the value-added tax would represent a possible solution. In order to reduce the regressive effect of such a surcharge on income distribution, which also requires the burden among member countries to be distributed according to their standard of living, agricultural products could be exempted from this surcharge. The surcharge would possibly appear acceptable to the consumer because, on the other hand, we would no longer have to finance the common agricultural policy indirectly through extremely high prices for agricultural products to anything like the same extent as before.

CONCLUSIONS AND RECOMMENDATIONS

1. If agriculture is not to remain a permanent burden on taxpayers and consumers at large, a substantial decline of employment in the sector, perhaps by as much as one third, is the price that has to be paid for achieving levels of income on a par with incomes in the industrial sector. Only a reduction in employment of such proportions is likely to bring

about the necessary increase in value-added per person working on the land.

2. There is a need for a great improvement in educational and training facilities in rural areas so that individuals can be fitted for employment in non-farm activities. Once its employment problem is resolved agriculture stands a good chance of catching up with other sectors.

3. The outward migration of the younger part of the population has deprived regions of rural poverty which are close to centres of industrial production of any long-term economic viability. In other regions of rural poverty it is only a matter of time before heavy under-employment will lead to an exodus. There is thus a strong inter-relationship between regional and agricultural policies.

4. There are promising considerations for agriculture which should not be overlooked. Certain uncompetitive rural areas could still experience a revival by providing a service to the urban population which is longing for open space, clean water for recreation and fresh air. This in turn could provide a new role for marginal farmers to protect the environment which, without subsidies, would have to be taken over by the state.

5. There is also a need for a policy which assists long-run development by raising the incomes of low-income farmers, while contributing to the short-run stability of prices and incomes. The measures taken, however, should not exempt farmers from changing the structure of production according to changes in the structure of demand.

6. The Community's political compromise on the instruments of the common agricultural policy, and the way in which it has been managed, was completely inappropriate for achieving its objectives. Basically the policy's failure results from the attempts to stabilize and improve incomes in agriculture by fixing minimum prices for many of the sector's products at common levels, providing at the same time an unlimited sales guarantee to producers.

7. Most agricultural goods moved freely in the Common Market until the series of currency crises began in 1969. The free movement of goods, however, only serves a useful economic purpose if it is allowed to induce a reallocation of productive resources in the direction of greater overall effici-

ency. In practice the management of the common agricultural policy prevented this from happening.

8. It can be safely said that apart from reducing the multitude of national interventions by establishing a common system, not much more has been achieved by the policy, unless it is a degree of short-run stabilization of prices. This last was only possible by isolating agriculture from the rest of the Community's economy and by suppressing market forces with an ever increasing number of *dirigiste* manoeuvres.

9. A series of deleterious effects were accepted in pursuit of the income objective through price support measures. Prices were supported far above what an open market would have supported, and the necessary reduction in agricultural employment was delayed. These high prices have largely benefited farmers already on high incomes, increasing income inequalities and contributing, thereby, to greater dissatisfaction in the farming community.

10. The average burden of expenditure for agriculture in the budgets of the six member countries was almost trebled in the period 1962/63 to 1969/70.

11. The steep rise in the cost of short-run stability prevented the Community from devoting sufficient resources to the long-run problems of structural adjustment. The solution to the structural problem was mostly left to the individual national governments which produced striking distortions in national farm-support programmes.

12. Further, since excess employment in agriculture tends to be concentrated in regions with no alternative employment opportunities, still greater emphasis was placed on price-support measures as the means for improving farm incomes.

13. Germany frequently complains about the burden she carries in respect of the Agricultural Fund. Her negotiators behave as if they do not realize that Germany's contributions are high because she has pleaded successfully for high prices to protect her farmers against more competitive farmers in other parts of the Community and elsewhere. In effect, Germany is paying for the protection of her own farmers; and by contrast to the intention of the common agricultural policy, she is conserving an inefficient structure of production instead of encouraging an efficient reallocation of resources.

14. In retrospect, it was only a matter of time before the Community's common agricultural policy collapsed. It became extremely difficult to isolate a whole sector from the rest of the economy by defending arbitrarily-decided common prices in terms of a third currency. When changes in exchange rates became unavoidable, member governments proved they were only prepared to accept the curious logic of the common agricultural policy as long as it suited what they felt to be their national interest.

15. The embarrassing surpluses of the Community have largely disappeared due in great part to world-wide poor weather conditions, the exhaustion of American stock-piles and a steadily growing demand for high-protein diets which combined to produce a world-wide shortage of a few basic agricultural commodities. Ministers and officials in the Commission are inclined to say these developments have proved that the common agricultural policy has been right in principle. We reject this interpretation of events.

16. As far as ministers are concerned, the reforms they envisage are largely cosmetic, aimed at improving the face of agricultural support, but really concerned with achieving self-sufficiency at almost any cost. The Commission, on the other hand, has scaled down its ambitions, mainly to altering a few relative prices and to thinking aloud about producers sharing the costs of surpluses which might still arise in the future. We do not share these attitudes.

17. Weather remains a major factor of uncertainty which from time to time helps cover up ill-conceived policies. A rational policy of maintaining buffer stocks of storable products to compensate short-term variations in production is preferable to an indiscriminate inducement, as a by-product of an inappropriate incomes policy, to surplus production.

18. Short-term developments ought not to be used to delay an urgent reform of the common agricultural policy. The Commission should resume the work it started in 1968 when it submitted the Mansholt Plan. The Plan pointed to the most important failure of the policy, namely its handling of the long-term adjustment problem, but left untouched the problem of absolute and relative prices for agricultural products. We would like to see a reform which goes further than this.

19. We find ourselves in agreement with proposals advanced by a study group of the Institut Atlantique des Affaires Internationales in Paris. Any reform of the Community's agricultural policy must ensure that price policy is not used as an instrument of an agricultural incomes policy. Absolute and relative prices be allowed to fulfil their appropriate functions, namely to guide the volume and structure of production. Only then will it be possible to stop the scandalous waste of resources in agriculture, to reduce protection and to bring about an adjustment according to the sector's long-term development prospects.

20. Income support should be provided by direct subsidies. This would not interfere with the price mechanism and would also be a more transparent procedure than a system of guaranteed prices because the public would have a better idea of how expensive the new common policy would be.

21. The new policy would also have to contribute to short-runs stabilization. In order to allow this the Community would have to develop a system of common bufferstocks in basic and storable products. Efforts would have to be made to organize international stabilization schemes and to set up and secure an international code of conduct for this market.

22. Producers would have to be compensated for a loss in their incomes which resulted from a change from the present to another system at a lower level of producer prices. Any compensation scheme would have to (i) guard against undesired expansion of production, (ii) bring about a reorientation of production and (iii) ensure that the poorest farmers are helped more than those who are better equipped to adjust to the long-term objectives.

23. Compensation would have to be paid only for the area under cultivation, or the number of livestock, at the beginning of the policy change. Additionally, compensation should be restricted to the present generation of farms, with a basis for computing compensation which automatically helps the poor farmers.

24. It appears necessary to narrow the long-run gap between Community prices and world-market prices in a number of stages. The management of buffer stocks, following a transition period, would represent a first administrative

problem. Structural change would probably still require a helping hand from the Community and member governments. And finally, in the interest of stabilization, not all agricultural prices should be left unprotected.

25. It is difficult to estimate the budgetary implications of a reform of the common agricultural policy. Maximum costs, however, cannot exceed the total reduction in the various prices multiplied by the corresponding production at the beginning of the reform. In any case, they would not be incurred at once, but according to the stages at which the reform was carried out.

26. If additional finance was necessary, though, a Community surcharge on the value-added tax would represent a possible solution. The surcharge would possibly appear acceptable to the consumer because he would no longer have to finance the common agricultural policy as much indirectly through high prices for agricultural products as before.

NOTES AND REFERENCES

1. For a comprehensive, and highly professional, analysis of the problems facing agricultural production in industrialized countries, see D. Gale Johnson, *World Agriculture in Disarray* (London: Macmillan, for the Trade Policy Research Centre, 1973). Also see Hermann Priebe, *Landwirtschaft in der Welt von morgen* (Düsseldorf: Econ Verlag, 1970), and Ugo Papi and Charles Nunn (eds.), *Economic Problems of Agriculture in Industrial Societies* (London: Macmillan, for the International Economic Association, 1969).

Reference should be made as well to four official reports: *Agricultural Adjustment in Developed Countries* (Rome: Food and Agriculture Organization, 1972); Group of Experts, *Agriculture and Economic Growth* (Paris: OECD Secretariat, 1961); and Panel of Experts, *Trends in International Trade*, Haberler Report (Geneva: GATT Secretariat, 1958).

2. In this connection, see Hugh Corbet, *Agriculture's Place in Commercial Diplomacy*, Ditchley Paper No. 48 (Enstone: Ditchley Foundation, 1974).

3. An excellent review of agricultural policies in Western Europe, set in historical context, can be found in Michael Tracy, *Agriculture in Western Europe: Crisis and Adaptation Since 1880* (London: Jonathan Cape, 1964).

4. As mentioned in Chapter 3, this inter-relationship is stressed in all three contributions — German, French and Dutch — to Priebe *et al.*, *Fields of Conflict in European Farm Policy*, Agricultural Trade Paper No. 3, (London: Trade Policy Research Centre, 1972). For an Italian

view, see G. W. Dean, Michele de Benedictis *et al.*, 'Potential Use of the Mansholt Plan for Restructuring Agriculture in the Italian Mezzogiorno', *European Economic Review*, Amsterdam, No. 3, 1972. Also see S. Cafiero, *Le zone particolarmente depresse nella politica per il Mezzogiorno* (Roma: Associazione per lo Sviluppo del Mezzogiorno, 1973).

5. G. G. Dell 'Angelo, 'Agricoltura difficile: progetti e problemi attuali', paper for the 25th Congress of Agricultural Science, Rome, 1969.

6. Such was the conclusion of the group of twenty two leading agricultural economists, from all over the European Community, that signed the Wageningen Memorandum: *Reform of the European Community's Common Agricultural Policy* (London and Wageningen: Trade Policy Research Centre and the Agricultural University of Wageningen, 1973), republished in *European Review of Agricultural Economics*, The Hague, Vol. 1, No. 1, 1973.

7. This brief description is based on the outline in Brian Fernon, *Issues in World Farm Trade*, Atlantic Trade Study No. 11 (London: Trade Policy Research Centre, 1970), pp. 43 and 44.

8. Although the common agricultural policy has been widely criticized, attention might be drawn to a number of representative independent views: Jacques Flavian, 'Dix ans de Marché Commun agricole', *Revue d'Economie Politique*, Paris, No. 7, 1968; Gabriel Browne, 'Vers une nouvelle Europe agricole', *Revue Marché Commun*, Paris, No. 17, 1968; T. E. Josling, *Agriculture and Britain's Trade Policy Dilemma*, Thames Essay No. 2 (London: Trade Policy Research Centre, 1969); and H. Niehaus, 'Die Krise der landwirtschaftlichen Preis- und Einkommenspolitik in der EWG', *Agrarwirtschaft*, Frankfurt, No. 18, 1969.

Also see *A New Agricultural Policy for Europe*, Report of a Study Group (London: Federal Trust for Education and Research, 1970); Adrien Zeller, *L'imbroglio agricole du Marché commun* (Paris: Calmann-Levy, 1970); Priebe, *op. cit.*; Claude Baillet, 'L'avenir de l'exploitation agricole dans la CEE', *Economie Rurale*, Versailles, No. 89, 1971; Adrien Ries, 'La politique agricole commune s'insère-t-elle davantage dans une véritable politique économique après les décisions du Conseil du 24 mars 1972', *Revue Marché Commun*, Paris, No. 155, 1972; Priebe *et al.*, *op. cit.*; Gian Paolo Casadio, 'Le politiche di sostegno agricolo', in *Negoziati Commerciali Internazionali: Conflitto o Cooperazione?* (Milan: Fiera di Milano, 1973); A. Hertitska, Pierre Malvé and Asher Winegarten, 'European Agricultural Policy', in Johnson and John Schnittker (eds.), *US Agriculture in a World Context* (Washington: D. C. Heath, for the Atlantic Council, 1974); Gunter Weinschenck, 'Issues of Future Agricultural Policy in the European Common Market', *European Review of Agricultural Economics*, Vol. 1, No. 1, 1973; and Giuseppe Barbero, 'L'Agricoltura nella politica economico-sociale della CEE', paper given to a conference of the Società Italiana di Economia Agraria', Bari, 30 November 1973.

9. Priebe, 'European Agricultural Policy: a German Viewpoint', in Priebe *et al.*, *op. cit.*, p. 6.

10. The gross inefficiency of price-support policies as a means of redistributing income to low-income farmers has been emphasized in a number of studies. In 1969 a report prepared for the French Government concluded that 'the system of agricultural price support, [which provides for] a price structure that does not correspond to the needs of the market, is the essential cause of the wrong orientation of production'. It went on to observe that 'the result has been to transform the productivity gains of agriculture into a charge on the general public'. This, the report added, has 'nearly exclusively profited a minority of farmers' since '20 per cent of the producers sell more than two-thirds of French production'. See *Prospective à long terme de l'agriculture Française 1968-85*, Vedel Report (Paris: Ministry of Agriculture, 1969). The conclusions of the Vedel Report were included in 'Rapport sur les principales options qui commandent la préparation du VIe Plan', *Journal Officiel*, Paris, 10 July 1970, p1.PL 135.

Income distribution under the system of 'deficiency payments' as it was administered in Britain, prior to her membership of the European Community, was also poor according to Josling and Donna Hamway, 'Distribution of Costs and Benefits of Farm Policy', in Josling *et al.*, *Burdens and Benefits of Farm-Support Policies*, Agricultural Trade Paper No. 1 (London: Trade Policy Research Centre, 1972), pp. 50-86. Broadly, the statistical analysis found that, on the basis of 1969 data, 48 per cent of the benefits went to the richest quarter of the farm population, while the poorest quarter received only 13 per cent. And it was found that with the shift to the import-levy system of support, under the European Community's regime, income distribution would be only marginally worse.

11.   M. G. Vedel *et al.*, *Rapport concerant les Politiques nationales de structure agricole dans la Communaté*, Vedel Report (Brussels: Commission of the European Community, 1972). Also see Denis Bergmann, 'European Agricultural Policy: a French Viewpoint', in Priebe *et at.*, *op. cit.*, pp. 23-39.

12.   M. Rossi Doria, 'Agriculture and Europe', *Daedalus*, Philadelphia, Winter, 1964.

13.   Josling, 'Exchange Rate Flexibility and the Common Agricultural Policy of the EEC', *Weltwirtschaftliches Archiv*, Kiel, January 1970.

14.   See the Lardinois Memorandum, 'Improvement of the Common Agricultural Policy', Supplement, *Bulletin of the European Community*, Brussels, No. 17, 1973.

15.   See Johnson, *op. cit.*, pp. 17-64 and 205-25.

16.   These three points are elaborated upon in Chapter 7.

17.   Instituto Nazionale di Economia Agraria, 'La riforma delle strutture agricole nella comunità economica europea', *Rivista di Economia Agria*, Vol. 2, No. 3, 1971.

18.   Pierre Uri *et al.*, *A Future for European Agriculture*, Atlantic Paper No. 4 (Paris: Atlantic Institute for International Affairs, 1970). A more complicated system of direct income support is proposed in J. F. van Riemsdijk, 'A System of Direct Compensation Payments to Farmers as a Means of Reconciling Short-run to Long-run Interests',

European Review of Agricultural Economics, Vol. 1, No. 2, 1973.
19. See 'Lo strumento della integrazione diretta del redditi', *Il dottore in scienze agrarie*, Rome, No. 9, 1973.

5 Industrial Development and Competition

Throughout the industrialized world governments have been increasingly exercising responsibilities for full employment, economic growth, regional development and industrial organization in ways that could, or do already, impose obstacles to trade with other countries. Yet they are committed, through adherence to the GATT and participation in the OECD, and in Western Europe through their membership of either the European Community or EFTA, to the reduction or elimination of barriers to trade. And they are also committed to the avoidance of policies which have a similar distorting effect. In this last respect, the relevant provisions in the European Community are Articles 92 to 94 of the Treaty of Rome, dealing with government aids to industry.

Two major factors have produced the apparent conflict in objectives between domestic and international economic policies.

(a) On the one hand there has been growing pressure on governments to assume greater responsibilities towards the social and economic welfare of their peoples.

(b) On the other, governments have failed to devise and implement adequate means for the adjustment of disequilibria in international trade and payments, until the forces of international currency markets obliged them to accept floating exchange rates as a fact of current life.

Governments appear to have been confronted with a choice between modifying the objectives of domestic policies or modifying their commitment to liberal trade. In practice, they have sought to reconcile the two courses, but domestic pressures are usually the first to tell — especially where there is no strong sense of international obligation.

Domestic pressures are invariably short-sighted, inward-looking and defensive. Ministers, being dependent on electoral support, are more likely to be influenced by such pressures, generated perhaps by the specific plight of a local industry unable to cope with import competition, than by the general damage that might be done in the long run to the international trading community through a beggar-my-neighbour measure.

But to achieve the benefits of trade liberalization, by exploiting comparative advantages through an international division of labour, policies need to be far-sighted, outward-looking and enlightened. In the past, successive rounds of GATT negotiations have provided intermittent relief from protectionist pressures, enabling governments to maintain countervailing pressures in a liberal direction. With the rapid integration of the world economy greatly accelerating the adjustment process, both domestically and internationally, there is a need for more or less continuous consultation and negotiation on the management of the international economic order. That is why we repeatedly stress the crucial importance of pursuing European economic integration in harmony with the integration of the world economy as a whole.

The reduction of tariffs on trade among developed countries in general, and the elimination of them in the European Community and EFTA in particular, has exposed the significance of non-tariff distortions of international competition. By these last are meant a wide variety of measures which either by design or accident protect or favour domestic producers *vis-à-vis* foreign suppliers — at the expense, incidentally, of domestic consumers and taxpayers. They include measures taken by private enterprises, referred to generically as 'restrictive business practices' — discussed later in this chapter in the context of competition policy. But non-tariff distortions are mostly public policies and practices. Many of them are measures implemented at the border by customs authorities, namely quantitative import restrictions (of concern mainly to developing countries), tariff quotas, anti-dumping duties, customs valuation procedures and so on. These are discussed in Chapter 7 below.

The non-tariff measures which appear to cause deepest

concern among developed countries, however, are those which are instruments of industrial policy — and are instruments also of other related policies. An industrial policy should embrace a number of inter-related objectives relating to the sectoral allocation of resources, the structural organization of industries, the development of technological innovation and the maintenance of regional balance. Among its instruments are government loans and subsidies, public procurement policies, technical standards and specifications, concessionary charges for public services and preferential tax treatment.[1]

INDUSTRIAL POLICY

For all intents and purposes, industrial policy in the European Community remains the prerogative of national governments, which greatly complicates the position of the Community in international negotiations on non-tariff barriers to trade. In fact, the Treaty of Rome does not envisage a common industrial policy in specific terms, but Articles 92 to 94 of the Treaty of Rome prohibit government aids which interfere with trade among the member countries. These provisions do allow, though, for exceptions in certain circumstances, most notably where there is regional unemployment.

With the close inter-relationship between regional and industrial policies it would be as well to clarify at this juncture the distinction between the two. The former, already discussed in Chapter 3 above, relates to public assistance which the producers of a particular region may obtain, no matter what they produce. On the other hand, the latter relates to public assistance which may be obtained by the producers of a particular line of product, wherever in a country they may be located. It is the latter with which the present chapter is concerned.

The common industrial policy of the European Community is still very much in embryo. In 1970 the Commission advanced proposals in the Colonna Memorandum.[2] But it was not until the 1972 meeting of heads of member governments that guide-lines were approved.[3] The elements stressed in the communiqué of the Paris summit, although published in a different order, call for

(a) the maintenance of fair competition as much within the Common Market as in external markets in conformity with the rules laid down by the treaties,

(b) the elimination of technical barriers to trade,

(c) the progressive and effective opening up of purchasing by the public sector,

(d) the transformation and conversion of declining industries under acceptable social conditions,

(e) the promotion on a European scale of competitive firms in the field of high technology,

(f) the elimination, particularly in the fiscal and legal fields, of barriers which hinder closer relations and mergers between firms,

(g) the rapid adoption of a European company statute, and

(h) the formation of measures to ensure that mergers affecting firms established in the European Community are in harmony with the economic and social aims of the Community.

These objectives are acceptable. And we would support them as far as they go. Continued endorsement would greatly depend on how they were implemented. Much careful scrutiny of each of the principles in turn is therefore required.

CONFORMITY WITH CONDITIONS OF FREE TRADE

Much depends, for a start, on what is meant by 'fair competition'. There is an obsessive and unfounded belief in some quarters, that for free trade to be effective it is necessary for all conditions of competition to be equalized, implying that all locational differences in costs of production and distribution are somehow trade distorting. But no division of labour through trade can take place if all competitive conditions are artificially equalized. For trade between countries is primarily based on cost *differences*. There is a wide gulf conceptually between

(a) eliminating distortions to competitve conditions resulting from government interventions, which would come under the heading of one non-tariff measure or another, and

(b) eliminating differences in competitive conditions resulting from differences in taxation, social benefits and company laws.

The first is necessary in any attempt to liberalize trade, on either a regional or a multilateral basis, and can be pursued effectively by inter-governmental means. The second, however, is not necessary to the liberalization of trade, but if an economic union is conceived an effective degree of supra-national authority is essential. This second group of measures is discussed in relation to fiscal integration, in Chapter 2, and in connection with European mergers and the development of a European company statute, dealt with towards the end of the present chapter.

Non-tariff Interventions

Within the first group of measures, however, fall the second and third elements in the framework of a common industrial policy, as set out above. Both the elimination of technical barriers to trade and the elimination of discrimination against suppliers in other member countries in the business of public purchasing could be supported as steps towards the elimination of competitive distortions that result from non-tariff interventions by governments.[4] They would be in line with the earlier mentioned principle, established in the Treaty of Rome, prohibiting government aids which interfere with trade, except *inter alia* for the purposes of regional development.

But these principles are only supportable if their implementation is accompanied, as envisaged in the Paris communiqué, by corresponding efforts on the part of member governments of the European Community to negotiate multilateral agreements with third countries on the elimination of the discriminatory aspects of technical standards and specifications,[5] public procurement policies and government subsidies.[6] Discrimination against the rest of the world cannot be countenanced as the basis of a common industrial policy.[7] For economic, political and strategic reasons – noted in Chapter 1 – the European Community is in no position to invite the antagonism, either of the United States or of other countries, that could be expected to ensue.[8]

As diplomatic efforts proceed in the Tokyo Round of multi-lateral trade negotiations, the European Community has a strong interest in the early establishment of a framework of international obligations with respect to non-tariff interventions, within which it could finalize a common industrial policy. The force of international obligations — undertaken in response to the threat to international economic order occasioned by world-wide inflation, commodity shortages and the energy crisis — might in any case facilitate the implementation of a common industrial policy. For inter-governmental action on non-tariff measures, whether in the European Community or in a wider context, is bound to exacerbate the sensitive issue of national sovereignty, such is the growing interdependence of nation states. Negotiations on non-tariff interventions are difficult in a global context — as they can be expected to be in the Community when it comes to formulating a common industrial policy — precisely because they impinge on national industrial policies. But then tariffs, too, are instruments of public assistance to industry. After all, in domestic terms commercial policies are also concerned with the industrial structure of countries, while internationally they are concerned with the location of production where there are comparative cost advantages.

ADJUSTMENT ASSISTANCE TO DECLINING INDUSTRIES

This leads to a consideration of the issues posed by the fourth element: 'the transformation and conversion of declining industries under acceptable social conditions'. The purpose of trade liberalization is to bring about a more efficient allocation of resources, both domestically and internationally, through greater specialization on particular industries or on particular product lines within industries. Adjustment to changing market conditions, on the demand side and on the supply side, is a normal and continuous process in market economies. It mainly takes place without the assistance of governments. But in certain circumstances governments intervene either (i) to help industries adjust or (ii) to alleviate the social consequences of adjustment.[9]

Now that tariffs have been reduced to low nominal levels,

and non-tariff measures are being broached in GATT negotiations, it is crucial that governments should place more emphasis on adjustment assistance. Indeed, there is almost an international consensus, reflected in numerous reports, on the need for adjustment assistance to be an integral part of 'escape clause' or emergency protection against sudden surges of imports (see Chapter 7 below).[10] As the European Community — along with other industrialized countries — comes under increasing pressure to accord greater market access to the products of developing countries, reinforcing the dynamic effects of internal trade liberalization, member governments should develop a more concerted approach to the provision of adjustment assistance to declining industries unable to compete in the face of growing imports or other changes in their business environment.

In developing a coherent policy towards declining industries, a clear distinction should be drawn between 'fair' adjustment assistance, on the one hand, and 'unfair' government aids on the other.[11]

(a) The appropriate form of adjustment assistance in a market economy aims to shift resources out of industries that are no longer competitive. There are occasions, of course, where such industries can be revitalized by the replacement of inefficient management, by the introduction of modern technological know-how and by the injection of fresh capital.

(b) The inappropriate form of government aid, which is merely a substitute for traditional forms of protection, aims to keep resources in an industry (through the provision of subsidized capital expenditures, subsidized research and development and subsidized skills). Such support is not amenable to legislative control, review and assessment and may therefore be more wasteful of resources than tariff or quota protection.

Most proposals for reforming the 'escape clause' of the GATT argue that temporary protection against sharp increases in import competition should be (i) degressive according to a definite time-table, (ii) allied with a programme of adjustment assistance and (iii) subject to multilateral surveillance. If international agreement is reached on those reforms, the European Community would have to coordinate, at least, the policies of member countries towards industries requiring the temporary imposition by the Community of import quotas or increased tariffs. But there is much to be said for the Community coordinating in any case the adjustment assistance policies of member countries. That could induce governments to develop coherent policies for assisting regions, firms and workers to adapt to changing economic circumstances.

What the European Community should do, to begin with, is secure agreement among member countries on the criteria and conditions for government assistance to industry. Those criteria and conditions should then be published and widely publicized. As experience has shown, if they are not publicly known and clearly enunciated, firms in competitive difficulty have an open invitation to exert political pressure for subsidy support or other special protection. It is not enough to depend on the usual checks and balances of inter-departmental responsibilities in governments to ensure that public resources are not squandered on economically unsound and inefficiently managed enterprises.[12]

In addition, as cases arise of government intervention in industry, at both national and supra-national level, the authorities should be required to consult a panel representing the public interest in the broadest sense, including consumer interests and the interests of other industries concerned, besides independent economic opinion. It is too late after the event for legislatures to find that public resources have not been deployed as effectively as they might have been.[13]

PROMOTION OF HIGH TECHNOLOGY

To date the attempts of the European Community to devise a common industrial policy have mainly been for the purpose of enabling European industry to develop technologically advanced capacities that are able to withstand American and Japanese competition. Therefore again, the fifth and sixth elements of the policy framework, as agreed at the Paris summit, have to be discussed in an international context. Technological innovation — the introduction of new technologies — plays an important role in the economic growth of nations. As a result, policies bearing on science and technology have become an important aspect of international economic relations, influencing both visible and invisible trade as well as foreign investment.

Since World War II almost all economies of Western Europe have enjoyed much more rapid growth than the economies of North America. To a large extent, this dynamism derived, as remarked on in Chapter 1, from the ability of Western Europe to imitate technological advances made in the United States — to exploit what has been rather loosely called 'the technological gap'. In the late 1960s, however, this particular source of growth has also become a source of friction between the European Community and the United States.

Technological Gap and Other Differences

Public opinion in the European Community has been subjected to a stream of dire predictions of a future dominated by American research and development, by American computer and automation techniques, by superior and continuously improving American managerial skills and, too, by the marketing strategies of multinational enterprises, all under American control. Such organizational prowess, so the argument has run, would ensure for the United States the commanding heights of modern technology and reduce the European Community to the permanent status of an industrial satellite.[14]

These predictions, widely purveyed by an uncritical press, might have been convincing if at the same time fears were not being expressed in the United States about the congenital inability of industries there to compete with the re-born industries of Western Europe and Japan. For many American commentators were predicting that the vast research-and-development effort of the United States would be cancelled by the acceleration in the international diffusion of technological innovation via direct investments which eventually might result in American firms being out-competed in their home market.[15]

The predictions on both sides of the Atlantic have been exaggerated. Two observations might be made about the mutual misunderstanding that seems to exist.

1. There are two distinct aspects of what is meant by a 'technological gap'.

(a) One aspect, or possible meaning, refers to labour-saving technologies for mass production that can be used in high-wage countries, but are not profitable in low-wage countries. It was bridging this technological gap that helped the economies of Western Europe to achieve their very high rates of growth in the post-war period.

(b) The second aspect relates to the difference in the rates of technological innovation that can be observed in different countries. As far as it can be measured at all, it is doubtful whether it lends itself to meaningful international comparisons, because it ignores for example the possibility that inventions made in one country may be put into practice in another. Many, if not most, of the basic scientific ideas implemented in the form of new technologies in the United States were originally discovered in Western Europe.

On the second aspect, the industrial research and development of the United States is heavily concentrated in the aerospace, nuclear engineering and electronics industries, but there are suggestions that in Western Europe probably more research and development is being done in all other industries. Not until more precise ways of measuring resources devoted to research and development have been elaborated will it be possible to obtain conclusive answers to questions of this kind. It should be taken into account, however, that those sectors dominated by American industry are of paramount importance for the future of economic development, because of their technological 'fall out'.

2. It has been obvious that expressions of the European 'technological inferiority complex' could not have been based on any recorded failing of West European industries in international competition. In 1960-70, American exports of products characterized by high wages and a high research-and-development content, although five times as large as the corresponding imports, were expanding at only half the annual average rate of the latter (10.4 per cent as against 19.6 per cent). It seems much more plausible to explain the

expressions of technological inferiority in terms of the unease felt in Western Europe over the growing frequency of American take-over bids for European companies in the late 1960s. The frequency of those bids was itself a predictable response to the under-valuation of some European currencies in those years and is now being corrected in a number of cases.

Discouraging Experience at Community Level

Like all industrial countries, the European Community, too, has to improve continuously its policies relating to science in general and to industrial research and development in particular. In spite of the high social return on investment which is generally expected in this field, both private and public funds for such purposes have tended to become scarce in recent years, due to the pressures on virtually all governments to reduce or restrict the growth of their budgets. But the problems associated with technological innovation in the Community go much deeper than lack of resources.

What has been happening? In the fields of nuclear, aerospace and related research, which on American experience could contribute to industrial development in the European Community through technological 'fall out', differing national policies have allowed the principle of *juste retour* to determine the course of events. Decisions have not been made on the basis of common Community interests. Instead they have been the product of inter-governmental negotiations — and sometimes only bilateral at that. Two separate institutions, ELDO and ESRO, were established in fields that were intimately related, and in the end they had to be merged.

The determination of every country participating in each venture to get back for its industry a fair return on its contribution has frequently thwarted a rational division of labour, invited costly national duplication and inspired telling tales of abortive collaboration at almost all levels. The basic problem of the European Community in its approach to advanced technology was summed up by the staff of ELDO following the Franco-German decision to terminate the *Europa II* project: 'It is clear that the failure of [European space] programmes is primarily due to the political incapacity of member states to define a common purpose and work together in a genuinely cooperative spirit.'[16]

Recent attempts to restructure European space programmes have been heavily handicapped by conflicts of national interest. France is chiefly interested in developing a rocket which, besides helping to launch satellites into space, would serve as a carrier of nuclear weapons. She is interested, therefore, in any means of spreading the financial burden of her *force de frappe,* but she insists on producing the rocket on her own in order to ensure independent control (for what it is worth in matters of collective security). Britain is chiefly interested in developing a satellite that would help to direct navigation. She is also interested in support for her geostationary technology satellite programme and is not unmindful of the interests of her electronics industry. And Germany hopes to help her industries more by joining the post-*Apollo* programme of the United States and thereby benefit from American experience and expertise.

The United States invited the European Community and other countries in Western Europe to join its post-*Apollo* programme for a manned laboratory in space, but set a deadline for the replies of governments, thereby putting them under pressure to respond. The response of the European Community is somewhat precarious. After fighting hard for their own projects, the United Kingdom, France and Germany decided to establish a European space agency, merging ELDO and ESRO. It is through this agency that the European contribution to the post-*Apollo* programme is to be channelled together with plans for a satellite launcher and a maritime satellite. The financial difficulties posed by governments in discussing this new beginning underscore the desolate state of common research endeavours.

Turning to the field of nuclear research, Euratom was from the outset divorced from the most important projects in the European Community, even though it was a Community institution. While France, the only source of basic knowledge among the original Six, did try to catch up with other nuclear powers, she restricted to her own industry the benefits of French weapons research. In the meantime, Euratom remained without a coherent research programme, which might

have made profitable the considerable investment in its research laboratories. Progress mostly took place outside
Community centres of research, creating new problems for
European cooperation in general and for the development, in
particular, of an efficient source of nuclear energy.

In this last respect, the most conspicuous clash has been
over the enrichment of uranium, where France's adoption of
the American technique of 'gaseous diffusion' is now competing
with the Anglo-Dutch-German 'gas centrifuge'. Faced with a
choice, the Commission decided that both projects should be
supported, adding that the Community should purchase and
stockpile any surplus enriched uranium that may result. In
spite of the potential burden it is likely to impose on the
Community, the Commission's admittedly lukewarm proposal was adopted by the Council of Ministers. If both
projects succeed, the Community could be faced with a
massive over-supply of uranium by 1980, even if the demand
for uranium is dramatically increased by an accelerated production of nuclear energy in response to the dramatic increase in the price of crude oil. Given the likely state of the
world market, the Community would probably have to buy
up the unwanted uranium, stocking it at very high cost. But
if the French project, or the other one, was to prove unsuccessful there would probably be pressure for it to be
supported out of Community funds.

So far, then, the efforts at Community level in the field of
advanced technology have contributed very little to the
common industrial base of the Common Market.

New Directions for Technology

Some idea of the direction in which a more efficient
European policy on science and technology might be
developed can be graphically illustrated by the case of computers. The world population of computers — of the first,
second and third generation — is being utilized at only a
fraction of its capacity. This indicates how much more
important the soft-ware is than the hard-ware. It also indicates that economically much more profitable opportunities
for research-and-development investment lie in the former
area. Needless to say the volume of capital required to

embark on effective research and development in these two areas differs by an astronomical order of magnitude.

Moreover, there is considerable scope on the human side of research in education, medicine and other similar fields, as pointed out in the Brooks Report for the OECD. In such fields it is almost true that there cannot be enough research. At any rate the scope for duplication is extremely limited.

At the present level of research and development in the European Community there is enormous scope for increasing its effectiveness through improvements in organization. Such improvements can, and have to be, achieved at three definite levels

(a) Improvements are needed in the political decision-making process at the level of national governments, in deciding on the optimal allocation of resources between pure and applied research.

(b) At the level of individual research establishments improvements could be achieved with greater regard for 'cost effectiveness'; that is, by improving the economic management of scientific research for which it is high time specialized post-graduate training was instituted.

(c) Finally, decision-making can be improved even at the level of the scientific community itself, which is by nature both national and supra-national. The scientific community should have the main, but not the exclusive, influence on decisions on the allocation of research resources among individual sciences (and industries).

To achieve these improvements it would clearly be necessary to obtain much closer — as well as more extensive and more formalized — involvement on the part of legislatures and the self-governing scientific community in the formulation of science and technology policies at national and Community level. What should be established for the purpose is a council on research and development. The need, in other words, is to reduce the relative influence on policy-making in this field of governmental and Communitarian bureaucracies and industries, which are usually more short-sighted than the scientific community and others.

Large areas of technology have been developed in the private sector. Governments generally, it should be pointed out, have been far less successful in encouraging advanced technology. Public responsibility does not have to be bureaucratic. It can be entrepreneurial.

Research in the private sector could be supported by the European Community, without provoking national rivalries, through a European university and related institutes. Not only could such institutions bring together qualified specialists from all member countries and act as a catalyst among different educational systems. There could be a vitalizing feed-back from practical experience to national universities. Furthermore, such scientific establishments could be located in economically backward regions, attracting science-based industries and inducing a higher standard of secondary education in the locality.

Opportunity of the Energy Crisis

The intensification of national scientific research which is being necessitated by the energy crisis provides an opportunity to move in the direction of wider involvement in policy-making. It should not be forgotten that in basic science there is a perfectly internationalized system within which knowledge, 'know-how' and talent move at minimum cost. And hence the internationally coordinated research effort which is necessary for meeting the energy crisis could be achieved with few formal negotiations, agreements or treaties.

In the long run, the suggested changes in the making of policy with respect to advanced technology could accelerate the trend, observable since the mid-1950s, towards an increasingly 'fine-mesh' international specialization in high technology industries. Part of that trend has been the transfer of technology through international direct investments. As the trend develops the possibility of any one country dominating trade in several of the strategic areas is likely to diminish steadily over the years.

PROMOTION OF EUROPEAN COMPANIES

Another part of the trend has been the role of multinational enterprises as agencies for the international transfer of capital, technology and managerial skill. The European Community could accordingly facilitate the development of technological innovation in the private sector by removing fiscal and legal barriers to closer relations and mergers between firms to form 'European companies'.[17] This could be assisted by the adoption of a European company statute, the seventh element of the Paris communiqué.

Differences in company laws and differences in corporate taxes pose serious problems for the establishment, transfer and merging of companies. Head offices cannot be transferred from one country to another without changing their juridical status. Branches and subsidiaries cannot be established in another member country without being subject to national laws that differ from those applying to their parent companies at home. Companies located in different member countries that are interested in integrating their operations are thus obliged to resort to a variety of legal strategems which, in the major and majority of cases, have not yet resulted in rationalizations of production.

Most of the mergers that took place after the formation of the European Community were therefore between firms of the same member country, rather than between firms in different member countries, although there were many mergers between member-country firms and foreign companies. Cooperation agreements were far more numerous than mergers, as Table 3 below shows, and the establishment

TABLE 3

Direct investments, cooperation agreements and mergers
in the European Community, 1961-69

Establishment of subsidiaries	
By member-country firms	2,300
By third-country firms	3,546
Cooperation agreements	
Between national firms	1,352
Between member-country firms	1,001
Between member-country and foreign firms	2,797
Mergers	
Between national firms	1,861
Between member-country firms	257
Between member-country and foreign firms	820

SOURCE: *Bulletin of the European Communities,* Commission of the European Community, Brussels, 1970, p. 30.

of subsidiaries was also on a substantial scale, but again the cases involving third countries far out-numbered those involving different member countries.

The main fiscal obstacles to trans-national mergers and to the establishment of subsidiaries in other member countries have included capital gains taxes on unrealized profits at the time of any merger and the double taxation of the profits remitted by subsidiaries to parent companies. The Commission has accordingly proposed that the taxation of capital gains should be postponed until they are realized. And it has also proposed the application of uniform rules throughout the Community in order to eliminate the double taxation of remitted profits.[18] Neither of the proposed directives has yet been approved by the Council of Ministers.

More generally, the Commission envisages the harmonization of corporate and other taxes, in order to eliminate distortions in the allocation of resources. While this is regarded as a long-term objective, there have been proposals for greater uniformity in the direction of the so-called classic system of taxation, involving the separation of corporate and personal income taxes, which would remove distortions created by the tax credit system of France and Belgium and the split rate system of Germany.[19] On the double taxation of dividends, the Commission has urged a generalized withholding tax in all member countries, replacing the network of bilateral double-taxation agreements that are by no means uniform and in any case are often ineffective. But again the Council of Ministers has still to give its approval.

Integration at company level has been further hampered by the lack of progress in developing an integrated capital market in the European Community. In accordance with Article 67 of the Treaty of Rome, calling for the free movement of capital between member countries, the Council of Ministers approved directives in 1960 and 1962 for relaxing foreign-exchange restrictions on certain classes of capital movements. Apart from the existence and risk of exchange controls, and the double taxation of interest and dividends, the free movement of capital in the Common Market is also obstructed by the unequal treatment accorded to stocks and shares issued in member countries. Securing the quotation of stocks and shares on the different *bourses* of member countries is a difficult and costly process. Various procedures are applied in the member countries to limit the quotation of stocks and shares by non-national companies. And then there are regulations which practically exclude the. purchase by institutional investors of stocks and shares issued in other member countries.

In 1966, the Segré Report recommended (i) the complete liberalization of all foreign-exchange transactions, (ii) the modification of fiscal regulations on interest payments and (iii) equal treatment for all stocks and shares issued in member countries.[20] But little or nothing has been done to implement the report's recommendations. In the direction of fiscal neutrality, the Commission has in the end come out in favour of a generalized withholding of tax on interest payments, as proposed on dividends.

Returning to the question of a European company statute, the Commission's proposals, submitted to the Council of Ministers in 1970, visualized the establishment of European companies that would be independent of national laws but subject to the control of the European Court. The shares of such companies would be quoted in national *bourses*. The companies would be taxed in the country where their head office was located, subject to the application of rules eliminating double taxation, for profits would be taxed in the countries where they were earned. The statute would also cover the constitution of supervisory and management boards, collective wage bargaining and 'worker participation'.[21]

The proposal for a European company statute has been widely discussed and several serious difficulties have been exposed:

(a) Provisions in the statute would conflict with provisions in national legislation. In less complex matters these differences might be overcome in due course. But in the realm of company legislation with all its technicalities they do appear seriously embarassing.

(b) If the provisions of the statute were less strict than those of national legislation, European companies would be accorded unfair advantages over national companies; and if they were more strict, the case for having a European statute would be greatly reduced.

(c) Then differences in rules relating to worker participation create further problems too involved to be reviewed here.

(d) Finally, the proposals for a European company statute have provoked resistance on the part of national governments, which are as reluctant in this matter as in others to cede any national sovereignty.

We would therefore recommend that member governments should concentrate on the harmonization of national company legislation in order to permit *inter alia* (i) the takeover of domestic companies by firms of another member country, (ii) the transfer of the head office of a company from one member country to another without change in juridicial status, (iii) the quotation on domestic *bourses* of stocks and shares issued in another member country and (iv) the harmonization of accounting practices so that company accounts can be comparable. In the process an effort might be made to adopt uniform provisions for the establishment of European companies. But we would not press this last course lest the best should become the enemy of the good.

COMPETITION POLICY

While trans-national mergers between firms can produce greater efficiency in production, including economies of scale, they can lead to the reduction or elimination of effective competition. Measures to encourage European mergers should therefore be accompanied by appropriate measures to ensure the maintenance of competitive conditions in the Common Market. On the subject of mergers there is thus a close inter-relationship between industrial and competition policies. This is particularly so where multinational enterprises are involved. For an early motivation for the European interest in encouraging mergers was concern over the ability of firms in the member countries of the European Community to compete with the subsidiaries of large American-based enterprises.[22]

MULTINATIONAL ENTERPRISES

What is a multinational enterprise? It is a group of affiliated companies which operates production facilities in more than one country.[23] Such groups are by no means all the same. They vary greatly. Nor are they all American based. Over half the major ones are based outside the United States. Indeed, the number of European-based multinational enterprises has been increasing, particularly in recent years. It should also be stressed in passing that there is no such animal in law as a 'multinational corporation'. The subsidiaries in a multinational enterprise are companies incorporated under national laws and thus subject to national controls. Governments can accordingly take whatever action they deem fit to safeguard national interests however defined.

There is a widespread belief that multinational enterprises represent a threat to national economies. That belief is often induced, it sometimes seems, by little more than nationalistic sentiments and a fear of big organizations.[24] But some concerns are understandable and even justified. Before discussing policy we want to comment briefly on the anxieties, and resulting allegations, aroused by multinational enterprises.

Before analysing the substantive issues relating to the operations of multinational enterprises we would like to dispel some of the misconceptions. For there seems to have developed a new form of protectionism against foreign firms that parallels the old form of protectionism against foreign products. Multinationality is a phenomenon that should not be confused with bigness *per se*.

Criticisms in Perspective

Many charges against multinational enterprises tend to assume that they are able to reallocate assets rather quickly in response to marginal changes in national policies. If sudden shifts in the location of productive assets could occur they might, indeed, create serious regional problems; and they might present a challenge to national governments in that such decisions may be taken outside their jurisdiction. The fact is, however, there are very few economic activities which permit such a high degree of mobility. Multinational enterprises invest in the expectation of long-run returns.

Multinational enterprises are repeatedly accused of being a disruptive influence in international currency markets through the generation of speculative movements of short-term capital. But no firm evidence to this effect has yet been established. In any case, to blame multinational businesses for contributing to disturbances in short-term capital markets, particularly through operations in the Euro-dollar market, is to confuse cause and effect. Given the acknowledged inadequacies of the present international monetary system, such operations provide a reason for changing the exchange-rate system, not a rationale for introducing costly controls. This is not to deny that safeguards may be necessary to prevent market instabilies in view of the large volume of liquid funds in the hands of multinational enterprises and a few other market participants. But this is only part of a much wider problem which must be resolved within an internationally-agreed framework.

Simple extrapolation of the growth of multinational enterprises, especially those of American origin, has produced a concern in certain quarters that some kind of take-over of the world economy by a few international oligopolists is imminent. But there were several specific reasons for the recent expansion of multinational groups outside their country of origin.

The under-valuation of most European currencies against the dollar throughout the 1960s made the acquisition of businesses in Western Europe an attractive proposition to American-owned companies with ready access to capital, either in their own reserves or by borrowing, at favourable rates, in European capital markets. Since 1971, however, the situation has changed with the realignment of currency exchange rates. Indeed, there has been a marked acceleration in the flow of direct investment in the United States by, among others, European-based companies.

Similarly, the very creation of the European Community, behind a wall of tariff and non-tariff barriers, also tended to attract investments from foreign firms anxious to preserve their position, or to establish a foothold, in the customs union. Direct investments from abroad should be regarded, incidentally, as a spur to competition which otherwise tends to flag in a sheltered market. The attractions of a single market in the European Community were stimulated by a rapid growth of incomes. Empirical studies have shown that market size and market growth are the most important determinants of foreign direct investments.[25] A further attraction was undoubtedly the generous regional-policy inducements and other investment incentives offered in some member countries. Another consideration was the intense competition in the American market which made it difficult for firms to expand their share of the home market.[26]

One reason why American-controlled multinational enterprises are thought to pose a threat to the European Community is the popular notion that bigness automatically ensures superior takeover ability. In practice this is not necessarily true. Even if size permits access to additional economies of scale, and beyond a certain level of output this is by no means assured, it is frequently the case that inefficiencies develop in the administration of big organizations. Large firms have been found to react slowly to changes in market conditions. And when large firms are confronted with structural crises, political problems develop simply because of the number of employees involved — leading very often to government intervention. But the problems of size have general implications that do not relate solely to international businesses. Under an effective competition policy it is as important to regulate mergers between Community firms as it is to regulate the operations of multinational enterprises.

A major advantage enjoyed by multinational enterprises is easy access to capital markets and a capacity to secure full and reliable information on investment opportunities. Accepted banking practice accords high credit ratings to large and powerful organizations. The Commission has suggested that such an advantage could be neutralized, so to speak, if an integrated capital market could be developed in the European Community to encourage the formation of large European companies. This would only make sense if capital markets could discriminate in favour of European enterprises (and therefore against non-European ones). Otherwise lending to low-risk American-based multinational enterprises would remain an attractive proposition. But markets cannot discriminate and any attempt to make them do so would probably provoke opposition from bankers and companies and retaliation, too, by governments outside the Community.

Real Sources of Tension

Tensions between multinational enterprises and national authorities have been increasing. The fault though has not been so much with the former as with the latter. For the source of these tensions lies in the divergencies between policies in different countries.[27] Those divergencies are apparent in systems of taxation, foreign-exchange controls, regional-policy incentives, competition policies and so on. The means by which those divergencies are exploited by multinational enterprises are well known. 'Transfer pricing', the administration of export markets and input-sourcing policies have perhaps attracted most attention. For example, by manipulating prices in trading between affiliates, profits can be shown in a low-tax country. Taxes on other transfers of income — royalties, licence fees et cetera — can be similarly avoided.

A network of affiliated companies differs from an independent company in that the latter ignores the losses suffered by its competitors whereas the former seeks to maximize the overall profits of the group. To that end the former, the multinational enterprise, may try to allocate markets.

Allocation of Markets

The allocation of markets is especially resorted to by multinational enterprises producing similar and competing products in different countries. The practice is hardly found in companies using domestic resources for the domestic market (as in insurance, banking and the distributive trade) where branches are established to serve local customers. Nor is the practice found in enterprises that produce components in various countries and assemble in one of them or in others that produce different lines of products in different countries for the world market. There should be a prima facie case against any restriction of exports unless the company can prove that total costs are reduced and no country's interests are harmed.

Transfer Prices

About one third of the trade of the free-enterprise world is

believed to consist of trade within groups of affiliated companies. Figures for the balances of payments of countries
therefore make little sense if the prices shown in transactions
within multinational enterprises are distorted. The problem is
that 'arm's length' prices — determined to reflect a 'market'
price — cannot always be applied when there is no comparable independent transaction. There is also the intrinsic difficulty of allocating overhead costs among the various
affiliates, particularly the cost of research, especially when it
is very hazardous. The problem of transfer prices is prevalent
in integrated industries and where the components of an
enterprise's products are manufactured in several countries. It
is also evident in groups where parent companies lend capital,
render services or provide 'know-how' to subsidiaries.

There are internal reasons why intra-multinational enterprise prices are distorted. The unequal degree of parent-
company participation in subsidiaries provides an incentive
for profits to appear in the books of wholly-owned subsidiaries or in those where the share of the equity is greatest.
This can only be prevented by high standards of disclosure in
company accounts and by the application of a principle of
non-discrimination.

There are also external reasons why intra-multinational
enterprise prices are distorted. One factor is the inappropriate
nature of government regulations or an absence of inter-
governmental coordination to prevent differences from being
exploited. Exchange controls, for instance, sometimes discriminate between the remittance of dividends and the
remittance of royalties. The main factor, however, is differences in taxation between countries.

Differences in Taxation

Companies are almost encouraged by their home governments to take recourse to 'tax havens' in order not to be at a
disadvantage *vis-à-vis* competing companies controlled from
other countries. This is done at the expense of the ordinary
taxpayer. At present most countries only tax profits earned
abroad at the time they are repatriated. If tax havens are to
be eliminated, world-wide profits of enterprises should be
taxed on an accrual basis, with deductions for taxes paid

elsewhere. Thus the less that is paid in tax havens the more there is that has to be paid in the home country. At the very least, profits made abroad should be taxed at the time they leave the host country, without waiting until they are remitted to the home country. In order to prevent companies from locating their headquarters in tax havens, the European Community should simply deny them the right of establishment.

Another real source of tension with multinational enterprises is the duality of authority — between local managements and head offices. It is too sweeping to complain that centres of business decision are outside a country. Any country engaged in international trade is affected by business decisions taken in other countries. But there is a specific problem over the contradiction between the internationalization of business and the continued compartmentalization of government action. Action by governments needs to be internationalized through greater coordination of policies and practices if differences between them are not to be exploited.

Finally there is a problem with international concentrations where a monopoly position develops. Either there is no action taken or there is extra-territorial application of a country's anti-trust legislation. Our proposals below on the control of concentrations suggest a way in which there could be agreement between the major industrial countries so that joint action could be feasible.

Opportunities to exploit differences in policies could be greatly reduced if systems of taxation and financial inducements to investment could be harmonized throughout the Community. Policy harmonization with respect to financial inducements would probably best be achieved by adjusting ongoing programmes to meet the special problems posed by the operations of multinational enterprises rather than attempt to formulate and implement a common policy. To seek a common policy could all too easily, and quite needlessly, provoke new problems in relations with multinational enterprises and with their home-country governments. With the process of international investment by European and Japanese firms accelerating, following recent realignments in exchange rates,[28] the interest of the European Community in the international regulation of foreign direct investment therefore shifted. Any discriminatory policies introduced by the Community would invite retaliation against European-based multinational enterprises and that could be costly in more ways than one. What the countries of Western Europe have to respond to is not *le défi américain;* rather it is *le défi technologique* that has to be addressed.

International Code of Conduct

Problems arising out of the operations of multinational enterprises can perhaps only be overcome gradually by securing adherence to international rules of conduct relating to investment incentives offered by governments and to divergencies in systems of taxation. In the course of putting its own house in order, the European Community should use its potential strength to obtain such a code, in which there appears to be widespread interest.

Turning to the conduct of multinational enterprises, a fundamental problem in countering tax avoidance through transfer pricing is the inadequate requirements regarding the publication of information on transfers between affiliated companies. Far greater disclosure of information about the activities of all companies will have to be required if there is to be any effective monitoring of the operations of multinational enterprises. The proposal for a European statute should include a general provision to increase disclosure by enterprises operating in the Community. The combined pressure of the Community countries should be applied to extending rules of disclosure on a multilateral basis that should be incorporated in the proposed code. With greater information, it should be possible to establish international rules to ensure that tax avoidance is minimized, if need be by a system for apportioning tax among the countries in which an enterprise operates. Such a course would show the Community measuring up to its international responsibilities because less developed countries, in particular, would probably be among the major beneficiaries.

SAFEGUARDING THE BENEFITS OF FREE TRADE

While the European Community has been encouraging mergers, that is concentrations of market power, it has also been seeking to ensure competition by limiting market power. This duality, it has been pointed out, is partly due to the bureaucratic separation in the Commission of industrial policy from competition policy, each the responsibility of a different directorate-general. More substantially it reflects the lack of a coherent policy on concentration and competition.[29]

In arguing the benefits, theoretically, of free trade within the European Community — and for that matter outside — it is usually assumed by economists that markets are competitive. But in practice that assumption has to be heavily qualified — as can be demonstrated in most countries. In many industries there is a high degree of competition between firms. In many others, however, firms seek to protect themselves from the rigours of a free and open market by means of inter-firm agreements — restrictive business practices.[30] The purposes of such agreements range from (i) the limitation of price competition to (ii) the geographical division of the available market, (iii) the pooling of research and purchasing facilities, (iv) the adoption of common attitudes to advertising and after-sales service and (v) the conclusion of exclusive distribution arrangements.

Only rarely though do conditions exist for a cartel or a monopoly to exploit successfully over an extended period its dominant position in a market. If the cartel maintains its prices at too high a level it will attract new entries to the industry. If it divides the market irrationally, traders will take action to adjust the situation. And if the cartel uses its strength to destroy smaller firms in a price war, imports from outside its markets will take their place as soon as it attempts to raise its prices to monopoly levels.

When a single enterprise attains a monopoly position, it sometimes pursues policies designed to exclude from the particular market any potential rivals, thereby protecting its monopoly profits. Or it may use the large profits earned on its 'safe' product lines, or in its 'safe' markets, to maintain a position in product lines or markets where there is strong competition from more efficient producers in other countries.

Although monopolies and cartels are limited in this way, there are lesser agreements aimed at rationalizing production, trade and distribution. They are promoted in the interests of producers, traders and distributors. They are not necessarily promoted in the interest of consumers. One of the principal objectives of free trade is to promote competition in the consumer interest. But one of the principal objectives of restrictive business practices is very often to reduce the impact of competition from imported supplies and/or of competition in export markets. Indeed, the conclusion of agreements with competing firms in other countries is frequently an important part of restrictive arrangements, the effects of which are in any case unlikely to be confined to the domestic scene.[31]

Restrictive business practices, especially those affecting international trade, thus frustrate the purpose of a common market. If the elimination of barriers to trade among the participating countries is to result in a redistribution of resources within and between those countries, the more efficient enterprises must be able, one way or another, to exploit their superior position and expand at the expense of less efficient firms.

But our concern for the maintenance of effective competition extends beyond purely economic considerations. Competition is one of the foundations of an open society in which all member countries of the European Community have a substantial stake.

Economic integration results in larger markets and favours the growth of firms capable of exploiting economies of scale. Larger firms may be compatible with competition since they are operating in larger markets. But that does not rule out the possibility of concentrations of private power not readily accessible to parliamentary control. In formulating competition policy, it is therefore necessary to weigh against the gains from industrial concentration the socio-political consequences of concentrations of private power, which could discredit property-owning democracy.

Several provisions have been made in the Treaty of Rome to ensure that the internal market of the European Community is reasonably competitive. But the implementation of the provisions has been very slow. After introducing a system for notifying restrictive practices, the Commission initially devoted most of its attention to vertical agreements between firms (a producer, its suppliers and/or its customers). Special interest was taken in exclusive distribution arrangements. More recently, attention has turned to horizontal agreements, those between enterprises engaged in the same line of products. Considerable thought has been given to how agreements, and particularly mergers, may lead to greater efficiency.[32]

FRUSTRATIONS AT COMMUNITY LEVEL

Since the enlargement of the Community, the Commission has made some significant progress in developing proposals, but there is no getting away from the fact that the impact of the Treaty of Rome's provisions for coping with restrictive business practices has been slight. What is preventing these provisions from being effective?

1. While the Treaty of Rome envisages a competition policy almost as demanding as the American anti-trust laws — although the break-up of existing monopolies is not required — it only establishes a set of basic principles. The Council of Ministers, together with the Commission, is left to devise appropriate rules and regulations, which have therefore been subject to the usual problems entailed in inter-governmental negotiations.

2. Some member countries have no national anti-trust legislation or, like Italy and France, have only weak provisions in this field of economic policy. Britain and West Germany, on the other hand, have relatively strong legislation in this field. Legal traditions also vary from country to country. These differences have added to the difficulties of reaching agreement on common rules and regulations. They also produce serious differences of opinion between the Commission and national governments.

3. Even though the Treaty of Rome places much emphasis on competition in trade between member countries, many measures of national governments designed to support sectors of industry, deemed to be in the national interest, infringe the common rules relating to competition. The resistance of governments to the harmonization of taxation, legal and institutional arrangements which inhibit increased competition, through the penetration of domestic markets by foreign

suppliers, is a further sign that they do not wish to surrender control to the European Community.

4. The powers of the Commission, as provided under the Treaty of Rome, to supervise the assistance given by member governments to firms, industries and regions are not strong enough to prevent distortions of competition, although this is a declared objective of the European Community. The ways in which national governments provide aid are far from 'transparent'. They are often based on general legal provisions and the allocation of support largely depends on discretionary decisions by governments which, having no clear concept, are prone to be influenced by immediate considerations (including pressure from vested interests). Our proposals for coordinating adjustment-assistance policies should help to induce a greater degree of transparency in government measures.

5. Not only is there limited information available to the Commission on public assistance to industry. Information on other infringements of common rules on competition is also severely limited. The Commission should be authorized to inform public opinion in member countries about specific cases where consumer interests are being overlooked. This might be achieved through reports to the European Parliament.

6. The Commission is required to decide (i) whether concentrations of economic power, in a corporate grouping of some kind, is acceptable because it helps to foster research and development, more efficient production or improved marketing to the benefit of society at large or (ii) whether it is unacceptable because it mainly restricts competition to the benefit of special interests. In this respect, the Commission has been interested in the creation of industrial and commercial enterprises of a size thought necessary to compete, both in the European Community and abroad, in the face of American-based multinational enterprises. It has found though that member governments have preferred to meet the challenge on their own by facilitating the restructuring of industries within their national framework — sometimes offering inducements to domestic firms to combine. But governments have also offered inducements, as noted in Chapter 3, to multinational enterprises to invest within their

borders, usually in backward regions. In this they have frequently rivalled each other.

REINFORCEMENT OF COMPETITION POLICY

Proposals for reinforcing the competition policy of the European Community have recently been advanced by the Commission. The existing rules on mergers, in particular, clearly need to be strengthened. Several mergers have had to be accepted over the last few years where, even if they improved the competitive position of the firms which merged, the benefits to society — in respect, say, of productivity — were by no means apparent.

The Commission is interested in developing a competition policy in the European Community which shares in principle the position of the Supreme Court in the United States on anti-trust legislation there: 'It is competition, not competitors, which the Act protects.' This means that there is no objection *per se* to the growth of firms and mergers between them, but competition must be preserved and, furthermore, the conditions of entry for new competitors must be safeguarded. In principle, therefore, we are in sympathy with the proposals of the Commission to obtain authority

(a) to control international mergers and, if necessary, to reverse any which contravene the requirements of competition, and

(b) to restore competition in industries where its conditions are no longer satisfied, even if this means dismantling large firms.

Precisely how preventive action should be taken poses a number of difficult problems. (i) By what procedure should firms be notified that the Commission intends to act against a proposed merger? (ii) Can criteria be laid down in order to limit the number of preventive actions to cases where effective competition is really likely to be jeopardized? On both questions the Commission's proposals encountered serious criticism.

In respect of the first question, it was considered that if all mergers which involved at least one Community-based firm and affected intra-Community trade had to be notified in advance to the Commission, this would delay them and introduce a costly element of uncertainty. Where publicly-quoted companies were involved it would be necessary to suspend stock-exchange dealings in the shares which would accordingly upset the whole market. In respect of the second question critics considered it too rigid a criterion for preventive actions to be confined to proposed mergers of firms whose combined sales of the products in question amounted to a certain percentage of total sales. A more acceptable set of criteria would relate to the performance of the firms taking part in the proposed merger.

In the light of these criticisms, we would suggest the following general rules to be applied:

First, it should be obligatory for all firms involved to announce their intention to embark on an international merger involving at least one Community-based firm, irrespective of whether it would be pursued through negotiations, a take-over bid or piecemeal purchases on the stock exchange.

Secondly, the Commission should be authorized to initiate proceedings to reverse, irrespective of its merits, any merger which has been concluded without the necessary announcement being made in advance.

Thirdly, the announcement of a proposed merger should be accompanied by a clear statement on its advantages for the economy as a whole.

Fourthly, the Commission should be accorded the right to investigate *ex post facto* whether a merger really achieved its stated objectives and whether it was satisfying the requirements of effective competition.

Fifthly, if the Commission finds that a merger has not achieved its stated objectives or is not satisfying the requirements of effective competition it should be authorized to initiate proceedings to reverse the merger.

Sixthly, exemptions from the principle to safeguard effective competition should be limited to cases which are in the public interest, relating for instance to regional development or adjustment in a declining industry.

These rules would protect the interests of employees and

shareholders in the firms involved as well as the public interest. In particular, the secret buying-up of shares would be outlawed, which has become an unacceptable aspect of capitalism. The proposed rules avoid the technical problems and possible disruptive effects that would be involved in powers to delay a merger. Instead they put the onus on firms to make sure that their post-merger activities will stand the test of official scrutiny. And in announcing in advance the plans for a merger they would immediately be confronted with the reactions of those likely to be affected. The requirement that proposals for mergers should be accompanied by a clear statement of its advantages for the economy as a whole should also serve to discourage the formation of conglomerates as far as they simply amount to asset speculation on a large scale.

Further Proposals on Competition Policy

There are a number of more detailed suggestions for reinforcing competition policy that might be considered.

We would support the Commission's proposal that it be entitled to initiate court proceedings aimed at dismantling enterprises which have acquired such a position in the market for their products that competition is severely restricted, either (i) because suppliers and consumers have little or no choice or (ii) because the conditions of entry for new competitors are too formidable.

The directorate-general for competition policy in the Commission should be made large enough to cope with the most important cases of potential violation of Community rules of competition. Because of this, and also because national competition policies in some member countries have not been developed, it may be useful to decentralize the directorate-general. Branch offices could be established in every member country and they could collaborate with national authorities where they exist.

Since public opinion can exert a positive influence on the competitive behaviour of firms, the Commission should be better placed to bring violations of competition policy to public attention, for which purpose there should be closer cooperation and exchange of information between the directorate-general and national authorities. Indeed, the directorate-general might be accorded the right to request information from national authorities; and it might be required to inform the European Parliament of refusals by member governments to cooperate in this way.

The cooperation of the directorate-general with other authorities concerned with competition policy might be extended beyond the European Community's borders. Here we chiefly have in mind the anti-trust office of the Department of Justice in the United States. Such cooperation would help in dealing with American-based multinational enterprises. But the Department of Justice would also be a useful source of experience.

The public sector should not be allowed to escape the surveillance of the directorate-general, which should be concerned with much more than government purchasing policies. Even more important are the activities of nationalized industries which, in most countries, do not appear to be required to conform to any particular standard of competitive behaviour.

In discussions in the European Community of competition policy the position of small businesses tends to be overlooked. Broadly there are two types of family business. There is the old worker who has become self-employed and, for the most part, has not been tutored in management. Then there is the business run by the heirs of the founder who share — or quarrel — about the functions of management.

Studies initiated by the Commission of the Community have demonstrated that certain features are prominent among small and medium-size firms.[33] Among them is inadequate distribution of functions, inadequate distinction between the firm's and the owner's resources, inadequate planning in the use of machinery, inadequate technological 'know-how' in production, inadequate attention to the market and inadequate financial forecasts. It has further been observed that small firms very often have no rational investment plan, little idea of future profits and, indeed, no forecasts beyond a few months or even a few weeks. While all these deficiencies are hardly ever present simultaneously, nearly all small or medium-size businesses exhibit some of them. This situation is particularly serious in France and Italy.

We suggest that consideration should be given to the establishment of an office in the Commission that caters for the interests of small businesses. Most important, small and medium-size firms need to be encouraged to specialize, but they can also be assisted with advice ranging from the keeping of accounts to the technological advances in their line of activity.

CONCLUSIONS AND RECOMMENDATIONS

In the development of industrial policy and competition policy in the European Community a conscious effort should be made to achieve between them a greater degree of intellectual coherence. Our recommendations are aimed in that direction.

1. Now that tariffs have been reduced to very low nominal levels, and non-tariff measures are being broached in GATT negotiations, the member governments of the European Community should place more emphasis on adjustment assistance. In fact they should develop a concerted approach to the provisions of adjustment assistance to declining industries unable to compete in the face of growing imports and other changes in their business environment.

2. Indeed, a common industrial policy should be formulated within a framework of international obligations relating to non-tariff interventions by governments in production and international trade and, also, to restrictive business practices.

3. In formulating a policy towards declining industries a clear distinction should be drawn between adjustment assistance, aimed at shifting resources into more competitive activities, and government aids which are merely substitutes for more traditional forms of protection.

4. The European Community should coordinate the adjustment assistance policies of member countries, thereby inducing governments to develop consistent policies for assisting regions, firms and workers to adapt to changing economic circumstances. Rules could be formulated as part of an international agreement on the reform of the 'safeguard' provisions in the GATT for temporary protection against sudden surges of imports.

5. In order to coordinate adjustment assistance policies, the Community should secure agreement among the member countries on the criteria and conditions for government assistance to industries. Those criteria and conditions should then be published and widely publicized.

6. When industries seek government assistance, the appropriate authorities at national (and supra-national) level should be required to consult a panel representing the public interest in the broadest sense, including consumer interests and the interests of other industries concerned, besides independent economic opinion.

7. These proposals should help to bring about increased 'transparency' in public assistance to industry the lack of which has hampered the implementation of an effective competition policy in the European Community.

8. The Commission should be asked to inform public opinion, perhaps through reports to the European Parliament, about specific cases where consumer interests are apparently being overlooked.

9. With respect to concentrations of industrial activity, we are in sympathy with the proposals of the Commission to obtain authority (i) to control international mergers and, if necessary, to reverse any which contravene the requirements of competition and (ii) to restore competition in industries where its conditions are no longer satisfied even if this means dismantling large firms.

10. Accordingly, we recommend that any contemplated merger involving at least one Community-based firm, and affecting intra-Community trade, should be announced in advance with a clear statement of its advantages for the economy as a whole. In the event of a merger not being announced in advance, the Commission should be allowed to seek its reversal.

11. Moreover, the Commission should be authorized to investigate mergers *ex post facto* to ensure that they have achieved their stated objectives and are satisfying the requirements of effective competition. If those stated objectives and requirements are not being met, again the Commission should be allowed to seek the reversal of the merger.

12. The only exemptions from the requirements of effective competition should be mergers in the public interest,

relating for instance to regional development or adjustment in a declining industry.

13. An early motivation of European interest in encouraging mergers was concern over the ability of firms in the member countries to compete with the subsidiaries of large American-based multinational enterprises.

14. Multinational enterprises are, in effect, agents for the international transfer of capital, technology and managerial expertise. Issues relating to them should be considered as issues relating to foreign direct investment.

15. The major sources of tension between multinational enterprises and national governments lie in the divergencies in the policies of different countries and are reflected in systems of taxation (particularly where 'tax havens' are concerned), foreign-exchange controls, regional-policy incentives, competition policies and so on. Opportunities to exploit policy differences would be greatly reduced if systems of taxation and financial inducements to investment could be harmonized throughout the Community.

16. Policy harmonization in respect of systems of taxation, investment incentives and company laws should be pursued by adjusting programmes to meet the special problems arising from the operations of multinational enterprises.

17. In the course of putting its own house in order, the European Community should promote adherence to an international code of conduct relating to investment incentives, systems of taxation and rules of disclosure. A fundamental problem in countering tax avoidance through 'transfer pricing' is the inadequate requirements regarding the publication of information on transfers between affiliated companies. Tax avoidance could then be minimized by a system of taxing the world-wide profits of enterprises on an accrual basis with deductions for taxes paid elsewhere.

18. In encouraging the formation of large industrial enterprises it has been found that differences, as between member countries, in company laws and corporate taxes pose serious problems for the establishment, transfer and merging of companies in the European Community.

19. Because of the difficulties in the way of implementing a European company statute at an early date, we

recommend that member governments should concentrate on the harmonization of national company legislation in order to permit *inter alia* (i) the absorption of domestic companies by firms of another member country, (ii) the transfer of the head office of a company without change of juridicial status and (iii) the quotation on domestic *bourses* of stocks and shares issued in another member country.

20. The policy for technological development that appears to be emerging in the European Community is just what might be expected to result from an almost exclusive interplay of bureaucratic and industrial interests.

21. Differing national policies have allowed the principle of *juste retour* to determine the course of events. Decisions have not been made on the basis of common Community interests. The determination of every country participating in each venture — whether it be in nuclear, aero-space or related research — to get back for its industry a fair return on its contribution has frequently thwarted a rational division of labour, invited costly national duplication and inspired telling tales of abortive collaboration at almost all levels.

22. Large areas of technology, it should be pointed out, have been developed in the private sector, whereas governments have been far less successful in encouraging advanced technology. Public responsibility does not have to be bureaucratic. It can be entrepreneurial.

23. At the present level of research and development in the European Community there is considerable scope for increasing its effectiveness through improvements in organization.

24. Improvements are needed in the political decision-making process at the level of national governments in deciding on the optimal allocation of resources between pure and applied research.

25. At the level of individual research establishments, improvements could be achieved with greater regard for 'cost effectiveness'; that is, by improving the economic management of scientific research for which specialized post-graduate training should be instituted.

26. Finally, decision-making can be improved even at the level of the scientific community itself, which is by nature both national and supra-national. The scientific community

should have the main, but not the exclusive, influence on decisions on the allocation of research resources among individual sciences (and industries), taking account of activities elsewhere.

27. In order to secure closer, more extensive and more formal involvement on the part of legislatures and the scientific community in the formulation of science and technology policies at both national and Community level, a council on research and development should be established on which all these interests should be represented.

28. Research in the private sector could be supported by the European Community, without provoking national rivalries, through a European university and related institutes.

29. There is considerable scope, too, for encouraging research on education, medicine and other areas concerned with improving human conditions, and without much risk of duplication.

NOTES AND REFERENCES

1. The scope of 'industrial policy' is open to a variety of interpretations. It can be conceived more broadly than in the present text to cover rights of establishment, freedom of capital movements and rules governing competition.

2. *Industrial Policy in the Community*, Colonna Memorandum (Brussels: Commission of the European Community, 1970).

3. The meeting of heads of government of the member countries of the European Community, together with those of the three prospective members, was held in Paris in November 1972.

4. The issue is succinctly posed in Goran Ohlin, 'Trade in a Non-Laissez-Faire World', in Paul A. Samuelson (ed.), *International Economic Relations* (London: Macmillan, for the International Economic Association, 1969).

On the subject of non-tariff interventions there has developed a considerable literature. The major reviews of the non-tariff problem have been Robert Baldwin, *Non-tariff Distortions of International Trade* (Washington: Brookings Institution, 1970); and Gerard and Victoria Curzon, *Hidden Barriers to International Trade*, Thames Essay No. 1 (London: Trade Policy Research Centre, 1970).

For an analysis of government intervention in Germany see Juergen Donges, Gerhard Fels and Axel Neu, *Protektion und Branchenstruktur der westdeutschen Wirtschaft* (Tübingen: J. C. B. Mohr, for the Institut für Weltwirtschaft an der Universität Kiel, 1973).

5. Technical standards and specifications are examined in Robert

Middleton, *Negotiating on Non-tariff Distortions of Trade* (London: Macmillan, for the Trade Policy Research Centre, 1974).

6. *Government Purchasing in Europe, North America and Japan: Regulations and Procedures* (Paris: OECD Secretariat, 1966).

7. There has been concern expressed in the United States, and in Japan, that when the European Community does set about agreeing on a common industrial policy, it might go to protectionist excesses against external interests — in order to satisfy the internal interests of all member countries — much as its common agricultural policy has done. See C. Fred Bergsten, 'Crisis in US Trade Policy', *Foreign Affairs*, New York, July 1971.

8. It is not altogether appreciated that much of the protectionist pressure that developed in the United States almost immediately after the successful conclusion in May 1967 of the Kennedy Round of GATT negotiations was provoked by the belief that foreign products, especially from Western Europe, were penetrating the American market with the aid of subsidies, either for their export or for their manufacture. For an account of the situation at that time, see *Constructive Proposals for US Import Quotas*, a Statement by the Canadian-American Committee (Washington: National Planning Association, 1968).

One specific and major source of difficulty has related to exports to the United States of heavy electrical engineering equipment, discussed in Horace de Podwin and Barbara Epstein, *The British Power Transformer Industry and its Excursions into the United States Market: a Case Study in International Price Discrimination* (New York: Institute of Finance, 1969).

9. Gerhard Fels, 'Meccanismi di aggiustamento', in *Negoziati Commerciali Internazionali: Conflitto o Cooperazione?* (Milan: Fiera di. Milano, 1973), a subsequent version of which appeared in *The Round Table*, London, July 1973.

10. This concensus was reflected in, for example, the report of the High-level Group on Trade and Related Problems, *Policy Perspectives on International Trade and Economic Relations*, Rey Report (Paris: OECD Secretariat, 1972), ch. 5, pp. 81-84. A detailed discussion of the shortcomings of the main 'escape clause' in the GATT — namely Article 19 — and how it might be reformed can be found in Jan Tumlir, *Proposals for Emergency Protection against Sharp Increases in Imports*, Guest Paper No. 1 (London: Trade Policy Research Centre, 1973).

11. Frank McFadzean *et al.*, *Towards an Open World Economy*, Report of an Advisory Group (London: Macmillan, for the Trade Policy Research Centre, 1972), pp. 28-30.

12. Geoffrey Denton and Seamus O'Cleireacain, *Subsidy Issues in International Commerce*, Thames Essay No. 5 (London: Trade Policy Research Centre, 1972), pp. v-vii.

13. In the United Kingdom, for example, it was ironic and even disturbing that when the Industry Act — which laid down no criteria or conditions for government subsidies — was going through the British Parliament, both the Expenditure Committee and the Public Accounts

Committee in the House of Commons were actually preparing and publishing reports that expressed grave disquiet over the way in which interventions in industry under previous governments had been managed. See *Public Money in the Private Sector*, Sixth Report of the Expenditure Committee (London: Her Majesty's Stationery Office, for the House of Commons, 1972), and *Third Report of the Committee of Public Accounts* (London: Her Majesty's Stationery Office, for the House of Commons, 1972).

14. This line of argument can be found in Jean-Jacques Servan-Schreiber, *Le défi américain* (Paris: Denoel, 1967). Also see Christopher Layton, *European Advanced Technology: a Programme of Integration* (London: Allen & Unwin, for Political and Economic Planning, 1969).

15. What is referred to here is the theory of the product cycle, developed by the Harvard economist, Raymond Vernon, in 'International Investment and International Trade in the Product Cycle', *Quarterly Journal of Economics*, Cambridge, Massachusetts, May 1966, pp. 190-207.

16. *The Times*, London, 15 June 1973.

17. Dennis Thompson, *The Proposal for a European Company*, European Series Paper No. 13 (London: Political and Economic Planning, 1968).

18. Proposed directives on both measures were submitted by the Commission to the Council of Ministers of the European Community on 16 January 1969. See *Journal Officiel*, Commission of the European Community, Brussels, No. C 39/1-10, 22 March 1969.

19. A. J. van den Temple, *Corporation Tax and the Individual Income Tax in the European Community* (Brussels: Commission of the European Community, 1970).

20. *Le développement d'un marché européen des capitaux*, Segré Report (Brussels: Commission of the European Community, 1966).

21. Colonna Memorandum, *op. cit.*

22. *La politique industrielle de la Communauté*, Colbrina Report (Brussels: Commission of the European Community, 1970).

23. For a range of definitions of a multinational enterprise, see *Multinational Corporations in World Development* (Geneva: United Nations, 1973).

24. M. D. Steuer *et al.*, *The Impact of Foreign Direct Investment on the United Kingdom*, Steuer Report (London: Her Majesty's Stationery Office, for the Department of Trade and Industry, 1973). In the report, initially commissioned by the British Board of Trade, many of the popular fears associated with foreign investment are put in perspective, both in economic and in social terms.

The operations of multinational enterprises have been subject to intensive professional study since the early 1960s, especially in the United States and in countries where American investment has been substantial, notably in Australia, Britain and Canada. From a vast literature on the subject, attention might be drawn to the following works: John Dunning, *American Investment in British Manufacturing*

(London: Allen & Unwin, for Political and Economic Planning, 1958); D. J. Brash, *American Investment in Australian Industry* (Canberra: Australian National University Press, 1966); A. E. Safarian, *Foreign Ownership of Canadian Industry* (Toronto: McGraw-Hill, 1966); Edith Penrose, *The Large International Firm in Developing Countries* (London: Allen & Unwin, 1968); Charles P. Kindleberger, *American Business Abroad* (New Haven: Yale University Press, 1969); and Y. Tsurumi, 'Profiles of Japanese-based Multinational Firms', *Journal of World Trade Law*, London, July-August 1972.

Among more general analyses of multinational corporate planning affecting 'national interests' might be noted: Murray C. Kemp, 'Foreign Investment and National Advantage', *Economic Record*, Melbourne, June 1962; J. N. Behrman, *National Interests and the Multinational Enterprise* (Englewood Cliffs: Prentice-Hall, 1970); M. Z. Brooke and H. L. Remmers, *The Strategy of Multinational Enterprise* (London: Longmans, 1970); Kindleberger (ed.), *The International Corporation* (Cambridge, Massachusetts: MIT Press, 1970); Raymond Vernon, *Sovereignty at Bay* (New York: Basic Books, 1971), Dunning (ed.), *The International Enterprise* (London: Allen & Unwin, 1971); J. M. Stopford and L. T. Wells, *Managing the Multinational Enterprise: Organization of the Firm and Ownership of Subsidiaries* (New York: Basic Books, 1972); and Dunning (ed.), *Economic Analysis and the Multinational Enterprise* (London: Allen & Unwin, 1974). Also see Pierre Uri, *L'Europe se gaspille* (Paris: Hachette Litterature, 1974), pp. 171-97.

On the balance-of-payments effects of outward investment, see W. B. Reddaway *et al.*, *Effects of United Kingdom Direct Investment Overseas* (Cambridge: Cambridge University Press, 1968); G. C. Hufbauer and F. M. Adler, *Overseas Manufacturing Investment and the Balance of Payments*, Tax Policy Research Paper No. 1 (Washington: US Government Printing Office, for the Treasury Department, 1968); and S. Lall, 'Balance of Payments Effects of Foreign Private Investment', TD/134 Supp. 1 (Geneva: United Nations, 1972).

For official, or quasi-official, enquiries, see the Colbrina Report, *op. cit.; A Foreign Economic Policy for the 1970s*, Part 4, The Multinational Corporation and International Investment (Washington: US Government Printing Office, for the Joint Economic Committee, United States Congress, 1970); Herbert Gray, *Foreign Direct Investment in Canada*, Gray Report (Ottawa: Queen's Printer, 1972); United States Tariff Commission, *Implications of Multinational Firms for World Trade and Investment and for US Trade and Labour* (Washington: US Government Printing Office, 1973); the Steuer Report, *op. cit.;* and the Group of Eminent Persons, *The Impact of Multinational Corporations on the Development Process and on International Relations*, Report for the UN Economic and Social Council (New York, United Nations, 1974).

The literature relating to multinational enterprises is comprehensively reviewed, according to the various policy issues posed by them, in Sperry Lea and Simon Webley, *Multinational Corporations in Developed Countries: a Review of Recent Research and Policy Think-*

ing (London, Washington and Montreal: British-North American Committee, 1973).

25. See, for instance, Brash, *op. cit.*, and Behrman, *op. cit.*

26. Report of the United States Tariff Commission, *op. cit.*

27. P. M. Goldberg and C. P. Kindleberger, 'Towards a GATT for Investment: a Proposal for the Supervision of the International Corporation', in *Law and Policy in International Business* (Washington: Georgetown University Law Centre, 1970). Also see Goldberg, 'The Determinants of US Direct Investment in the EEC', *American Economic Review*, 1972.

28. Cf. Stephen Hymer and A. R. Rowthorne, 'Multinational Corporations and Oligopoly: the Non-American Challenge', in Kindleberger (ed.), *The International Corporation* (Cambridge, Massachusetts: MIT Press, 1970). In addition, see Thomas Horst, 'Firm and Industry Determinants of Decisions to Invest Abroad: an Empirical Study', *Review of Economics and Statistics*, Cambridge, Massachusetts, May 1972.

29. Bela Balassa, 'Industrial Policy in the European Common Market', *Banca Nazionale del Lavoro Quarterly Review*, Rome, December 1973.

30. The OECD has maintained a long-standing interest in restrictive business practices. See, for example, *Guide to Legislation on Restrictive Business Practices* (Paris: OECD Secretariat, 1972), a looseleaf publication in six volumes with supplements. Also see other OECD publications: *Glossary on Terms relating to Restrictive Business Practices* (1965); *Refusal to Sell*, Report of the Committee of Experts on Restrictive Business Practices (1969); and *Market Power and the Law* (1970), a study of restrictive business practice laws of OECD countries and, too, of the European Community and the ECSC dealing with market power.

In addition, see Adrienne Szokoloczy-Syllaba, *EFTA: Restrictive Business Practices* (Bern: Verlag Stämpfli, 1973), and John S. Lambrinidis, *The Structure, Function and Law of a Free Trade Area* (London: Stevens, for the London Institute of World Affairs, 1965).

31. Hans Liesner, 'Harmonization Issues under Free Trade', in Harry G. Johnson (ed.), *Trade Strategy for Rich and Poor Nations* (London: Allen & Unwin, for the Trade Policy Research Centre, 1971), pp. 146-49.

32. See, for example, *The Problem of Concentration in the Common Market* (Brussels: Commission of the European Community, 1966); and *The First Report on Competition Policy* (1972) and the second report (1973) of the Commission.

33. Referred to in Uri, *op. cit.*, pp. 192-97.

6 Social Environment for Change

Material prosperity is not an objective to be pursued at any price. There are qualitative aspects which cannot be ignored. Indeed, there are three major and complementary aspects that need to be considered, the first of which was discussed in the previous chapter.

(a) Competition must be ensured and reinforced in order to contribute to (i) greater individual freedom by controlling economic power, (ii) increased price stability which is threatened by sellers' market power and (iii) smoother adjustment in industry to changes in economic circumstances.

(b) The protection of the environment must rest on common principles and partly on a common policy designed to (i) prevent producers and consumers from making socially unacceptable choices when faced with decisions between production or consumption and environmental damage, and (ii) prevent the use of the environment, which increasingly grows in importance as a social good in affluent societies, from leading to serious inequalities in standards of living.

(c) There should be a common effort to achieve social progress throughout the Community so that (i) economic burdens placed on individuals when adjusting to changing economic circumstances are reduced, (ii) conditions of work are continuously improved, (iii) workers are more closely involved in the development of firms and (iv) existing inequalities in individual opportunities to prosper are significantly reduced.

In this chapter the discussion will focus on environmental protection and social progress.

ENVIRONMENTAL PROTECTION

The protection of the environment has been virtually neglected in the European Community since the first days of the Six. The Treaty of Rome includes a declaration to improve living conditions, but there has been no legal basis established. Thus in cases relating to the preservation and improvement of the environment the Commission could only recommend resort to Article 235. This article, however, is interpreted as authorizing Community action, following a unanimous decision of the Council of Ministers, in cases not specifically provided for by the Treaty of Rome.

In fact, the Commission did not take any action in this field until July 1971,[1] after which a comprehensive programme was put forward in March 1972.[2] The Commission's proposals reflected a lack of political interest in environmental problems and had to be presented again after the Paris summit meeting of October 1972, where they had been overlooked. This same lack of concern has been noticeable since the end of World War II when, in the wake of destruction and shortages, the objective everywhere in Western Europe was material growth. At that time superiority of socio-economic systems was measured in terms of growth of GNP per head. Only since the late 1960s has concern grown over the future of the environment.[3]

(a) It has slowly been acknowledged that growing economic maturity has brought about a change in social values which have led the public not only to ask that the further degradation of the environment be prevented but to demand its improvement;

(b) As a result of this change in values, and with more information on environmental problems available, the financial sacrifices for the battle against pollution are likely to be more readily accepted;

(c) Present institutions and fiscal arrangements must be adapted to deal with environmental problems and this might mean significant changes in the traditional political and economic framework.

POLLUTION CONTROL

Environmental policy was established as a field for common action at the Paris meeting of heads of government in 1972. Two questions now need to be asked. First, how can environmental control be fitted into a comprehensive and consistent economic policy programme for the Community? Secondly, what action is required at Community level? In order to answer the first question it is necessary to examine the various ways in which environmental control would touch other policies. Four aspects need to be considered.

First, the various sectors of production will receive incentives, as well as disincentives, to accept environmental control policies. This indicates inter-relationships between environmental policy and industrial policies.

Agricultural policies affect the landscape particularly where cultivation is abandoned. This leads to land erosion, steppe formation and so on. Against a concern for public 'goods' — for which agricultural lobbies rarely fail to claim subsidies — one must weigh the public 'bads' produced by this sector.[4] For example, the use of pesticides, like DDT, not only affects agricultural products to a perilous extent but may upset whole ecological sub-systems throughout the world.

Another policy aspect is that there are areas in Western Europe which, while no longer economically viable for continued agricultural production, still possess an environment suitable for tourism and recreation. These areas could contribute to the improvement of the overall quality of life.

Industry is one of the sectors in which a rather limited number of activities produce the most obvious environmental damages — the pollution of the air and water. The use and disposal of many industrial products also creates serious problems. Well-known examples are pollution from motor cars and detergents and the disposal of consumer durables. Environmental controls in these instances can be expected to have a feed-back on production and employment and hence may be resisted. Already there is an increasing demand though for products and manufacturing techniques (recycling) that prevent or reduce environmental damage.

A second aspect of the problem is that the seriousness of the dangers produced by environmental neglect is still uncertain and this may partly explain the note of hysteria emanating from some of those working in this field. We do not know enough about the structure of the various ecological systems which are affected by the fact that 'to live is to pollute'; and further the assimilative capacities of nature and the possibilities to strengthen this capacity have still to be assessed.

We need to know more about the possibilities of introducing non-polluting methods of production and consumption which could be immediately explored if the environment were not provided at a zero price.[5] Policy instruments must be devised to reallocate resources. The present misallocation of resources stems from the fact that pollution, as a joint product of production and consumption, is insufficiently priced, thereby setting wrong market signals. Research and development in this field promises to provide a high rate of social return if the environment could be valued as high as it appears to be in the more mature economies.

The third aspect of the problem that needs to be considered is that the distribution of pollution is largely determined by the geographical concentration of production and consumption. The inter-relationship between environmental and regional policy is therefore evident. We have already discussed the extent to which discrepancies between private and social costs of production contribute to agglomeration and congestion. In the context of the environment, for example, public expenditure on the disposal of waste of all kinds is not recovered by charging the (incremental) costs. In many cases the extent to which these services are used is neglected by charging flat rates. Still more serious are those cases in which the use of the environment, especially water and air, is allowed at a zero price. The most obvious examples of such pollution are the numerous instances of untreated wastes from industry and households which are fed into rivers and lakes and the uncontrolled emission of noxious gases from industrial plants, heating systems and private motor cars.

This gross negligence in respect of the environment contributes to a spatial situation where regions with a high income and a depleted and over-utilized environment co-exist with low-income regions which offer good environmental qualities, including an under-utilized although limited natural capacity to assimilate pollution. This means that even if one does not assume that the inhabitants of the poor regions are probably prepared to accept heavy environmental losses for gains in income, a net total environmental gain could be recorded if a decentralization of economic activities were successful. Any attempt to bring some relief to the regions which suffer from environmental degradation would clearly support the efforts in regional policy and vice versa.

The fourth aspect of the problem is that the growing awareness of pollution in developed countries presents an opportunity to the less developed countries to specialize more in polluting types of industry. To take on the world's dirty work, as an economist recently phrased it, is indeed a matter of social choice. The less developed countries, however, in view of their under-utilized environmental capacity to assimilate pollution would not suffer from this to the same extent as the already industrialized countries. Alternatively they have the opportunity to gain from an increase in tourism. Industry, though, could well be relocated to those countries which have spare environmental capacities and are under-developed. Needless to say, the less developed countries — in most cases — cannot have it both ways. They cannot industrialize and at the same time attract tourism simply because both activities compete for environmental services.

A more serious problem concerns the inter-relationship between environmental control and international economic relations.[6] In many cases pollution does not stop at national borders. Air and water, goods as well as animals and even human beings act as carriers of pollution. Under such conditions a country or group of countries — like the European Community — may not be prepared to import freely products which violate national pollution standards. Barriers to imports, whose production contaminates the importer's atmosphere and waterways, may be justified as creating national external costs. Similarly imports may have to satisfy the pollution standards of the importing country. This measure would be in line with the GATT if import substitutes are to be treated alike. Finally, health certificates may appear to be impediments to the free movement of people across borders.

AREAS FOR COMMUNITY ACTION

Having explored the position of environmental control within the wider framework of economic policy, we now turn to the question of what the division of competence should be between the Community, its member countries and other authorities when dealing with matters of environmental policy. At first glance the Community's responsibilities appear to be rather obvious.

(a) It is the Community's responsibility to set the pattern for agreements on regional border-crossing pollution between the member countries.

(b) The Community should also protect those resources which are of crucial importance to the ecological future of the member countries as a whole.

(c) The Community should aid the development of common enforceable standards or other instruments to limit the manufacturing of polluting products not only as a measure in avoiding cross-border pollution, but irrespective of its country of origin.

(d) In accordance with the Community's international responsibilities, common initiatives should be taken to deal with problems of cross-border pollution between the Community and neighbouring countries and to protect and improve the world's environment.

(e) Finally, it should be the Community's responsibility to aid the common cause of research and development and, as well, to promote the exchange of information in the field of environmental protection and improvement.

Possible Solutions to Problems

Cross-border pollution appears at first glance to be a rather clear-cut case. This is true particularly in view of such striking examples as the pollution of the Rhine river, the pollution of the seas which form part of the borders of the European Community and the pollution of border regions within the Community. It is perhaps politically feasible to restrict common action — as is suggested by the Commission — to these and similar types of cases. There are other carriers of pollution, however (particularly the air), which require greater common action. Here what is required at the very least is an agreement on common standards or other devices to control particularly the emissions from highly pollution-intensive productions and for the consumption of most forms of energy.

It is extremely difficult to achieve an agreement of self-restraint between the polluters and the corresponding national governments. Efforts were made as early as 1960 — in the case of the Rhine river — when a multinational commission was set up. Little has been achieved, except that the pollution of the Rhine has now reached extraordinary proportions. The results in this instance are quite in line with other attempts to achieve agreement on effective multinational programmes. To make matters even worse, while common sense suggests that the polluter should be financially responsible for preventive measures, almost all countries — especially France — tend to negotiate from a position which implies that the polluter should be subsidized by those who have to bear the burden of pollution. Visible progress in dealing with this and similar pollution problems would be a clear test of the cohesion and solidarity of the Community.

It is questionable whether environmental quality standards, accepted directly or indirectly, will be established. Experience has shown that — in view of the fact that pollution intensive production by the few is combined with small individual pollution by the many (that is, the consumers) — efforts to improve the quality of the environment will primarily have two consequences. Either the few will resist a rise in costs through paying for or preventing pollution, leaving it to the many to improve the quality of the environment by acting alone or perhaps even by subsidizing the few to do something. Or nothing will happen at all.

The scope for independent regional decisions must be reduced if inter-regional problems are to be solved. In such circumstances the central government is the only authority the many can turn to if anything is to be accomplished. The government will be immediately faced with the argument that it can hardly put the national economy at a competitive disadvantage in external trade; and although this argument is at best only temporarily valid, it has proven quite successful in preventing or delaying measures to control the externalities of production.

The protection of common natural resources is also a difficult area to handle. Although some cases, like the destruction of common river and off-shore fishing grounds appear to be easily attacked, there still remain intriguing problems. For example, should a member country be free to reduce its forest-land although such action will have climatic and hydrological consequences which will not stop at its borders? Or should there be an agreement about how such an asset must be managed throughout the Community? If the member countries could agree on a general outline of how the Community's land should be used (as we contemplated when dealing with regional policy) this and other related problems would not arise.

Protection could be made much more effective by establishing in the European Community a natural conservation trust which would (i) supervise the use of common natural resources, (ii) have a right either through an initiative of its own or following an appeal from private citizens or public authorities to uphold any national or regional decisions which are likely to reduce these resources, and (iii) be responsible to the European Parliament. The rationale for handing over some responsibility in this field to the Community must be viewed in the light that there are still existing differences in the material standard of living within the Community. Not all member countries can afford to devote their resources to this purpose to the extent which may be desirable in the long run.

The development of standards for products — the use of which may cause severe pollution — appears to be well advanced throughout the world. The European Community, however, is far from being the most progressive in the field of pollution control. Sufficient illustrations include the protracted discussions over the future maximum weight of lorries allowed within the Community (provoked by widespread concern over juggernauts thundering through peaceful villages), the comparatively low standards imposed on the exhausts and the noise levels of motor cars and airplanes and the continuously delayed action in the various member countries to reduce the emission of noxious gases through fuel heating. The slow progress made in these areas can be partly explained by a national fear of losing international competitiveness. But even more important may be the resistance of producers who fear for their sales if anti-pollution devices make products more expensive. Economists have obviously not been very successful in this area. The fact is that present practices cause society to subsidize those who use polluting products and, at the same time, society bears indiscriminately the external costs of a consumption which varies between individuals.

The European Community's international responsibility in environmental matters was put to the test in 1973 at a meeting of the members of the European Council. It was suggested at this conference that the Council should be more closely involved in environmental matters for the very reason that pollution stops neither at national or Community borders. France, in particular, strongly resisted a solution which could have reduced the sovereignty of the member countries and the final result hardly measured up to the Community's responsibilities.

It is clear that the European Community, in a world-wide context, is far from setting a good example or taking a sincere initiative in the field of pollution control. Community members, for example, are among those who do not hesitate to over-fish the seas and use these same waters as a huge dust bin.

Our final point concerns common research and development and is, perhaps, the area least prone to problems. Admittedly knowledge of this field is still rather limited. Many causes of environmental depletion are known though. To mention but one example, we now know quite a bit about the interaction of the various pollutants within the ecological system. Similarly, the major instruments to combat pollution are known. These range from prohibition, compelling standards, special levies and tradeable certificates which entitle the holder to a certain amount of pollution. Their major strengths and weaknesses are largely explored in theory and without their being put into use a final verdict is not possible.

What we are attempting to point out is that there is nothing to gain from waiting any longer. At the outset, however, it should be made clear that environmental policy, perhaps more than other policies, is bound to be a kind of social experiment which will require revision as more and better information becomes available and when measures prove to be unsuccessful.

SOCIAL PROGRESS

We now turn to the third major qualitative aspect of economic development which relates to social progress.[7] Reassurance is given in the Paris summit communiqué that 'the heads of state or of government attach as much importance to vigorous action in the social field as to the achievement of an economic and monetary union'. The Treaty of Rome (Article 117 *et seq.*), as well as the treaty creating the ECSC, clearly stipulate a common social policy. And most of the aims of such a policy are defined in the Treaty of Rome. It is difficult, however, to dismiss the idea that within the EEC social matters as such took a back seat. Admittedly, within the narrow field covered by the ECSC, some efforts were made to deal with the social problems of an industry in conversion and decline. The Commission of the European Community has tried to ensure that the provisions of the Treaty of Rome were put into practice and that these provisions were exploited, given the meagre financial help administered by the Community's Social Fund. Following the Paris summit of 1972 social policy still remains a rather vague area, although those in charge of European integration now appear to be aware of the importance of social progress.

The proposals submitted by the German Government to the Paris summit include six major issues for Community action in the field of social policy:[8]

(a) The principle of free mobility of labour within the Common Market (Article 117) should be complemented by coordinating step-by-step the national policies dealing with the labour market. It was suggested that national employment agencies be set up to communicate the actual labour market situation in the Community as well as development perspectives.

(b) Conditions of work should be improved, including

the prevention of accidents and the protection of health. The exchange of experiences and information in health and safety fields should help to formulate common and binding minimum standards.

(c) Employees should be able to participate effectively in the decision-making process of the enterprises in which they are employed. (No specific suggestions were put forward, presumably because the issue of participation or co-determination is one in which the individual member countries show extreme differences.)

(d) In view of the plans to create a European Company statute, the German Government tentatively suggested an examination in cooperation with the labour market organizations as to whether a common framework for wage-negotiations and contracts between unions and employer organizations should be established.

(e) The national systems of social security should be coordinated according to common principles and a continuous improvement of its related services should be tied to the economic progress of the individual member country. The Social Fund is suggested as an instrument to help coordinate and communicate the progress in this area to the Community.

(f) Inequalities in professional career opportunities should be reduced. Common perspectives in the area of professional training and in adult education should be developed and would be complementary to the principle of free mobility.

The proposals submitted by the Commission to the Council after the summit meeting are basically in line with the suggestions above and hence can be discussed simultaneously.[9]

HELOTS OF WESTERN EUROPE

A primary social problem — that of migrant workers — is related to the Community's principle of free mobility of labour and consequently to migration. A Community-wide solution is urgently required. Experience has shown that the

Community must consider not only migration within its borders but also migration primarily into the Community from third countries. The most obvious reason is that at present, of the more than six million (mostly temporary) migrants living and working in the Community, only one sixth to fifth of these are the result of intra-Community migration. The impact of such large-scale migration is even greater because migrants are concentrated in the most developed regions of the Community. And from an economic as well aas a social point of view both the receiving countries and the countries of origin are becoming increasingly aware that migration on such a scale represents, at the very least, a mixed blessing.

The Community must weigh the contribution to domestic economic growth of cheap and frequently underpaid foreign labour against several factors.

(a) The necessary reduction in agricultural employment will be delayed because the supply of foreign labour acts as a substitute for domestic labour — which would otherwise have come from the agricultural sector — to allow further growth of the industrial and the service sector.

(b) The locational spread of industry will be retarded. Hence the objectives of regional balance and the reduction of environmental pressures in industrial areas are more difficult to achieve because foreign labour is readily inclined to move into the agglomerations and to live there frequently under poor conditions.

(c) The volume and locational concentration of migrants produce massive strains on the local provision of public services because the foreign labour inflow fosters the growth of agglomerations and pushes the corresponding social costs up.

(d) Poor living conditions and the low social status of migrants are sources of social unrest. It is only a matter of time until migrant workers become dissatisfied with their under-privileged status and begin to react against unequal conditions.

(e) Primarily inward migration from third countries, in general, results in a clash of cultures which, because the foreign labour force is concentrated in a few regions, leads to racism. And because this clash is combined with the creation of a helot class available to do menial jobs other parts of the population scorn, attitudes of superiority and disdain are developed which, under pressure and strain, can produce racial conflicts. This is increasingly the case throughout Western Europe.

Equally important, the countries supplying the migrant workers must weigh the (i) reduction of domestic employment problems, (ii) the support given to their balance of payments and to their national income through remittances from migrated nationals, and (iii) the improvement in the quality of their labour force when migrant workers return against several social factors.

(a) In many cases, migrants are among the supplying country's best workers. As these workers leave the rural areas in large numbers they leave behind the weak and the old and reduce domestic agricultural production.

(b) Some countries are left with a growth-impeding specific or general labour shortage. The first is observable in the exodus of professional people who are scarce in numbers anyway and the second is illustrated by the fact that Spain, Italy and Greece are now attracting workers from North Africa.

(c) Returning migrants frequently cannot find jobs which enable them to use their acquired skills. In addition, they are alienated from the agricultural sector (where most of them worked before their departure). Therefore they are likely to turn to the few urban centres, increase the number of unemployed or underemployed and act as a source of social and political unrest, which in turn reduces the attraction of such countries as locations for foreign investments.

The migration problem, as sketched above, immediately raises three policy questions. First, what can be done to improve the lot of the migrant? Second, is heavy inward migration avoidable without increasing unemployment in the regions or countries of origin? And third, is migration warranted at all?

First, even as far as intra-Community migration is concerned, member countries are still far from securing for migrant workers the same rights and opportunities as those given to their own nationals. And this is in spite of Article 48, Section 2, which provides for the removal of any discrimination as to employment, pay and other conditions of work. That the Commission finds it necessary to propose that migrants should enjoy the same social security as the nationals of the host country, illustrates once again that the Treaty of Rome (in this case Article 51), largely remains an unfulfilled promise. Education and housing facilities are two other items on the Commission's list of proposals. But not much has been achieved. Given the present geographical concentration of migrants it is hard to see how such a proposal could be put into effect in the near future without serious financial strain.

What is questionable, however, is the Commission's suggestion that the policy towards migrants from third countries should be treated separately. Here we see a serious danger. The Community would create three types of citizens: nationals, migrants from other member countries who might eventually be treated like nationals and migrants from third countries whose initial negotiating position is particularly weak. The consequences of such a policy are almost predictable. It may perhaps be debatable whether any restrictions should be imposed on inward migration from third countries. Social justice, however, demands that those who are allowed in should be protected against any form of discrimination.

Secondly, as to reducing inward migration, strong interrelationships with regional and foreign economic policy exist and could be favourably exploited. If a common regional policy were to succeed in removing, and thus preventing, congestion in central areas, providing at the same time attractive new urban centres in backward areas capable of self-sustained growth, at least intra-Community migration would be reduced and inward migration partly redirected. Inward migration would be reduced as well since an effort to narrow the gap between social and private costs of production within the Community would also induce production to move beyond Community borders to locations where labour is still cheap and land less scarce. And if the Community were to no longer defend the production of goods which could become exportables of the lesser developed countries, the pressure in those countries to migrate because of unemployment would be further reduced. To some extent this liberalization of trade is also complementary to a policy whose objective is to relocate Community production in lesser developed countries. Such relocation would mean that production would have to be allowed to flow back into the Community on competitive terms.

Finally, the answer to the question — is migration warranted — is a positive one. The Treaty of Rome goes even further, for example, by suggesting that member states foster the exchange of young people, according to a common programme (Article 50). This is another point on which the Commission's proposal represent a telling reminder for the member states. There is no need to explore at length the economic benefits of free mobility within a large labour market such as the Community. Beyond these benefits, however, which are similar to those of free trade, the Community must have an interest in mobility because it can promote its cohesion. This is only the case, though, if migration is not a one-way street from the periphery to the centre, and if it is not the only alternative available to people in their struggle for economic survival.

OTHER NEGLECTED COMMITMENTS

Before leaving the subject of migration, it might be well to point out another suggestion included in the proposals made by the German Government at the Paris summit and, consecutively, by the Commission. Both suggest that national labour-market policies be coordinated, information exchanged about the state and perspectives of the individual labour markets and that a common information centre be created to this respect. Once again we must recall that the Treaty of Rome (Article 49) foresaw most of these elements in its common social policy. Moreover it is well known that most of these elements were among the leading ideas which inspired Community regulations on migrant labour.

Looking at other proposals mentioned earlier, and at the Treaty of Rome, further omissions in social policy come to the fore. This is the case particularly for work conditions, health and safety standards at work, social security and the relationship between the labour-market organizations on a Community level. Article 118 of the Treaty of Rome asks the Commission to foster cooperation between the member countries and to initiate research and inquiries in this field. If sufficient progress had been made, it would hardly have been necessary for the German Government to rephrase this article in terms of proposals which were also taken up by the Commission. Without going into specifics related to the proposals above (which we would largely endorse) at least one of them is partly questionable.

The German proposal concerning the coordination and improvement of the national systems of social security ties the improvement to the economic progress of the individual member country. A similar position is taken in Article 117 of the Treaty of Rome which also rests its hopes for assimilation on the progress of individual member countries. Such a hope is only justified if the Community succeeds in removing the still existing differences in income per head between member countries and between regions. So far there is little hope that this will happen in the near future. But the proposal, and as well the Treaty, imply that those parts of the Community which are behind in this respect must wait until they can afford to provide social services similar to those provided in other parts of the Community. Since social security standards, however, affect the attractiveness of the various regions as locations of economic activity, the proposal contributes another element to the vicious circle in which the backward regions are caught. It is little consolation that the Social Fund provides at least some relief to the social budget of the weaker partners of the Community. As emphasized earlier, we would like to see established a transfer system for the Community which would allow all her partners to provide a similar quality of social services. The transfer system must, however, be constructed in such a way that it does not negatively affect the beneficiaries' propensity to work, a danger which may arise if in weaker regions unemployment benefits come close to earnings in low-paid jobs.

A FIELD FOR EXPERIMENTATION

A more general comment should be made regarding the proposal that workers should be more closely and effectively involved in the decision-making process and the development of firms. As a matter of principle, this proposal is gaining ground throughout the Community. But as already mentioned, in some member countries the discussion has only just begun, while in others it is more advanced or has already led to the introduction of various schemes (as in the case of Germany). In view of this situation, social progress would probably be delayed if one were to ask for a common model to be worked out and constructed. To us this field is well suited to experimentation and diversification, particularly when the differences in social structures and in labour relations of the various member countries are also taken into account.

A similar view must be taken of the problems raised by work organization in factories. It is well known that the organizational structures of industrial firms are dominated by a high degree of specialization, with work fragmented by the demarcation lines drawn between industrial skills. This fragmentation is not diminished but reinforced by the introduction of new 'know-how', although there has been a progressive improvement in working conditions and a growth in the relative importance of technicians and skilled workers on company payrolls. Industrial development has made possible general social progress alongside the extreme division of labour on the production line; and this has entailed, on the one hand, a progressive reduction in available reserves of unskilled labour (as, for example, in agriculture), and, on the other hand, a tendency for the school leaving age to rise, for a general improvement in economic and cultural conditions and, not least, for greater· awareness of the rights of individuals.

These changes make for increasing dissatisfaction with the present system of work organization. Theoretical discussion on priorities for bettering the social structure consistently with that system acquires in this context an extremely concrete meaning and is likely to become increasingly important as a result of the tensions caused by congestion. The question is whether the increased productive potential of contemporary society should be directed increasingly towards the enjoyment of leisure within limits set by other consumer needs, or whether it is not possible to make leisure for recuperation less necessary through the introduction of new forms of work organization. For the time being, this can only be the subject of research and study.

FACING UP TO INEQUALITIES

The Community will be successful in the eyes of its own citizens only if it manages to improve the conditions of life and of work and, also, to reduce social inequalities more effectively than any of its member countries.[10] Most of the attempts so far have limited themselves to raising low wages or increasing other allowances in money terms. As long as there are no effective means of reducing other demands, such attempts are quickly translated into rising prices and the former inequalities are re-introduced, only at a higher price level. An effective social policy requires a completely different approach. It must go to the roots of inequalities which are based on structural factors on the one hand, and on institutional factors on the other.

Throughout this report, we emphasize the structural disparities between regions, between branches and between firms. A great many of our recommendations are directed towards a reduction of such disparities. This is the meaning of an effective regional policy as well as of continuous adjustment aid substituted for the blind application of protections. Part of what we have to say about international economic policy is designed to attain the same objective.

But institutional factors cannot be ignored. Three main ones require special attention.

One is the access to higher education. Even when public education is completely free, a good many families cannot afford to do without the additional income which can be earned by young people if they can go to work. Moreover, the absence of general schooling at a very early age makes children extremely dependent on the family environment. These two factors explain the extraordinary distortion between the share of the various social categories in the active population and the participation of their children in higher education. Sons and daughters of public servants almost all go to university and only a very small number of children of small farmers or industrial workers do so. A fundamental reform will not only establish equality of opportunity but will tend to reduce the spread between the lower wages and the higher salaries as it will make unskilled labour more scarce while promoting the growth of technical and managerial talents.

Another barrier to equality relates to the way in which credits are provided for private undertakings. Because credits are based on a discounting of the proceeds of sales or on a matching direct contribution or guarantee by the beneficiaries, they tend to confirm established positions. As a consequence newcomers are severely hampered. This not only reduces the overall chances for individuals to prosper but also presents a barrier to entry. This situation reinforces the monopoly power and the level of profits as compared with wages and salaries. It can hardly be assumed that the creation of a West European capital market would increase the chances for the newcomers. What appears essential is the multiplication of specialized subsidiaries of banks which would extend credits to people on the basis of their capacity and the value of their creative ideas.

The third and most important institutional factor of unjustified inequalities is the way in which inheritance is treated in the member countries. Whatever the differences between them, the main feature is the very profound difference between the rate of taxation for the successions going from parents to children and the other cases. In other words wealth is automatically devolved in a dynastic way without any practical possibility of redistribution through bequests. Concrete examples will highlight the injustice and absurdity of the present systems. A child of five who becomes an orphan is subject to the same rate of inheritance duties as a man of fifty who is a multi-millionaire in dollars. A land labourer who inherits a cottage from his uncle is subject to such high duties that he cannot keep it but must sell it to pay them. This calls for a complete overhaul of the taxation system on inheritance. Whereas there should be reduced rates for children who have not come of age, the differences according to the degree of kinship should be drastically reduced. The basic allowances should in all cases be enlarged. And the duties should be made highly progressive with the wealth of the inheritor. This would give a greater incentive to savings, due to the greater freedom to dispose of one's wealth. It would also give an extremely strong inducement to the redistribution of this wealth either to charities or to people with a modest income rather than rewarding it to the wealthier. This would also eliminate the possibility that people might own and manage a firm by right of birth.

USES AND ABUSES OF THE EMPLOYMENT OBJECTIVE

All efforts to ensure equality of opportunity in achieving individual prosperity are useless if there are not sufficient employment opportunities. The Commission places considerable emphasis on the objective of full employment as a guiding principle for the Community's social policy. This objective has been interpreted only too frequently in a rather questionable way. For instance, there is a fundamental difference between sufficient employment opportunities and an employment guarantee.

Nearly all member countries have to face the problem of dealing with adjustment assistance. The Community, through the Social Fund and the Agricultural Fund, has taken at least limited responsibility in this area. If, however, under pressure from some groups adversely affected by structural change, the employment objective is more or less disguisedly interpreted as a specific job guarantee, structural conservation with its inflationary, protectionist and growth-retarding consequences is the price that will be paid.

Regional policy is high on both the agenda of the Community and individual member countries. If regional policy is interpreted as beginning with the principle that work should always be brought to the workers, the employment objective as a locational employment guarantee either disregards completely the social costs incurred if this guarantee produces spatial misallocations of resources, or the interpretation assumes at least that the human burden of migration is always higher than the allocational advantages.

All governments are well equipped with instruments to manage demand in a way which avoids serious recession. If, however, the sellers of goods as well as the sellers of labour can rely on a general employment guarantee, one must not wonder that, freed from the risk of pricing themselves out of the market, the way is paved for an inflationary distribution struggle.

CONCLUSIONS AND RECOMMENDATIONS

1. Concern has grown over the preservation and improvement of the environment only over the last few years. The public — responding to a growing economic maturity which has brought about a change in social values — has begun to demand not only that the further depletion of the environment be prevented but that the environment be improved.

2. This change in social values, plus the increase in information on environmental problems, suggests that financial sacrifices for the battle against pollution are likely to be both more readily made and accepted.

3. Additionally, because present institutions and fiscal arrangements must be adapted if we are to deal with environmental problems, significant changes are forecast in the traditional political and economic framework.

4. There are at least four major sectors which would be affected by environmental policy controls: (i) the various sectors of production; (ii) research and development, owing to the fact that we still know very little about the environment itself (ecological systems, assimilative capabilities of the environment et cetera); (iii) the inter-relationship between regional policy; and (iv) international economic relations.

5. The European Community's responsibilities in the area of environmental protection appear to be quite obvious. It is the Community's responsibility to control regional border-crossing pollution between member countries, to promote the use of common natural resources and protect these same resources which are of crucial ecological importance to the Community as a whole.

6. Along these same lines the Community should help develop common enforceable standards to limit product-pollution irrespective of country of origin and, in accordance

with its international responsibilities, the Community should promote common initiatives to deal with cross-border pollution between the Community and neighbouring countries.

7. Finally, the Community should aid the common cause of research and development and promote the exchange of information in the field of environmental protection.

8. Visible progress in dealing with pollution problems would be a clear test of the cohesion and solidarity of the Community.

9. If the problems of cross-regional pollution are to be solved the scope for independent regional decisions must be reduced. This area and two others — environmental quality standards and the protection of common natural resources — are difficult fields to handle. It remains to be seen whether or not individual member countries will relinquish control in these areas to a central authority for the benefit of the Community as a whole.

10. Environmental protection could be made more effective if the Community were to set up a conservation trust to supervise the use of common natural resources. The rationale for handing over some responsibility in this field to the Community must be viewed in the light of the existing differences between member countries in the material standard of living. Not all member countries can afford to devote their resources to the protection of the environment to the extent which is desirable in the long run.

11. The Community is not very progressive in the field of pollution control. Slow progress in this area can in part be attributed to the fact that producers fear for their sales if anti-pollution devices make products more expensive. The fact remains, though, that present practices cause society to subsidize those who use polluting products and at the same time bear indiscriminately the external costs of a consumption which varies between individuals.

12. It is also clear that the Community, in a world-wide context, is far from setting a good example or taking a sincere initiative in controlling pollution. Community members, for example, are among those who do not hesitate to over-fish the seas and pollute these same waters by using them as huge dust bins.

13. There is nothing to gain from waiting any longer to

implement controls in the field of pollution control. At the outset, however, it should be made clear that environmental policy is bound to be a kind of social experiment which will require revision as more information becomes available and when measures prove to be unsuccessful.

14. We endorse the proposals on social policy which the German Government presented at the Paris summit. These proposals include the coordination of national policies dealing with the labour market, the improvement of working conditions (accident prevention and so forth), employee participation in the decision-making process and coordinating national systems of social security.

15. A primary social problem confronting the Community is that of migrant labour. From an economic as well as a social point of view, the receiving countries and the countries of origin are becoming increasingly aware that migration on a large scale represents, at the very least, a mixed blessing. The Community must weigh the contribution to domestic economic growth of cheap foreign labour against several factors. These include the delay in reducing domestic agricultural employment, regional imbalances, and the probability of racial clashes and social unrest.

16. Equally important are the problems facing those countries supplying the Community's migrant workers. Again, there are several factors they must weigh against the reduction of their domestic employment problems and the support given to their balance of payments and their national income through remittances from migrated nationals. These negative factors include the fact that many returning migrants are unable to find jobs enabling them to use newly acquired skills, some countries are left with a specific or general labour shortage and in many cases migrants are among the supplying country's best workers and as they depart the rural areas they leave behind the aged and the weak.

17. Even as far as intra-Community migration is concerned, member countries have not yet obtained for migrant workers the same rights and opportunities as those given to their own nationals. And this is even though the removal of any discrimination as to employment, pay and other conditions of work was agreed upon within the EEC. That the

Community finds it necessary to propose that migrants enjoy the same social security as the nationals of the host country illustrates that the Treaty of Rome (in this case Article 51) largely remains an unfulfilled promise.

18. We see a serious danger in the Community's proposal that migrants from third countries be treated separately. The Community might be inclined to create three types of citizens: nationals, migrants from other member countries who might eventually be treated like nationals and migrants from third countries. The consequences of such a policy are almost predictable.

19. Migration, including that of young people, that is not a one-way street, that is from the periphery to the centre, or that is not the only alternative available to people in their struggle for economic survival is in the interest of the Community as it can promote the Community's cohesion.

20. We would like to see a transfer system established within the Community for the purpose of allowing all member countries to provide a similar quality of social services. At present those member countries which lag behind in social services must wait until they are economically prepared before they can provide similar services. Since social security standards affect the attractiveness of the various regions as locations of economic activity, it is all too evident that the Community's proposal to tie the improvement of national systems of social security to the improvement of the economic progress of the individual member country is but another element in the vicious circle in which the backward regions are caught.

21. Workers should be more closely and effectively involved in the decision-making process of the firms in which they work. To us, this field is well suited to experimentation, particularly when the differences in social structures and labour relations of the various member countries are taken into account. The more general conclusion is that the Community may require in some cases centralization and in others harmonization through common rules and regulations.

22. We believe that while improving the access to education, training and retraining undoubtedly helps to reduce the inequalities which face individuals seeking to improve their standard of living, this alone is not sufficient. We see at least

two other institutional barriers to a more equitable distribution of income. The first is the way in which inheritance is treated in the member countries. In general the total legacy is taxed and not the inheritor. A more equitable way would be to tax the inheritor progressively, taking into account the wealth he might have accumulated. The second barrier concerns the way in which credits are provided for private undertakings. Here we see a chance for improvement via moving towards a European capital market where safeguards are introduced to improve the allocation of resources.

23. All efforts to ensure equality of opportunity are useless if there are not sufficient employment opportunities. The Commission places considerable emphasis on the objective of full employment as a guide principle for the Community's social policy. Social policies should be designed in such a way, however, as not to affect negatively the propensity of beneficiaries to work. This danger may arise if in weaker regions unemployment benefits come close to earnings in low-paid jobs.

NOTES AND REFERENCES

1. *Bulletin of the European Communities*, Brussels, Supplement 11, 1972.
2. *Bulletin of the European Communities*, Supplement 3, 1973.
3. In this connection, see D. H. Meadows *et al.*, *The Limits of Growth* (New York: Potomac Associates, 1972), known as the Report of the Club of Rome. As a further reflection of growing concern for the state of the environment, see Edward Goldsmith *et al.*, 'Blueprint for Survival', *The Ecologist*, Weybridge (England), Vol. 2, No. 1, 1972. A critique of the Report of the Club of Rome can be found in W. D. Nordhaus, 'World Dynamics: Measurement without Data', *Economic Journal*, London, December 1973.
   Also see H. Berg, *Zur Funktionsfähigkeit der Europäischen Wirtschaftsgemeinshaft* (Göttingen: Vandenhoeck & Ruprecht, 1972); and Wilfred Beckermann, 'Economists, Scientists and Environmental Catastrophe', *Oxford Economic Papers*, Oxford, No. 24, 1972.
4. Harry G. Johnson, *Man and his Environment* (London, Washington and Montreal: British-North American Committee, 1973).
5. J. H. Dales, *Pollution, Property and Prices* (Toronto: University of Toronto Press, 1968).
6. For a discussion of the implications of environmental measures on industrial development, see Giuseppe Petrilli, 'Community Ecological Policy: Consequences of Action to Improve the Environment on Indus-

trial Development', *The Science of the Total Environment,* Amsterdam, No. 1, 1972-73.

The issues relating, more specifically, to the impact of environmental controls on international relations are surveyed by Ingo Walter, 'Environmental Control and Patterns of International Trade and Investment: an Emerging Policy Issue', *Banca Nazionale del Lavoro Quarterly Review,* Rome, March 1972.

In addition, see *Industrial Pollution Control and Industrial Trade* (Geneva: GATT Secretariat, 1971); Allen V. Kneese, Sidney Rolfe and Joseph Harned (eds.), *Managing the Environment: International Economic Cooperation and Pollution Control* (New York: Praeger, 1971), and W. J. Baumol, *Environmental Protection: International Spillovers and Trade,* Wicksell Lectures (Uppsala: Almqvist & Wiksell, 1971).

7. For a discussion of social policy issues, see *Rapport sur la Capacité Concurrentielle de la Communauté Européenne par un Group de Travail Institué par la Commission,* Uri Report (Brussels: Commission of the European Community, 1971). A summary of the report is contained in Annex I.

8. 'Vorschläge der Bundesregierung auf der Pariser Gipfelkonferenz,' Bulletin No. 147, Press und Informationsamt der Bundesregierung, Bonn, 20 October 1972.

9. *Bulletin of the European Communities,* Supplement No. 4, 1973.

10. See Pierre Uri, *L'Europe se gaspille* (Paris: Hachette Littérature, 1974), pp. 341-42.

7 International Economic Policy

The way in which the European Community pursues its commercial and other economic interests, even if it just temporizes and does nothing, is bound to exert a profound influence on the world economic (and political) order. If the process of European economic integration is to be promoted in harmony with the integration of the world economy as a whole, the interest of the Community lies very much in the maintenance of a multilateral system of trade and payments that is open and non-discriminatory, one governed by explicit and internationally-agreed rules and principles.[1]

EXTERNAL COMMERCIAL RELATIONS

It is on this basis that the discussion in this chapter deals with tariff and non-tariff barriers to trade, in both manufactured and agricultural goods, with relations with developing countries as well as with East-West trade and, in the final section, with international capital movements.

Internal considerations have also weighed heavily in our review of the European Community's external commercial relations. For the isolation of industries, both manufacturing and agricultural, from international competition generally serves to keep labour in low-wage activities. In this sense, it is the entrepreneurs, not the workers, who are protected by tariffs and other impediments to trade. Studies have shown that very little unemployment has resulted from trade expansion over the last two decades.[2] The freeing of trade and capital movements endows social benefits that should not be overlooked.

INDUSTRIAL TARIFFS AND ECONOMIC ORDER

With political perceptions of economic needs tending in any case to lag behind reality, governments have been experiencing greater difficulty than is perhaps normal in placing what they perceive as commercial policy problems in a contemporary context, such has been the rapidity of change in the world economy over the last decade or so. For the way problems are perceived and understood is influenced by past experience. And the policy experience which has guided governments in their preparations for the Tokyo Round of GATT negotiations was derived from years of trading under an international system characterized by acute and growing exchange-rate disequilibrium. It is thus understandable that countries hope, and will probably attempt, to resolve through the negotiations many problems — which although experienced as trade problems — have been a reflection of exchange-rate disequilibrium that is being corrected in the reform of the international monetary system.

Flexible exchange rates are being incorporated by the force of events into the new monetary order. They remove the balance-of-payments rationale for tariff protection. This is not to suggest that tariffs no longer matter. They remain for the European Community and other industrialized countries a distorting factor in the allocation of resources by affording some domestic producers a higher price premium over foreign producers than others. In this respect, however, the tariffs of the European Community do not present a serious obstacle to the low-priced (and high-quality) exports of Japan or to the high-technology exports of the United States.

Social Benefits of Tariff Reductions

In any attempt to put extant tariffs in perspective it is not enough though to stress how low *on average* they are nowadays (see Table 4 below). Averaging tariffs conceals the high rates payable on certain products in the American, Canadian and Japanese schedules. Moreover, low *nominal* tariffs, particularly on semi-manufactures, can represent high *effective* levels of protection.[3]

TABLE 4
Tariff averages[a] of all industrial products, 1972[b]

Country	All items, including duty-free items[c]				Dutiable items only[c]			
	No. 1	No. 2	No. 3	No. 4	No. 1	No. 2	No. 3	No. 4
EEC (Six) common external tariff	6.9	6.0	3.9	6.0	7.5	8.0	8.0	8.1
United States	10.9	7.1	6.1	6.2	11.9	9.0	8.5	8.2
Canada	9.2	6.4	6.4	6.9	15.2	13.0	14.1	12.6
Japan	10.1	9.7	5.7	9.6	11.1	11.5	10.7	11.6
United Kingdom	9.3	7.6	5.5	7.1	10.7	10.2	10.5	9.9
Switzerland	4.7	3.5	3.2	3.2	4.8	4.5	3.7	4.1
Sweden	5.8	4.1	4.8	4.0	7.8	5.9	7.7	5.7
Denmark	4.5	3.3	4.0	3.6	8.2	5.7	8.6	5.9
Austria	11.0	10.3	11.8	11.3	13.6	13.5	16.9	14.8
Norway	8.4	5.0	3.7	4.7	11.5	9.2	10.6	8.8
Finland	8.8	5.2	5.8	5.4	13.6	8.5	10.7	8.8
Eleven tariffs combined	8.1	6.2	5.5	6.2	10.5	9.0	10.0	9.0

SOURCE: *GATT Basic Documentation for the Tariff Study* (Geneva: GATT Secretariat, 1971).

[a]The comparability of tariff levels, and in particular of their practical incidence, is affected by differences in methods of valuation for customs purposes.

[b]Although the European Community was enlarged in 1973, the figures are for 1972, following the implementation of the Kennedy Round agreement, since the tariffs of the new members are adjusting to the common external tariff over a transition period.

[c]Each of the four columns gives a tariff average according to a different method of calculation.

Average No. 1 is a simple (unweighted) arithmetic average of all MFN rates of duty applying to those tariff lines relevant to the general category of products being considered.

Average No. 2 has been calculated in two steps. First, a simple (unweighted) arithmetic average of the tariff lines was compared for each relevant BTN heading. Then, each of these averages was weighted by total world trade for the BTN heading, and an average of all BTN headings was calculated.

Average No. 3 is a weighted average, in which the duty rates for each of the tariff lines in Average No. 1 is weighted by each country's MFN imports on that line.

Average No. 4 has also been calculated in two steps. First each tariff line was weighted as in Average No. 3, and averages were computed for each BTN heading. Then, each of these individual averages was weighted by total world trade for that heading, and overall averages were taken.

The products considered here are those represented by Chapters 25-99 of the BTN. They fall into three groups: raw materials, semi-finished manufactures and finished manufactures.

Following on from the previous chapter, the further reduction and elimination of tariffs would afford considerable social and economic benefits. While tariffs do affect the international distribution of income, it is highly questionable whether they do so in any desired or, indeed, foreseeable way. What is much easier to demonstrate is that tariffs affect the distribution of income within the society they are supposedly protecting. If a national tariff were averaged and made uniform across all imports it would represent a purely fiscal or financial device and its influence on the allocation of resources between industries would be minor. Only levels of protection that are above the average can be said to impart actual protection. What the above-average protected industries gain is obtained at the expense of industries which enjoy less than average protection. And they all gain at the expense of consumers.

At this point it is relevant to ask whether tariffs redistribute income from capital to labour or vice versa. On this question, the European Community's tariffs — like the tariffs of other industralized countries — afford the highest protection to the relatively old, relatively labour-intensive and relatively low-wage industries. Among these are textiles and clothing, footwear and leather products, toys and sports goods, wood products and ceramics. In many — notably textiles, clothing and footwear — the comparative advantage of the labour-abundant and capital-poor developing countries is already so pronounced that it easily defeats tariffs at any politically acceptable level.[4] Protection to the corresponding industries in the high-income countries therefore has to be provided by non-tariff measures — usually quantitative import restrictions.

Where fiscal and monetary policies (including exchange rates) are conducted sufficiently well to maintain overall full employment, labour organizations do not have a rational interest in a tariff policy, or in a non-tariff course, that ties a significant proportion of the work force of a country to low-wage occupations. They would, or at any rate should, prefer a policy of gradual trade liberalization, the result of which would be an equally gradual shift of labour into the more modern, more skill-intensive and thus higher-wage industries and occupations.

Labour displacement by imports, even if the latter are growing and the high rates which have come to be regarded over the last decade as normal, represents only a small fraction of the annual retirements of (aged) workers from any industry. With adequate adjustment policies, which would among other less important things provide new entrants into the labour force with the skills required in high-productivity industries, the dismantling of protection need not bring about much if any unemployment at all.

These considerations gain additional force when employment statistics are examined. To varying degrees of precision, they show that throughout the European Community the *bulk* of foreign labour in the manufacturing sector that is imported from low-wage countries works in the relatively more protected industries.[5]

Impact of the Energy Crisis

The energy crisis makes it necessary to carry a stage further the analysis of motives for, and effects of, the patterns of protection that are prevalent not only in the European Community but in all industrial countries. The growing comparative advantage of the developing countries in the industries discussed above has been making itself felt over the last two decades or so; and, indeed, the developing countries concerned have been encountering in the process a growing multiplicity of non-tariff barriers.[6]

In virtually all cases, increased protection has been explained as temporary action intended to give the import-competing industry time to adjust by increasing its productivity in order, in due course, to become competitive again. But in most cases the 'temporary' measures became permanent. For the innovations of the import-competing industries that were introduced to increase productivity were quickly adopted, and often adapted, by the export industry in the developing countries. The industrialized countries react by again stepping up their research effort. As a result of this escalation, made possible by protection, the world economy has channelled an unjustifiably large part of its scarce research-and-development resources into the creation of unnecessarily capital-intensive, and hence also energy-intensive, technologies in order to supply consumers with such mundane goods as fabrics and clothing.

To express the problem in fashionable terms, it would be energy-saving to eliminate tariffs and let the low opportunity-cost man-power in developing countries produce standard consumer manufactures by simpler technologies. In this way the research-and-development resources of the European Community could be freed from a hopeless rear-guard action against a virtually inexhaustible reservoir of labour available at very low rates of pay and could instead be employed on genuine innovation for which there is now a sharply increased need.

The energy crisis also has serious implications of more immediate concern for the maintenance of the world economic order to which the smaller powers have to look for their interests to be safeguarded. As remarked in Chapter 1, the dramatic increase in crude oil prices is expected to generate in the hands of the oil-producing countries liquid assets of around $70,000m a year, the size of the problem depending on the movement of prices and, too, on the quantity of oil in demand and the availability of supplies. But it is not the size of the problem that is the cause of concern. It is the handling of the ensuing transfers that matters.[7]

By 1980 an 'oil-debt overhang' of several hundreds of billions of dollars — a multiple of the volume of the Euro-dollar market at the present time — could have accumulated, but the oil-producing countries will not be in a position to absorb real transfers of goods, as a counterpart to this debt, for many years to come. The financial flows that result will be far greater than anything ever experienced before. The full impact of those financial flows has yet to be felt. All too easily, though, they could have a distorting effect on the structure of exchange rates, tempting or even obliging countries to resort to autarkic policies in order to achieve a balance in their current accounts. Competitive devaluations, import restrictions or domestic deflations could lead to the destruction of the system of trade and payments on which post-war prosperity and security have been based. The danger is all the greater because of the tensions that had already developed in the system before the energy crisis was precipitated.

Undermining Influence of Preferences

Where tariff policies are concerned, the influence of the European Community, it should be recognized, has not always been beneficial and there is accordingly much to be repaired. Let us emphasize straight away, however, that the creation of the European Community did in no way infringe on, or violate, the principle of most-favoured-nation (or equal) treatment, as expressed in the GATT. Nothing in the philosophical content and historical analysis of that principle can be construed as a presumption against the elimination of tariffs among a group of countries willing to surrender, and merge, certain significant aspects of their national sovereignty. The parallels often drawn with the creation of the United States of America or of modern Germany are quite legitimate.

But the subsequent development of a galaxy of discriminatory trading arrangements around the European Community is an altogether different story. The

(a) association with the Community of a host of developing countries on the basis of multi-tiered preferential tariff agreements,

(b) crowned by a range of free trade agreements between the enlarged Community and the remaining EFTA countries,

(c) on which is superimposed a far from general though 'generalized' scheme of tariff preferences for all developing countries,

has created an exceedingly complex system of customs regulations which inevitably creates interminable friction between affected countries. Not only has friction been created between the European Community and other developed countries across the Atlantic and further away.[8] No less adverse to the political interests of a new Europe is the friction being created between the Community and the developing countries which are granted tariff preferences with such varying degrees of generosity.[9]

The political tensions generated by multiple trade discrimination, for no visible economic benefit, are likely to worsen unless countervailing action is taken. It appears that

the only way out of the situation is for the European Community to negotiate with its major trading partners the
gradual elimination of substantially all tariffs on manufactured products traded among developed countries.[10] In due
course arrangements with 'associated' countries in the Third
World should come to be confined to financial and technical
assistance. Over what period the elimination of tariffs on
developed-country trade would be scheduled is of secondary
importance. Even if it were only completed by the year
2000, the main political achievement – effective immediately
– would be the relief and relaxation of tensions which would
follow the recognition that henceforth tariffs were to be
regarded simply as a transitory instrument of policy. To see
in the European Community's common external tariff, and in
the protection provided by it, a necessary bond holding the
nine menbers together is to debase the European idea.[11]

In the first draft of the European Community's initial
bargaining position for the Tokyo Round negotiations, the
Commission asserted that 'tariff-free trade is impossible without international organization and harmonization of national
policy considerations – for instance, taxation, social legislation and measures to stimulate economic development'.[12]
The passage was among those eliminated from the document
finally agreed by the Council of Ministers. But the miscon-
ception keeps recurring in public discussion.[13]

The point has been discussed in Chapter 5 where it is
pointed out that no division of labour through trade could
take place if all competitive conditions are artificially equalized. After all international trade is induced on cost differences and tends to equalize them. Conceptually there is a
clear distinction between (i) ruling out distortions to competitive conditions resulting from government interventions,
which would fall into the category of one non-tariff measure
or another, and (ii) ruling out differences in competitive conditions resulting from differences in taxation, social benefits
and company laws. The first, we have stressed, is a feasible
and necessary part of any attempt to liberalize international
trade. The second is neither feasible nor necessary among
countries not aspiring to economic and political union.

With respect to differences in wage levels between
countries, a reservation is entered here over the concern

reflected in the Havana Charter, which all GATT signatory countries are expected to observe, relating to situations where wages are not set by free bargaining, but are set by repressive or discriminatory systems. Countries where such circumstances are evident should be obliged to prove that wages in the industry in question are commensurate with the level of productivity and with the level of employment.

Optional Negotiating Techniques

An agreement to move towards tariff-free trade in industrial products among developed countries would rid the European Community of the worst diplomatic and political difficulties in its external economic relationships. That objective also commends itself when the optional negotiating techniques are closely examined — as they have been in several studies, articles and reports.[14]

Item-by-Item Bargaining

Previous rounds of GATT negotiations have been based on reciprocal item-by-item bargaining with all tariff concessions, as negotiated between two or more signatory countries, extended unconditionally to all other adherents to the General Agreement. This last has been required under the MFN clause[15] which has thus served to limit the progress of negotiations to the pace of the least willing participants. In order to overcome this resistance to progress, the Kennedy Round negotiations sought across-the-board or linear reductions, but on the most sensitive items they reverted to item-by-item bargaining. Before these negotiations were completed it was evident that in future negotiations a different approach would have to be employed. Since most of the tariffs that remain are unlikely to yield to conventional negotiating techniques, another traditional GATT round could well be encumbered with long lists of 'exceptions', enough to sap the political will of countries to see the negotiations through to a successful conclusion.

Tariff Harmonization

In order to overcome the problem of 'tariff disparities' (see Table 5), the European Community has shown interest in negotiations aimed at the harmonization of tariffs, whereby countries with high rates of duty in their tariff schedules would be required to make larger concessions than countries with more even rates of duty. The very idea implies a rejection of the principle of reciprocity at a time when on all sides renewed emphasis has been put on reciprocity in multilateral trade negotiations. To what level, anyway, should tariffs be harmonized? The question inspires many answers that could take an age for negotiators to resolve. And some answers could result in an increase in protection for some industries!

TABLE 5

Frequency distribution of most-favoured-nation imports of industrial products according to the level of duty[a]

Countries	Level of Duty[b] Duty-free	0.1– 5%	5.1– 10%	10.1– 15%	15.1– 20%	20.1– 25%	Over 25%
EEC (Six)[c]	51.1	12.9	24.8	8.0	3.1	0.1	–
United States	27.9	35.8	21.2	5.1	4.1	1.9	4.0
Canada	54.4	2.0	16.4	10.9	12.2	2.5	1.6
Japan	46.8	7.6	17.1	23.6	3.3	0.9	0.7
United Kingdom	47.2	5.1	27.6	12.5	6.5	1.1	–
Sweden	37.5	27.1	24.3	10.0	0.8	–	0.3
Denmark	52.9	12.6	18.7	12.1	1.8	1.9	–
Norway	65.3	10.3	12.2	5.1	4.2	2.2	0.7
Finland	46.2	12.0	24.7	8.2	3.1	2.6	3.2
Switzerland	12.2	62.0	18.4	5.7	1.2	0.5	–
Austria	30.2	5.1	16.5	13.4	17.1	6.7	11.0
Eleven tariffs combined	42.9	17.5	20.2	10.4	5.2	1.9	2.0

SOURCE: Derived from *Basic Documentation for the Tariff Study* (Geneva: GATT Secretariat, 1971).

[a]This table shows the percentage of the total value of a country's imports falling within each range of tariff levels. The imports considered here are MFN imports of all industrial products (Chapters 25-99 BTN), including raw materials, semi-finished manufactures and finished manufactures.

[b]The comparability of tariff levels, and in particular of their practical incidence, is affected by variations in valuation methods for customs purposes.

[c]Since the new members of the European Community are moving to the common external tariff over a transition period, the tariffs for the Six and for Britain and Denmark (Ireland excluded) are shown separately.

Sector-by-Sector Negotiations

Negotiations on a sector-by-sector or on an industry-by-industry basis, enabling tariffs and non-tariff measures to be taken together, have been proposed by Canada. Exploration of the technique — going back a number of years — suggests very strongly that it has little practical applicability. For there are very few industries in which the nature of the trade is such as to make bargaining possible among advanced countries, on a reciprocally advantageous basis, without considering the effects on the competitive positions of related industries. Discussion could get bogged down over the precise definition of industries with the attitudes of countries very much depending on the competitivity of their firms operating in the 'grey area' between one industry and another.

Linear Reductions

The major objectives of the above approaches could be achieved in negotiations for an agreement on progressive, linear and automatic reductions over an agreed period, along the lines that the European Community pursued the elimination of tariffs among its member countries. Such an agreement would satisfy the principle of reciprocity since it would entail an equal commitment from all parties. It would also serve to overcome in due course the 'tariff disparities' problem and to contain the problem of 'exceptions' from trade liberalization.

What is more the approach would provide the basis for an imaginative counter to protectionist pressures at a time when the momentum of trade liberalization is in need of restoration. This would be especially so, allowing the most willing participants to set the pace, if the technique was applied on a conditional MFN basis. Such a basis would be possible under the GATT's Article 24 which provides for exceptions from unconditional MFN treatment (expressing the principle of non-discrimination) where countries are embarking on free trade among themselves. Paradoxically, a conditional MFN approach to the phased elimination of tariffs among developed countries could help to reassert the principle of non-discrimination, in that it would forestall the development of preferential trading arrangements. By using Article 24, the developed countries would not be abandoning the general principle of non-discrimination, which if it was to be discarded altogether could result in the outbreak all round of world of discriminatory trading arrangements among small groups of countries and in small groups of products.

In recommending the adoption of this approach, we envisage the multilateral negotiations on tariffs, in the Tokyo Round discussions, focusing first of all on the timetable of the progressive, linear and automatic reductions. The transition to zero tariff positions might run over ten, fifteen or more years. And it might be divided into two stages with provision at the end of the first stage for a legislative review before authority is given for the second stage to be embarked upon. Some industries might be permitted a longer transition period in which to adjust to international competition.

Having agreed a formula for across-the-board reductions, the negotiations would then focus on the industries to be excepted from the general movement towards tariff-free trade among developed countries. In short, the zero-tariff objective should be subject to strict provisions for 'exceptions' and to provisions, also, for 'safeguards' against 'market disruption' — as discussed below.

TRADE WITH DEVELOPING COUNTRIES

As for the future of the European Community's trade with developing countries, there should be no illusions about the generalized schemes of tariff preferences introduced by various countries, even after all the amendments recently put into effect and still contemplated. The schemes cannot bring about the indicated changes to anything like the degree necessary. They are open to criticism on two points.

1. Exclusions from Preferential Scheme

Less than half the dutiable imports entering the European Community from developing countries qualify to benefit from its scheme of generalized preferences. Exclusions from the Community's scheme, and from other schemes, were dictated by fears that preferential imports might create problems (i) for the corresponding domestic industry, (ii) for the trade of other developed countries and (iii) for the exports of developing countries with whom a special trading relationship already existed.

Although there are differences in the exclusions under the various schemes, most are concentrated in the textile, leather and petroleum-product sectors. The European Community only includes in its scheme textile and clothing imports from countries which have agreed to a quantitative limitation of their exports under the recently concluded Arrangement Regarding International Trade in Textiles.[16] Most of the relatively labour-intensive manufactures of the poorest developing countries are thus excluded from generalized preferential treatment.

2. Limits and Insecurity of Preferential Access

Some nine-tenths of imports presently benefiting from generalized preferences are imported under schemes which limit preferential entry by tariff quotas and ceilings. Given the formulae for calculating these quotas and ceilings, and the rate of growth of total imports of manufactures from developing countries in recent years, it is very likely that the main beneficiaries will fill their preferential quotas and then continue to export across the MFN tariff. Where preferential entry is unlimited in principle, the donor country retains the right to invoke a special escape clause allowing the re-imposition of the MFN tariff in those cases where a continued growth of imports under the preference would create a serious adjustment problem for domestic industry. Since generalized preferences are a unilateral action the judgment as to the 'seriousness' of the problem is likely to be equally one-sided.

Two conclusions can be drawn from these criticisms. First, in their present form, generalized preferences do little to stimulate trade. They could permanently raise the rate of growth of exports from developing countries only if they are *assured* of unlimited preferential access. With preferential quotas filled, additional exports face the MFN tariff. (It therefore follows that the reduction of the MFN tariff in these cases represents a net benefit, not an 'erosion of prefer-

ential advantage', to the exporting less-developed countries.)
Thus, at the margin where it counts, the schemes as such
provide no incentive for extra export effort. And, more
fundamentally, even those tariff lines on which unlimited
preferential access is offered in principle cannot furnish any
additional incentive for investment in export capacities.[17] For
given the uncertainty inherent in the unilateral 'escape
clauses' in the schemes, the scarce capital available to
developing countries can, in all conscience, be committed
only to investments whose products can be profitably sold
across MFN tariffs. (With guaranteed unlimited preferential
access, one could expect much of the new export-oriented
investment to be financed from preference-granting countries.)

Second, by excluding manufactures which the poor
developing countries are best suited to export, generalized
preferences become another factor making for an increasing
disparity between the more advanced (already industrializing)
and the less advanced developing countries. And precisely
because they are biased in favour of the former group, whose
export capacities and competitiveness are growing rapidly,
generalized preferences are unlikely to be improved by any
provision of stronger guarantees of preferential access. The
problem of the industrializing countries is increasingly one of
securing assurances of unlimited access *across the MFN
tariffs*.

TRADE IN AGRICULTURAL PRODUCTS

In the past ten or fifteen years, it has been the European
Community's agricultural-support policies that have provoked
the most strident protests and objections from other trading
countries, particularly from those which have traditionally
been large agricultural exporters.[18] While there are good
reasons for criticism, it is important to put these problems in
perspective, especially in the perspective of recent developments in the world market for agricultural products. For
these developments seem to offer an opportunity for a
mutually satisfactory settlement of the outstanding problems
between exporting countries and countries that find it necessary to support their farmers.[19]

The European Community's common agricultural policy,

while different in its instruments, has not substantially
differed in its effects from policies pursued by other industrial countries, specifically by the United States and the
United Kingdom. Even formally, the device of variable
import levies, the main instrument of the common agricultural policy, is comparable with the quota-system used for
the protection of American agriculture. The administration
of the common agricultural policy, as explained in Chapter 4,
proceeds from an estimate of internal supply likely to be
generated at the guaranteed domestic price, to setting the
import levy at a level which will prevent commodities from
entering in a volume which, added to domestic production,
would make supply exceed demand. Quotas in the United
States are set in the same way.

While the former British system of maintaining farm
income was based on the radically different device of 'deficiency payments', it should be noted that, over the past ten or
fifteen years, the United Kingdom achieved a higher degree
of replacement of agricultural imports by domestic production than did the Community of Six. The obvious conclusion
to be drawn is that it is not so much the mechanism of
agricultural policy as the overall objectives towards which the
mechanism is administered that influences foreign trade in
agricultural products.

During the period 1962-72, the European Community's
agricultural imports subject to variable levies first showed a
relatively sharp decline, but recovered afterwards; the 1972
imports exceeded those of 1962 in value, although they were
somewhat less in volume. Given the difficulty of calculating
the rise in prices, the change in volume can only be esti-
mated, but it hardly reached one-third. What is more, the
European Community's agricultural imports, from third
countries, of agricultural products not subject to levies increased rapidly from 1962 to 1972. During this period the
volume of world trade in agricultural products rose by about
40 per cent. It is also true that agricultural-producer prices in
the Community were significantly higher than those prevailing on world markets until about mid-1972. Since then,
however, world prices increased so fast that by January 1974
they exceeded, in several products, the Community's guaranteed domestic prices.

Strategy for Negotiations

As long ago as 1958, the Haberler Report concluded that there would be substantial gains from the liberalization of agricultural trade, but the rising trend of protection continued. Since commodity prices have been buoyant, relieving governments of the pressures normally associated with depressed prices, the general climate for negotiations has improved. The situation, however, was never likely to last for very long. For income-benefits from high prices tend to be capitalized into higher values on farm assets which farmers soon take for granted.

Before circumstances (for trade liberalization) change again for the worse, governments should endeavour in the Tokyo Round talks to reach a measure of understanding on a concerted, though gradual, approach towards overcoming the problems of agricultural trade. As a principle underlying the discussion, it might be accepted that governments should limit the extent to which the burden of domestic adjustment in the agricultural sector is shifted, through trade measures, to producers in other countries. Negotiations should therefore focus on the measures which have been most disruptive of international trade.

Governments should have no difficulty, for a start, in reaching an agreement on the use of export subsidies — especially if tight markets persist. Whereas governments are biased towards import controls, in order to underpin other farm-support measures, they are biased away from export subsidies however much they may resort to them from time to time. Export subsidies are used as devices to boost farm incomes. But they have none of the advantages of import controls. For they are expensive in terms of government expenditure. They are politically vulnerable to the charge, too, that foreign consumers benefit at the expense of domestic taxpayers. It should be more satisfactory all round and easier to remove export subsidies on a multilateral basis rather than by unilateral decision where the fall in export sales is likely to be greater. They should be replaced by stockpiling surpluses along the lines discussed below.

Just as export subsidies disrupt markets when supplies are plentiful, so also do export controls when supplies are tight. Several countries, not only the United States, have stopped or rationed exports of key commodities when shortages developed, creating uncertainty in world markets and in policy-making circles everywhere. Reaching an understanding on export controls will be more difficult in a period of shortage. With the likelihood of rising inflation, resort to export controls, not only of agricultural products but of minerals and other raw materials, can be expected to increase.

Commodity shortages have made importing countries realize that they must be prepared to share the responsibility, and therefore the cost, of stockpiling instead of leaving it all to the exporting countries. Until the early 1970s, the world benefited from the reserves built up mainly by the United States, unintentional as those stockpiles may have been. In retrospect, it is recognized that American stocks helped to maintain a reasonable balance between supply and demand, as well as meet the obvious requirements of famine relief.

With the importing countries interested in the security and stability of supplies, the Tokyo Round negotiations should be able to reach agreement on the financing and management of reserve stocks of storable commodities, mainly grains. There is already emerging a substantial degree of consensus on the objectives and principles governing such reserves.[20] They would be aimed at

(a) mitigating wide swings over periods of several years in the availability of supplies and therefore in prices,

(b) moderating year-to-year fluctuations in the volume and value of international trade in farm commodities, and

(c) developing strategic reserves against the threat of famine in developing countries.

With the cost of world reserves being shared by both exporting and importing countries, the management of them would have to be by international agreement, involving consultation and negotiation for which it would be necessary to introduce firm procedures.

Having established a framework in which some semblance of order might be achieved in agricultural trade, the negotiations should take up, and carry a stage further, the *montant de soutien* proposals of the European Community at the time of the Kennedy Round negotiations. Instead of arguing about appropriate and inappropriate *methods* of support, the negotiations should concentrate on the *levels* of support, leaving governments to decide for themselves the form of support that is most appropriate in their circumstances. What this would involve first of all is agreeing a basis on which to determine the level of effective protection afforded to agricultural producers by the various methods of support. Those levels might then be 'bound' and afterwards gradually reduced by negotiation.

In the course of consultations and negotiations, which should be a more or less continuous process, the effectiveness of farm-support policies could come to be questioned more closely so that reforms might be induced. To what extent are they fulfilling their objectives?

(a) How much have agricultural policies increased net farm income?

(b) What effect have agricultural policies had on farm output and on domestic consumption of farm products?

(c) How much do agricultural policies cost taxpayers and consumers?

(d) How are the economic benefits of agricultural policies distributed between high and low-income families in agriculture?

(e) What part of the total costs borne by consumers and taxpayers actually accrues to farm people as additional income?

These are the questions that need to be answered if ever the fundamental problems of agricultural trade are to be overcome.

Those problems will not be overcome by negotiating arrangements for maintaining the *status quo*. That has been the implicit objective of most commodity agreements. The purpose of these agreements has not been the liberalization of international trade. Not that commodity agreements should be ruled out of the question. Much depends on what is contained in them. If they were to cover the above elements a commodity approach could provide unity and continuity.

NON-TARIFF INTERFERENCES

The diminishing importance of tariffs has attracted attention to the various non-tariff means of protection which have, since time immemorial, supplemented the protective effects of customs duties. Here a clear distinction should be drawn between two categories of devices:

(a) the 'hard' ones, non-tariff *restrictions,* whose main or sole purpose is to protect; and

(b) the 'soft' ones, such as customs valuations and other administrative procedures, industrial, health and safety standards, public procurement practices, government subsidies, prior import deposits, border-tax adjustments and many others.

These last are legitimate in themselves, but can be abused for protective purposes or, even without any administrative intent, cause serious distortions of trade. Government subsidies and public procurement practices are increasingly used in the United States and the European Community to support the development of the technologically-advanced industries in which the more traditional forms of protection (tariffs and/or quantitative restrictions) are ineffective or attract foreign investment.

Clearly it is the first category that calls for priority attention. The 'soft' devices, and the distortions they cause, can only be brought under control by gradually securing adherence to negotiated codes of conduct through GATT procedures for complaints, consultation and arbitration.[21] The development of a framework of international obligations, urged in Chapter 5, might be broached in stages. First, general rules should be negotiated to cover, where appropriate, the various categories of non-tariff intervention in international trade. The point at this stage should be to secure the commitment of governments to a set of obligations. The basic principle underlying all codes of conduct should be that governments do not pass on to other countries the costs of their adjustment policies. Later the general rules should be elaborated upon in what would amount to a continuous process of consultation and negotiation. These rules should supplement those already contained in Part II of the General Agreement which have been rendered nugatory by the so-called 'grandfather clause'. This last has permitted those policies and practices which existed before the General Agreement was signed in 1947 to continue in force. The Protocol of Provisional Application should therefore be terminated.[22]

The liberalization of the 'hard' restrictions is all the more urgent since in this area there has been, in the past decade or so, a proliferation of a dangerous new device, the so-called 'voluntary self-restraint' on exporters. (Most recently, a mirror-image of this device has been observed in markets where supply has become short and the exporter has shied away from the opprobrium that imposing an export-embargo would be sure to bring him: in these cases, individual importing countries were coerced into importer's 'self-restraint'.) Since in the case of voluntary exports restraints, the government of the exporting country has to force its industry to police its exports, what the device amounts to is the creation of export cartels. Even before the onset of the oil crisis, the insight was slowly gaining ground that the two most talked-about features of the contemporary economic scene, namely (i) the burgeoning phenomenon of the multinational enterprise and (ii) the increasing resort to negotiation for protective purposes so-called voluntary export restraints, imply a spreading cartellization of the world economy. The success of the petroleum cartel increases the same danger where raw material supplies are concerned. While in the past, in other words, competition inside and among national economies was taken for granted, and trade negotiations were essentially about equalizing the conditions of competitive access, it is now time to realize that the very maintenance of competition is a matter of international responsibility.

The restrictions already in existence are unlikely to be liberalized through the process of multilateral bargaining. For each represents a more or less 'neuralgic point' for the country imposing it and there do not exist reciprocal relations in this respect among the main trading countries that would permit 'equivalent swaps'. The only way to bring these proliferating restrictions under control, and eventually to eliminate them, is in agreements to institute policies designed to bring about an adjustment of the protected industries. There would have to be a mechanism for multilateral supervision of such policies. It is through this mechanism that the issue of existing non-tariff restrictions is intertwined with the issue of safeguard mechanisms against sudden surges in imports.

IMPROVED 'SAFEGUARDS' ON IMPORTS

Reforming the existing multilateral safeguard system, embodied in Article 19 of the GATT, into one better adapted to the high rates of trade expansion — present and anticipated — poses difficult and complex problems.[23] But they can be described fairly simply. They divide into two parts. The first is to make the rules sufficiently flexible to cover all situations in which a country might need emergency protection. Here the purpose would be to eliminate the incentive for large importing countries to act unilaterally or bilaterally in situations where import-absorption problems emerge for individual industries. The second step entails reforms that, as proposed in Chapter 5, would make the safeguard system an instrument of industrial adjustment and thus raise the import-absorption capacity of the participating economies in the long run.

The difficulty with the first step is in calibrating the degree of permissiveness in the rules governing safeguard action. Too permissive a safeguard clause would destroy security of access which has been the central purpose of the General Agreement. On the other hand, provisions so strict and rigid as to impose 'unbearable' costs on the invoking country would have a similar effect, because they would force countries in emergency situations to act outside the framework of agreed principles and multilateral control. The problem is therefore one of establishing a balance of rights and obligations under multilateral control, a solution which demands some surrender of national sovereignty, but no greater than governments are willing to make.

While the first step relates essentially to a reformulation of the safeguard or escape clause provisions existing in national legislations and international contracts, the second issue represents a conceptual innovation. It ought to be recalled that the existing provisions, agreed upon and enacted a quarter of a century ago, embody the experience and wisdom of a much slower and in some respects a much more stable world. The existing safeguard provisions were meant for exceptional and essentially temporary (mainly cyclical) emergencies. They are limited to provisions for *emergency* protection. In view of the current and anticipated growth of export capacities, the new system cannot be conceived of as one for exceptional situations. It has to be an instrument for the continuing transformations and accommodations that are going to be increasingly required. The objective of this part of the reform is to ensure, therefore, that the safeguard action will provide only a temporary respite from 'excessive' import pressure, a period during which something will be done to solve the problem which gave rise to the request for protection. To be effective in this regard, the safeguard mechanism should combine the right to impose temporary protection with an obligation of the protecting country to prepare, discuss with its trading partners and put into effect a convincing adjustment programme for the industry under import pressure.

The most important institutional arrangement for regulating emergency protection measures concerns the procedure by which an injury of a national industry by a sudden surge of imports would be established. Since the first complaint would be made to domestic authorities, it would be in the interest of the European Community to propose a procedure for which an international precedent already exists in the GATT Anti-Dumping Code, to which the Community has subscribed.

The procedure specified in this Code, and equally applicable to a code on safeguard or emergency protection measures, provides for the creation — at national or at Community level — of a standing body responsible for the determination of injury. Upon receiving a request for emergency protection, and following a preliminary investigation, this body would arrange for a *public hearing* in which all parties related to, or affected by, the case would have a full opportunity to defend their interest, including the opportunity to cross-examine the representatives of other interests. The interested parties should include:

(a) the domestic industry, that is both enterprise and labour;

(b) the trade, that is foreign exporters, domestic importers and the distributive trade;

(c) all industries which are users of the produce in question; and, last but not least,

(d) the consumer interest.

This last interest should be taken into account by a requirement that a panel of independent economists presents an estimate of the effect on retail prices of the product in question of the various possible forms, extent and duration of emergency protection. The findings of such a body — a tribunal, commission, or a standing panel of experts and officials — would then be submitted for a review to an international commission representing the country's trading partners.

We believe that the sectional protectionist interest, still strong in many Community countries and industries, can be kept at bay only by procedures of this kind; that is, procedures which in a democratically 'transparent' way can be seen by all to give an objective and adequate consideration to all the social interests involved.

NEW 'SAFEGUARDS' ON EXPORTS

Recent developments have given rise to concern about market disruption through a shortage of supplies from abroad. This is a counterpart of the more familiar concern, just discussed, of market disruption through an excess of supplies from abroad. Whether this concern is exaggerated remains to be seen. But it has underscored the need for an international framework in which to deal with situations where a government imposes, for internal purposes, a restraint on the exports of a particular commodity. There are three areas in which governments could agree on more concerted action.

First of all, under the GATT the imposition of export controls is prohibited, but exceptions are allowed in respect of exhaustible resources, commodities in short supply and national security. These exceptions, combined with the general terms in which the rules are expressed, has meant that the GATT has not been effective in this situation. The European Community should therefore seek, in negotiations with other countries, a more precise definition of the conditions under which 'exceptions' are permitted. If the articles cannot be amended, a separate protocol should be negotiated covering the major trading countries, if not all GATT signatories.

Secondly, a separate 'safeguard' mechanism on exports might be negotiated, similar to the safeguard mechanism on imports proposed above. Again the underlying principle should be that governments, in seeking to assist the adjustment of domestic producers and consumers to supply shortages, should not pass all the burden of adjustment to foreign producers and consumers.[24] Governments taking action to restrain exports should be required to consult with the governments of importing countries. They should also be induced to take domestic measures to alleviate the situation.

Thirdly, some governments have been exploring the possibility of negotiating commitments on access to supplies, in much the same way as commitments on access to markets have been negotiated in the past. The European Community could perhaps negotiate with other countries access to their supplies of a commodity in exchange for access to the Common Market for other commodities. Putting into effect such agreements could involve commitments on access to government stockpiles, on production controls, on export taxes and on price agreements.

EAST-WEST TRADE

Non-tariff restrictions, mainly quotas, are deemed necessary for coping with imports from the state-trading countries of Eastern Europe and East Asia, if only because of the difficulties of determining when products are being 'dumped' or otherwise sold with the help of 'subsidies'. Quota restrictions are also deemed necessary for the purposes of reciprocal bargaining. But the insistence on reciprocity should not conceal the fact that East-West trade is just as beneficial to the welfare of domestic consumers as trade with other countries if goods can be obtained relatively cheaply and on a reliable basis. What makes trade with state-trading countries subject to a degree of risk is the possibility of sudden restrictions on supplies.

Since supplies from state-trading countries only account for a small proportion of the European Community's imports from third countries, neither increases nor decreases in supplies should pose a serious 'market disruption' problem for member countries. Even though there are marked differences in the objectives of state-trading countries, all of them are interested in reliable sources of supply, which means that the Community should be able to negotiate long-term contracts for raw material and energy supplies. In return the Community could offer increases in quotas for other goods.

Reliance on quantitative restrictions as a means of thwarting the dumping of East European products in the European Community could offer increases in import quotas.
should be allayed when transactions are conducted at world market prices or at the prices of market-economy competitors.

In considering the problems of East-West trade a distinction has to be drawn between the Soviet Union and the countries of Eastern Europe. Czechoslovakia, Poland, Rumania and Hungary are members of the GATT whereas the Soviet Union is not. An agreement has been reached with Poland within the GATT whereby quantitative increases in Polish imports can be negotiated against a reduction in duties by market-economy countries. The formula should be applicable in negotiations with other East European countries.[25]

The state-trading countries are likely to ask for credits to finance purchases of machinery and equipment with a high technology content. To prevent intra-Community competition over the terms of such credits, minimum rules should be established. Interest rates should be tied to those in the free capital market.

INTERNATIONAL CAPITAL FLOWS

Flowing on from the earlier discussion in the previous section of trade policies towards developing countries, we will first discuss in this section the problems of financial assistance to the under-developed parts of the world, before dealing with the problems of the international monetary system.

FINANCIAL ASSISTANCE TO DEVELOPING COUNTRIES

If the total flow of economic aid from industrial to developing countries over the last decade, in the definitions used by the OECD, were properly deflated for the price changes that have taken place in this period, it would be found that the real volume of official development assistance has stagnated if it has not absolutely declined. In the same period the population of developing countries increased by about one third. The recent changes in the price of petroleum, as well as other basic food-stuffs and raw materials (even though these prices may eventually decline), will add a charge to the balance of payments of the net-importing less-developed countries which will practically offset all their official development assistance receipts.

Several reports and studies have appeared in recent years criticizing the ways in which the industrial countries distributed their aid.[26] Much of this criticism has been justified and a number of changes in these practices, which should not be politically difficult to obtain, would considerably increase the effectiveness of such assistance as the industrial countries can make available. There seem therefore to be two main objectives to guide the European Community's development assistance policy: first, increase the total amount of assistance transferred and, second, raise its effectiveness by improving its distribution both among the recipient countries and among the uses to which it can be put.

It would be desirable to see a more rapid progress in the centralization of the Community's development assistance policy, preferably by keeping the volume of bilateral assistance constant and rapidly increasing the volume of assistance channelled through the European Development Fund. The 918m u.a. distributed by this Fund in the 1970-74 period was clearly insufficient, given the needs even of the signatories to the second Yaoundé Agreement, the sole recipients of the Fund's assistance.[27] What the Fund distributes annually amounts to less than 0.1 per cent of the Community's GNP.

By improving its development assistance, the European Community could assert itself in an important field of foreign policy. A common policy could make financial aid both more effective and less discriminatory. The distribution of aid should be determined less by historical and political ties than by economic criteria. One such criterion should focus on subsistance aid, particularly in food, aimed at keeping people alive. Another emphasis should be placed on improving the economic infra-structure of developing countries so that private direct investment can be attracted. Emphasis should also be put on giving incentives for investments in labour-intensive lines of production so that unemployment can be reduced.[28] Aid to agricultural extension, the provision of technical advice, can both provide more productive employment and prevent hunger.

Should aid be distributed on the basis of merit or on that of need? Distribution on merit, that is more aid to those who can make the most of it, tends to maximize both growth and inequality. But distribution on the basis of need, does not necessarily sacrifice growth if the quantitative re-adjustment in favour of the poorest countries were combined with a qualitative re-adjustment concerning the projects to be financed.

Comparing the relative magnitudes of development assistance and private capital flowing from developed to developing countries, and especially the relative magnitudes as they might be in a decade or two, it would seem necessary to scrutinize very carefully the development assistance to be devoted to the creation of industrial capacities which private capital does not find it profitable to undertake in order to make sure such assistance is not wasted. The objective, in most general terms, should be to create an environment in which private capital can be found and employed for industrial production. This is the crucial problem for development assistance. For such an environment is a matter of social organization, efficient administration (particularly in such services as the provision of security and justice, agricultural extension, tax collection) and an organization of educational systems geared to development needs. The difficulty is that these are areas where aid must be essentially technical.

It is this insight that accounts for the recent emphasis which is being placed in project allocation of financial assistance, mainly by the World Bank but increasingly also by individual donors in their bilateral commitments, on agriculture and, in this area, on projects aimed specifically and verifiably at improving the productivity and incomes of the poorest peasants. This effort has been explained and defended as arising out of the concern about equality of income distribution *within* developing countries. In some discussions it has been presented as a pragmatic scaling-down of the unsustainable ambitions of the earlier objectives of development assistance: 'if we cannot do much to increase aggregate growth, we should at least try to do something about absolute poverty'. If such policies succeed in improving the income situation (productivity) of the poorest and most numerous class, the peasants, they will increase the marketable surplus of agriculture, the size of which is the main determinant of the scope of investment in the long run. Finally, beyond this economic prospect, there is a political hope. If experience under an assistance programme of this type convinced the largely apathetic peasantry of the possibility of progress, there would be a hope of a gradual improvement in the administrative and political systems as well.

There are two more specific points that should be stressed. The first point concerns an issue that attracted considerable attention in the mid-1960s but has since been almost forgotten. As monetary and balance-of-payments difficulties began to develop under the system of fixed-exchange rates, the countries granting development assistance reacted, one by one, by tying an increasing proportion of their bilateral assistance to purchases in their domestic markets. It was interesting to observe that, in the process, all were loudly decrying the necessity of doing so, explicitly recognizing the reduction in the real transfer of resources implied by this practice which they were introducing in response to severe — though by their nature temporary — balance-of-payments problems.

Having corrected the most serious parity disequilibria, and moving towards a more stable international monetary system in which corrections of balance-of-payments problems will be effected more easily, the assistance-granting countries should realize that the original justification for tying their aid is rapidly diminishing. A speedy liberalization of assistance would have two very substantial beneficial effects. For the recipient who is a good 'comparison shopper', untied aid stretches much further. The second effect should be considered even more important. The untying of aid would eliminate the influence of supplying firms in the donor country on the planning of individual projects in the recipient country. The elimination of the well-known, and socially very unhealthy, 'aid-politicking' (including bribery) could greatly improve the efficiency of development project planning.

A second very important way in which the members of the European Community have exercised influence over developing countries has been through their policies concerning the immigration of labour. There can be no doubt that the result of these policies, the massive inflow of foreign workers — first from Southern Europe, but progressively from farther afield — into Western Europe has helped the economies of the countries of emigration. They have been receiving a large and growing flow of remittances. The limits to further expansion of this type of 'assistance', however, are now becoming clearly visible. It has to be asked how efficient a form of assistance it has been. The problem of efficiency should be viewed from both sides: that of the countries of immigration, as well as that of the countries of emigration.

In the first group of countries, the excessive availability of low-cost labour has in effect slowed down the inevitable transformation of industrial structures, has distorted the wage patterns, has caused under-investment in certain important industries — and, last but not least, has generated dangerous social friction which in several instances verges on the emergence of a new racism. In the countries of emigration, the same process has also distorted wage patterns, and in several instances caused shortages of specific industrial skills. It has furthermore contributed to inequality in the internal distribution of income which has led to social friction. And, finally, it has in several cases influenced the pattern of gross fixed investment in an unanticipated and — from the viewpoint of economic growth — inefficient direction. Both sides would have been better off if, instead of bringing labour towards capital, capital had been moved towards labour and the resulting products had been exported to the investing countries.

In order to encourage private capital flows and a net resource transfer to less developed countries, the latter should be permitted to have 'under-valued' exchange rates in relation to the industrialized countries, including the European Community and the United States. An under-valued exchange rate represents a uniform tax on all imported goods and a uniform subsidy to all exports, thereby increasing demand for the production of less developed countries and attracting foreign investors to them. To the extent that imported capital goods become more expensive in local currency, exchange-rate under-valuation also weakens the tendency to adopt capital-intensive methods of production, which contributes to the perpetuation of structural unemployment in these countries. Finally, the rise in foreign exchange reserves which would be implied by under-valuation would represent a social saving, which later on could be used for investment, public or private, and a higher growth of the economy.

REFORM OF THE WORLD MONETARY SYSTEM

By the middle of 1973, the situation on the international money and capital markets, and the prospects for the reform of the international monetary system, were in a sufficiently crystalline state to be described in a few simple propositions.

(a) As a result of past deficits in the American balance of payments, official and private holders abroad had accumulated what was then called a large 'dollar overhang'. Since the authorities in the United States would not guarantee 'ultimate' convertibility, the private holders were increasingly unwilling to hold dollar balances; and since the central banks were unwilling to add to their dollar reserves, the exchange rate of the dollar *vis-à-vis* most other currencies floated downwards between February and July. In the course of the summer, however, enough became known about the accruals of export orders to American firms, and about the flow of long-term investment toward the United States, for this movement to be arrested.

(b) The rapid expansion of the Euro-currency market, together with the large liquidities of multinational enterprises, and the constant possibility of changes in leads and lags on a large and rapidly growing volume of international trade, provided instruments for devastatingly large and abrupt shifts of short-term capital. In this situation central banks became virtually incapable of maintaining fixed-exchange rates in the face of concerted market expectations. It should be added that the central banks added to the disruption as market participants.

(c) Massively concerted expectations, however, were likely to be formed only with respect to the dollar, sterling and the lira. With these three currencies on a relatively free float, the 'European snake' had a good life-expectancy, the basic economic conditions of the currencies within it being unlikely to undergo a rapid change relative to each other.

(d) It was thus possible to speak of relative stabilization providing an opportunity, a breathing space, for work on the basic reform of the international monetary system to be completed. There was a gradual convergence of thinking on the main points of the reform. The question of the future role of gold was clearly subordinate to the problem of the definition or valuation, and the proper criteria of issue, of the paper *numéraire* (the SDR, perhaps under another name). The question of the composition of reserves, essentially the question of funding the dollar overhang, was recognized to be changing its nature. Thus the adjustment process was coming to be generally seen as the main problem of the reform. The problem concerned the criteria and the means by which pressure could be brought on countries in persistent surplus.

Towards the end of the summer, it became possible to expect the current account of the United States to turn out a surplus for the year as a whole. The first expert forecasts appeared, indicating a large surplus, around $7,000 million, for 1974. And the observable balance-of-capital flows indicated a still larger surplus on the balance of payments as a whole. It was these perceivable developments that changed the nature of the 'dollar overhang'. It was not that dollars had been 'valueless paper', as so many economic journalists had been tempted to maintain in the period of the large American deficits; even then dollars could buy goods in the United States, except that the same goods could be had for less from somewhere else. In this sense the dollar, although possessing some value, had been 'unwanted' in the period of excess; and its relative desirability changed with its exchange rate. Now there were few places outside the United States where the goods in demand could be obtained more cheaply. For Western Europe, the turn-around on both the current and the capital account of the American balance of payments meant that the United States was beginning to repay its heavy short-term indebtedness incurred in the recent inflationary years, the repayment being partly in current goods and services, partly in property titles.

The sharp upsurge in commodity prices since mid-1972 has been in conflict with the stabilizing forces described above and, given a fillip by the oil crisis, brought about in the late fall of 1973 a complete turn-around in the situation. The petroleum and other price increases will have a smaller negative impact on the current account of the United States, a large primary producer, than on the trade account of any other industrial country. This consideration, coming on top of the forecast large improvement in the American trade account in response to the depreciation of the dollar from July 1971 to July 1973, has already brought about a significant appreciation on technical grounds alone. Furthermore, for both private and official holders liquid dollar balances are becoming still more desirable in view of their increased fuel bills, and of the petroleum exporters' preference for dollars (and, in lesser amounts, the German mark and the sterling) as a vehicle for placing those funds which they are unable to spend on current imports. In consequence, the dollar appreciated particularly sharply against those currencies, such as the yen and the French franc, whose governments were primarily concerned with improving their current account position and did not provide support in the exchange market.

The French break-out from the 'snake' not only demon-strated the impossibility of maintaining even a limited monetary union in the absence of a common agreement on the main aims of national trade policies. In its potential as an example to be followed, it threatened to throw international trade relations back to the 1930s. The European Community, and the OECD countries as a group, must realize that there is no way for them to earn an extra $35,500m, by running surpluses with each other. In particular, France and the United Kingdom, the main proponents of separate mutually convenient deals with the petroleum producers, should realize that they have so far been acting on sufferance of the more responsible members of the OECD group. Are they not aware, in their rush to conclude long-term agreements at what are probably unsustainably high prices, that in a free-for-all scramble they would be hopelessly bid out of any possible deal by the United States and Germany?

In the situation as it existed in 1974, the Committee of Twenty could not do anything but shelve the reform of the international monetary system, given the impossibility of foreseeing the extent of the adjustment problem posed by the rise and uncertainty of petroleum prices. As for global concerns, two issues are pre-eminent now:

1. Ways have to be found by which the increased oil payments bill can be financed without importing countries being forced into competitive devaluations entraining a world recession. This implies, as a stop-gap measure, a large-scale re-cycling of petro-funds in favour of countries which do not benefit from a spontaneous capital inflow, and a correspond-ingly intensified coordination of the monetary and fiscal policies of the major industrial countries. We must not, however, get drunk on the magic word 're-cycling', keeping in mind that re-cycling means borrowing. Unless certain import-ant industrial economies are willing to go on borrowing short-term billions of dollars year after year, the only lasting solution to the problem posed by the permanently increased cost of energy is to be found in the creation of new monetary and real assets in which the petroleum producers would be willing to invest the 'currently unspendable' part of their increased export earnings in productive capacities. It is important to stress the crucial distinction between borrowing

to finance consumption and borrowing for investment.[29] The less developed countries suggest themselves as a logical place for the creation of such new real (industrial) assets.

2. If the short-run financing problem can be solved through a multilateral re-cycling scheme, such as the IMF has proposed, the long-term adjustment will still be fraught with risks of balance-of-payments crises. The European Community, mainly concerned with the return of the wayward currencies into the 'snake', should now press, in the interest of self-preservation, for agreement in the IMF on the general criteria for, and generally preferred measures of, balance-of-payments adjustment. Even aside from the special Community problems, this is where the main stress in international relations will be felt in the next few years. The European Community should insist that any 'adjustment surveillance body', whether established in the IMF or any other organization, should contain not only monetary but also trade experts. A provision for countries. to be represented by treasury and/or central bank officials as well as economy and/or trade ministry officials would furthermore ensure and improve the national policy coordination in these matters, and thus greatly facilitate European integration.

CONCLUSIONS AND RECOMMENDATIONS

In summarizing our conclusions and recommendations on international economic policy, there can be discerned the elements of a strategy that, while strengthening the international system of trade and payments, could promote the economic integration of the European Community.

1. If the economic integration of the European Community is to be promoted in harmony with the integration of the world economy as a whole, the interest of the Community lies very much in the maintenance of a multilateral system of trade and payments that is open and non-discriminatory, one governed by explicit and internationally-agreed rules and principles.

2. But since the mid-1960s the international economic order has been subject to increasing strains and is now in need of repair and strengthening. The situation has been

worsened by the balance-of-payments implications of the dramatic increase in crude oil prices at the end of 1973.

3. In order to avoid further internal disruption brought about by external 'shocks' — inflation, monetary turmoil, commodity shortages, trade restrictions — the European Community should focus greater attention on the reform of the international system of trade and payments. Because of the differences between them, the countries of the Community are affected differently by global problems, which means that in the absence of Community initiatives their governments are bound to react in different ways.

4. In any case, the European Community could develop a distinct political identity, as between the United States and the Soviet Union, by advancing bold initiatives for the reconstruction of the international economic order. Waiting to react to initiatives from others only invites internal dissent. For the reactions of member countries are likely to differ and thus, even before discussions begin at Community level, individual governments are 'digging themselves into positions'. The reluctance of governments to work out external initiatives therefore impedes integration and makes the search for identity more difficult.

5. What also needs to be emphasized are the social effects of international trade. For the isolation of industries, both manufacturing and agricultural, from international competition generally serves to keep labour in low-wage activities. In this sense, it is the entrepreneurs, not the workers, who are protected by tariffs and other impediments to trade. It appears that very little unemployment has resulted from trade expansion over the last two decades.

6. Turning, then, to more specific issues, the influence of the European Community where tariff policies are concerned has not always been beneficial to the international system, which is to say there are principles to be reasserted. The complex array of customs regulations that have been built up around the Community have created friction between the affected countries: (i) between the Community and other developed countries; (ii) between the Community and developing countries; and (iii) between developing countries that have been granted tariff preferences by the Community with varying degrees of generosity.

7. An agreement among developed countries on the substantial elimination, over an appropriate transition period, of tariffs on industrial products traded among them would rid the European Community of the worst diplomatic and political difficulties in its external relationships. Even if the elimination of tariffs was phased over fifteen or twenty years, the main political achievement would be effective immediately, in that henceforth tariffs would be regarded simply as a transitory instrument of policy.

8. To see in the European Community's common external tariff, and the xenophobic protectionism vested in it, a necessary bond holding the nine members together is to debase the European idea. Efforts must be made to develop a more constructive approach to European unity.

9. The European Community's tariffs afford the highest protection to the relatively old, relatively labour-intensive and relatively low-wage industries. And what the protected industries gain is obtained at the expense of industries which enjoy less than average protection. The gradual elimination of tariffs would result, equally gradually, in a shift of labour into more modern, more skill-intensive and thus higher-wage industries and occupations.

10. With appropriate provisions for adjustment assistance, as discussed in Chapter 5, the dismantling of protection need not bring about much, if any, unemployment.

11. It would also be energy-saving to phase out tariffs on industrial products traded among developed countries and let the low opportunity-cost man-power in developing countries produce standard consumer manufactures by simpler technologies. The European Community's research-and-development resources would then be freed from a hopeless rear-guard action against a virtually inexhaustible reservoir of labour available at very low rates of pay and could instead be employed on genuine innovation for which there is now a sharply increased need.

12. We recommend that the substantial elimination among developed countries of tariffs on industrial products should be pursued by progressive, linear and automatic reductions, in the way that tariffs were eliminated within the European Community. Discussion in the Tokyo Round of GATT negotiations should focus first of all on the timetable

for such reductions. The objective might be approached in two stages with provision at the end of the first stage for a legislative review before authority is given for the second stage to be embarked upon.

13. Having agreed a formula, the Tokyo Round negotiations could next concentrate on the industries to be allowed a longer transition period, or even exempted altogether from the general movement towards tariff-free trade among developed countries. But strict criteria should be established for 'exceptions' — as well as for 'safeguards' against 'market disruption'.

14. The approach we suggest would provide a basis for an imaginative counter to protectionist pressures at a time when the momentum of trade liberalization plainly needs to be restored. This would be especially so, allowing the most willing participants to set the pace, if the linear technique was applied on a conditional MFN basis.

15. Conditional MFN would not be applied, however, to developing countries, which should continue to be accorded preferential access on a non-reciprocal basis to the markets of developed countries as long as tariffs are retained by them. It should be pointed out, however, that developing countries would gain more from *free* access to industrial markets than they are obtaining under preferential trade arrangements.

16. The European Community's generalized scheme of preferences in favour of developing countries — like the schemes of other countries — is open to criticism on two points. First, more than half the dutiable imports into the Community from developing countries are excluded from the scheme and, secondly, those that are benefiting from preferences are severely limited by quotas. Thus little or no additional incentive is offered to new exporters or new investors in developing countries — which rather defeats the purpose of preferences in the first place. What is more, by excluding industrial products which the developing countries are best able to produce and export, generalized preferences have become another factor in increasing the disparity between the more advanced and the less advanced developing countries.

17. The problem of the industrializing countries of the Third World is increasingly one of securing assured and un-

limited access across MFN tariffs to the markets of developed countries.

18. It is implicit in our discussion of generalized tariff preferences *per se* that they could be improved by extending the commodities covered and enlarging — even better, removing — the quotas on them. More explicitly, we suggest that in due course the European Community's economic arrangements with 'associate' countries in the Third World should be confined to financial and technical assistance.

19. The diminishing importance of tariffs has attracted attention to the various non-tariff means of protection which have, since time immemorial, supplemented the protective effects of customs duties. In this respect, 'hard' non-tariff restrictions whose main or sole purpose is to protect, namely quantitative restrictions on imports and restraints on exports, should be considered separately.

20. The 'soft' non-tariff interventions — customs valuations and other administrative procedures, technical standards, public procurement practices, government subsidies, prior import deposits and so on — can only be brought under control by gradually securing the adherence of governments to negotiated codes of conduct through GATT procedures for complaints, consultation and arbitration.

21. Hard non-tariff restrictions, however, are unlikely to be liberalized through the process of multilateral bargaining. For each represents a more or less 'neuralgic point' for the country imposing it and there do not exist reciprocal rules in this respect among the main trading countries that would permit 'equivalent swaps'. The only way to bring these proliferating restrictions under control, and eventually to eliminate them, is an adjustment of the protected industries. There would have to be a mechanism for multilateral supervision of such policies.

22. It is through such a mechanism that the issue of existing non-tariff restrictions is intertwined with the issue of safeguard mechanisms against sudden surges in imports.

23. The first objective in reforming the existing multilateral safeguard system, mainly embodied in Article 19 of the GATT, should be to make the rules sufficiently flexible to cover all circumstances in which a country might need emergency protection. Here the purpose should be to

eliminate the incentive for large importing countries to act unilaterally or bilaterally in circumstances where import-absorption problems emerge for individual countries. The second objective should be to make the safeguard system an instrument of industrial adjustment and thus raise the import-absorption capacity of the participating countries in the long run.

24. We believe that the sectional protectionist interest, still strong in many Community countries and industries, can be kept at bay only by procedures which in a democratically 'transparent' way can be seen by all to give an objective and adequate consideration to all the social interests involved.

25. The European Community should seek to establish an international framework in which to deal with circumstances where a government imposes, for internal purposes, a restraint on the exports of a particular commodity. There are three areas in which governments could agree on more concerted action. First the Community should seek a more precise definition of the conditions under which 'exceptions' to the prohibition in the GATT against the imposition of export controls are permitted. Secondly, a separate 'safeguard' mechanism on exports should be negotiated, along the lines of the safeguard mechanism on imports as proposed in this report. Thirdly, the European Community could negotiate with other countries access to their supplies of a commodity, in exchange for access to the Common Market for other commidities.

26. Non-tariff restrictions are necessary when dealing with the state-trading countries of Eastern Europe and East Asia if only because of the difficulty in determining when products are being 'dumped' or otherwise sold with the help of 'subsidies'. What makes state-trading countries subject to a degree of risk is the possibility of sudden restrictions on supplies. The European Community should be able to negotiate long-term contracts for raw material and energy supplies in return for increased quotas for other goods.

27. With the imbalance between supply and demand that has developed in world agriculture, it is in the interest of all that the largest agricultural-producing countries should allow the forces of comparative advantage to influence to an increasing degree the patterns of their production, and so

optimize their combined agricultural output. This can best be done by adjusting agricultural price structures to the price-relatives prevailing in the world market — which indicate relative scarcities *vis-à-vis* the pattern of global demand. The general inflation of agricultural prices should facilitate such an adjustment.

28. Because commodity prices have been bouyant, relieving governments of the pressures normally associated with depressed prices, the general climate for international negotiations on problems in international agricultural trade has greatly improved. The situation, however, was never likely to last very long. For income-benefits from high prices tend to be capitalized into higher values on farm assets which farmers soon take for granted. Before circumstances change again for the worse (from a negotiating standpoint), governments should therefore endeavour in the Tokyo Round negotiations to reach a measure of understanding on a concerted, if gradual, approach towards overcoming the problems of agricultural trade.

29. As a principle underlying the discussion, it might be expected that governments should limit the extent to which the burden of domestic adjustment in the agricultural sector is shifted, through trade measures, to producers in other countries.

30. Multilateral negotiations should therefore focus on the measures which have been most disruptive of international trade. Governments should have no difficulty, for a start, in reaching an agreement on the use of export subsidies — especially if tight markets persist. Similarly, an understanding on export controls should also be pursued, although here the task could be more difficult.

31. Commodity shortages have made importing countries realize that they must be prepared to share the responsibility and therefore the cost, of stockpiling instead of leaving it all to the exporting countries. With the importing countries interested in the security and stability of supplies, the Tokyo Round negotiations should be able to reach agreement on the financing and management of reserve stocks of storable commodities, mainly grain.

32. Having established a framework in which some semblance of order might be achieved in agricultural trade,

the negotiations should take up, and carry a stage further, the *montant de soutien* proposals that the European Community first advanced during the Kennedy Round negotiations. Instead of arguing about appropriate and inappropriate *methods* of support, the negotiations should concentrate on *levels* of support, leaving governments to decide for themselves the form of support that is most appropriate in their circumstances. What this would involve first of all is agreeing a basis on which to determine the level of effective protection afforded to agricultural producers by the various methods of support. Those levels could then be 'bound' and afterwards gradually reduced by negotiation.

33. In the course of consultations and negotiations, which should be a more or less continuous process, the effectiveness of farm-support policies could come to be questioned more closely so that reforms might be induced over time.

34. In assisting by financial means the development of developing countries, the European Community should agree a common policy, which could make such assistance both more effective and less discriminatory. The distribution of aid should be determined less by historical and political ties and more by economic criteria. Emphasis should be placed on improving the economic infra-structure of developing countries so that private direct investment can be attracted. Attention should also be given to incentives for investment in labour-intensive lines of production so that unemployment can be reduced.

35. The 'liberalization' of financial assistance would have substantial and beneficial effects. It would enable untied aid to stretch much further for the recipient who is a good 'comparison shopper' and eliminate the influence of supplying firms in the donor country on the planning of individual projects in the recipient country by untying bilateral aid.

36. The European Community has 'assisted' developing countries through the immigration of labour, but both sides would be better off if, instead of bringing labour towards capital, capital was moved towards labour and the resulting products were exported to the investing countries.

37. We would also recommend that in order to encourage

capital flows and a net resource transfer to less developed countries, the latter should be permitted to have 'undervalued' exchange rates in relation to the industrialized countries, including the European Community and the United States.

38. Following the dramatic increase in crude oil prices towards the end of 1973, the only lasting solution to the problem posed by the permanently-increased cost of energy — unless certain industrial countries are prepared to go on borrowing short-term dollars in large quantities year after year — is for new monetary and real assets to be created in which the petroleum producers would be willing to invest the 'currently unspendable' part of their increased export earnings in producing capacities. (In this respect it is important to stress the crucial distinction between borrowing to finance consumption and borrowing for investment.) The less developed countries suggest themselves as a logical place for the creation of new industrial assets.

39. Even though the short-run financing problem posed by the increase in oil prices may be resolved through a multilateral re-cycling scheme, the long-term adjustment will be fraught with risks of balance-of-payments crises. The European Community should press, in the interest of self-preservation, for agreement in the IMF on the general criteria for, and generally preferred measures of, balance-of-payments adjustment.

40. Further, the European Community should insist that any 'adjustment surveillance body', whether established in the IMF or any other organization, should contain not only monetary but also trade experts. A provision for countries to be represented by treasury and/or central bank officials as well as economy and/or trade ministry officials would furthermore ensure and improve the national policy coordination in these matters and thus greatly facilitate European integration.

NOTES AND REFERENCES

1. In the European Community there appears to be something of a conceptual vacuum with respect to the management of the world economy. This was amply demonstrated by the declaration which the

Council of Ministers was pleased to issue after its meeting in Copen-
hagen in September 1973. For the statement begged far more questions
than it answered.
2. See, for example: Stephen P. Magee, *The Welfare Effects of Restrictions on US Trade,* Brookings Paper on Economic Activity No. 3
(Washington: Brookings Institution, 1972); *Adjustment Assistance
Measures,* TD/121/Supp. 1 (Geneva: UNCTAD Secretariat, 1972);
Robert E. Baldwin and John H. Mutti, 'Policy Problems in the Adjust-
ment Process', in Helen Hughes (ed.), *Prospects for Partnership:
Industrialization and Trade Policies in the 1970s* (Baltimore: Johns
Hopkins University Press, for the International Bank for Reconstruc-
tion and Development, 1973); Peter Isard, 'Employment Impacts of
Textile Imports and Investment: a Vintage-Capital Model', *American
Economic Review,* New York, June 1973; and Seamus O'Cleireacain,
*The Impact of Trade Expansion on Employment in the United
Kingdom,* Staff Paper No. 5 (London: Trade Policy Research Centre,
1974).
3. The concept of the effective rate of protection — which, in
measuring the degree of protection afforded to an economic activity in
terms of the value added to that activity, takes into account the duties
levied on material inputs — is discussed in W. M. Corden, 'The Structure
of a Tariff System and the Effective Protective Rate', *Journal of
Political Economy,* Chicago, June 1966. Also see Harry G. Johnson,
'The Theory of Tariff Structure, with Special Reference to World Trade
and Development', in Johnson and Peter Kenen (eds.), *Trade and
Development* (Geneva: Librarie Droz, 1965). In addition, see Corden,
The Theory of Protection (Oxford: Clarendon Press, 1971).
4. The structure and level of tariffs in developed countries, after the
implementation of the Kennedy Round agreement, is analysed in Jan
Tumlir, 'Trade Negotiations in the Field of Manufactures', in Paul
Streeten (ed.), *Trade Strategies for Development* (London: Macmillan,
for the Cambridge Overseas Studies Committee, 1973), pp. 280-87.
5. One notable exception, in this respect, is the German car-making
industry, where 'guest workers' are increasingly being employed.
6. Caroline Pestieau and Jacques Henry, *Non-Tariff Trade Barriers as a
Problem in International Development* (Montreal: Private Planning
Association of Canada, 1972). The PPAC has since become the C. D.
Howe Research Institute.
7. The point is emphasized in the statement of a group of European
businessmen and economists, McFadzean *et al., Reform of the International Commercial System,* Bellagio Memorandum (London: Trade
Policy Research Centre, 1974).
8. See, *inter alia,* the widely noted statement by Sir John McEwen, as
Deputy Prime Minister of Australia, in the House of Representatives,
Canberra, 20 August 1970, republished as 'European Negotiations:
Need for a "Third Party" Initiative', *The Atlantic Community Quarterly,* Washington, Winter, 1970-71. In the course of the statement, he
said: 'Australia's interest — and, we believe, the world's interest — is to
try to ensure that trading *blocs,* where they exist, and countries outside

such *blocs*, return to the principles and rules laid down in the GATT. Only by the rule of law,' Sir John argued, 'can small countries hope to receive a fair deal in world trade. Only by observance of the rule of law can the big prevent or avoid disruption and loss to themselves, as well as to others, of all the gains made since World War II in the field of international trade.'

The attitude of the United States towards the proliferation of discriminatory trading arrangements was crystallized in Special Assistant to the President for International Economic Affairs, *A Foreign Economic Perspective*, Peterson Report (Washington: US Government Printing Office, for the Executive Office of the President, 1971). This report was drawn on extensively in the preparation of *Towards a New World Economic System: the Goals of US Policy* (London: United States Information Service, 1973).

American official attitudes towards discriminatory trading arrangements are not determined by their economic impact, which is small; rather they are determined by the way they are undermining the principle of non-discrimination. In this connection, see Harald B. Malmgren, 'The New Posture in US Trade Policy', *The World Today*, London, December 1971.

9. Sidney Golt, 'Access for the Exports of Developing Countries', in Hugh Corbet and Robert Jackson (eds.), *In Search of a New World Economic Order* (London: Croom Helm, for the Trade Policy Research Centre, 1974), pp. 240-45. Mr Golt was chairman of the high-level group established by the OECD to prepare recommendations on the implementation of generalized tariff preferences in favour of developing countries.

10. This course has been urged by, among others, Giovanni Agnelli, president of FIAT, the Italian automobile manufacturer, in an address to the National Foreign Trade Convention, New York, 14 November 1972, subsequently published as 'Economic Relations Across the Atlantic: an Agenda for Cooperation', *The Atlantic Community Quarterly*, Spring 1973.

Also see the statement of the Director-general of the Confederazione Generale dell' Industria Italiana, Franco Mattei, 'L'Industria Europea e il Nixon Round', in *Negoziati Commerciali Internazionali: Conflitto o Cooperazione?* (Milan: Fiera di Milano, 1973), which also argued for the substantial and gradual elimination of tariffs on industrial products traded among developed countries.

Other study groups involving varying degrees of European participation have concluded in favour of the phasing out of industrial tariffs: *Reshaping the International Economic Order* (Washington: Brookings Institution, 1972), a tripartite report sponsored by the Brookings Institution, the Institut de la Communauté Européenne pour les Etudes Universitaries and the Japan Economic Research Centre; Frank McFadzean *et al.*, *Towards an Open World Economy*, Report of an Advisory Group (London: Macmillan, for the Trade Policy Research Centre, 1972), hereafter cited as the McFadzean Report; the Maidenhead Communiqué, signed by twenty businessmen, economists and labour leaders from Western Europe, Japan and North America, and published in *Weltwirtschaftliches Archiv*, Kiel, Band 9; Heft 2, 1973; and the Bellagio Memorandum, *op. cit.*, prepared by a group of fifteen European businessmen and economists.

11. Yet, as mentioned in Chapter 1, the Council of Ministers wrote into the European Community's initial bargaining position for the Tokyo Round negotiations a stipulation that *inter alia* the customs union 'may not be called in question'. See note 40 to Chapter 1.

For general discussions of the shape of an external policy that *inter alia* embraces the phasing out of the common external tariff, see Theo Peeters, *A Foreign Trade Policy for the EEC* (Leuven: Centrum voor Economische Studien, Katholieke Universiteit Leuven, 1972); Also see M. E. Streit, 'European External Economic Policy at the Crossroads', *Konjunkturpolitik*, Berlin, No. 4, 1973.

12. Document COMM (73) 556, Commission of the European Community, Brussels, 4 April 1971. This document has been widely disseminated and therefore requires comment.

13. See, for example, the address by Theo Hijzen, as the European Community's Representative to the GATT, to the European-Atlantic Group, London, 22 October 1973.

14. Corbet and Harry G. Johnson, 'Optional Negotiating Techniques on Industrial Tariffs', in the McFadzean Report *op. cit.*, pp. 57-72.

15. Article 1 of the General Agreement requires tariff 'concessions' negotiated between two or more countries to be extended *unconditionally* to all other signatory countries.

16. Agreement was reached on the arrangement on 20 December 1973 and entered into force on 1 January 1974.

17. Richard N. Cooper, 'The EEC Preferences: a critical Evaluation', *Intereconomics*, Hamburg, April 1971, a fuller version of which was published as 'The European Community's System of Generalized Preferences: a Critique', *Journal of Development Studies*, London, July 1972.

For a further examination of generalized tariff preferences, see Tracy Murray, 'How Helpful is the Generalized System of Preferences to Developing Countries', *The Economic Journal*, London, July 1973; and by the same author, 'UNCTAD's Generalized Preferences: An Appraisal', *Journal of World Trade Law*, London, July-August 1973.

On the subject of the European Community's special tariff preferences, under the Yaounde Convention, see Alassane Outtara, 'Trade Effects of the Association of African Countries with the EEC', *IMF Staff Papers*, Washington, July 1973

18. Political statements apart, numerous professional papers can be cited on this score, among them being: Gerald I. Trant, David L. MacFarlane and Lewis A. Fischer, *Trade Liberalization and Canadian Agriculture* (Toronto: University of Toronto Press, for the Private Planning Association of Canada, 1968); Malmgren and David L. Schlechty, 'Technology and Neo-mercantilism in International Agricultural Trade'. *American Journal of Agricultural Economics*, New York, December 1969; Byron Bernston, O. H. Goolsby and C. O.

Nohre, *The European Community's Common Agricultural Policy* (Washington: United States Department of Agriculture, 1969); Brian Fernon, *Issues in World Farm Trade: Chaos or Cooperation?* (London: Trade Policy Research Centre, 1970); and J. Price Gittinger, *North American Agriculture in a New World*, Report for the Canadian-American Committee (Washington: National Planning Association, 1970).

Attention might be drawn to two official, and formidable, reports in the United States, namely: Presidential Commission on International Trade and Investment Policy, *United States International Economic Policy in an Interdependent World*, Williams Report (Washington: US Government Printing Office, 1971), ch. 7, pp. 141-68, and the accompanying Compendium of Papers, Vol. 1, pp. 791-910; and Assistant to the President for International Economic Affairs, *Agricultural Trade and the Proposed Round of Multilateral Negotiations*, Flanigan Report (Washington: US Government Printing Office, for the Senate Committee on Agriculture, United States Congress, 1973).

19. Edward R. Fried *et al.*, *Toward the Integration of World Agriculture*, Report of Fourteen Economists from North America, the European Community and Japan (Washington: Brookings Institution, 1973), sponsored by the Brookings Institution, Institut de la Communauté Européenne pour les Etudes Universitaires and the Japan Economic Research Centre.

20. Among proposals made for food reserves and stockpiling are the following: Fred Waugh, 'Reserve Stocks of Farm Products', in Presidential Commission on Food and Fiber, *Food and Fiber for the Future*, Technical Papers Vol. V (Washington: US Government Printing Office, 1967); T. E. Josling, *An International Grain Reserve Policy* (London, Washington and Montreal: British-North American Committee, 1973); *World Food Security*, Proposal of the Director-General of the FAO (Rome: Food and Agriculture Organization, 1973); Fried *et al.*, *op. cit.*; and J. S. Hilman *et al.*, *The Impact of an International Food Bank* (Washington: US Government Printing Office, for the Senate Committee on Agriculture, United States Congress, 1974).

Also see D. Gale Johnson, *World Agriculture in Disarray* (London: Macmillan, for the Trade Policy Research Centre, 1973).

21. On this there has developed a broad international consensus. The problem of non-tariff intervention is surveyed in Robert E. Baldwin, *Non-tariff Distortions of International Trade* (Washington: Brookings Institution, 1971), and in Gerard and Victoria Curzon, *Hidden Barriers to International Trade*, Thames Essay No. 1 (London: Trade Policy Research Centre, 1971); Also see Malmgren, *International Economic Peacekeeping* (New York: Quadrangle, for the Atlantic Council of the United States, 1972), and Ingo Walter and Jae W. Chung, 'The Pattern of Non-tariff Obstacles to International Market Access', *Weltwirtschaftliches Archiv*, Kiel, Band 108, Heft 3, 1972.

For more detailed country studies, see Brian Hindley, *Britain's Position on Non-tariff Protection*, Thames Essay No. 4 (London: Trade Policy Research Centre, 1972); Klaus Stegmann, *Canadian Non-tariff*

Barriers to Trade (Montreal: Private Planning Association of Canada, 1973); Anthony Scaperlanda (ed.), *Prospects for Eliminating Non-tariff Distortions of International Trade* (Leyden: Sijthoff, for the Kennedy Institute, University of Tilburg, 1973), which covers the Benelux countries; Peter Lloyd, *Non-tariff Distortions of Australian Trade* (Canberra: Australian National University Press, 1973); Stanley D. Metzger, *Lowering Non-tariff Barriers: US Law, Practice and Negotiating Objectives* (Washington: Brookings Institution, 1974), and Juergen B. Donges, Gerhard Fels, Axel D. Nev *et al.*, *Protektion und Branchenstruktur der westdeutschen Wirtschaft*, Kieler Studien 123 (Tubingen: J. C. B. Mohr, for the Institut fur Weltwirtschaft an der Universitat Kiel, 1973).

An attempt is made to devise a method for measuring the impact of non-tariff devices in Hans Glisman and Axel Neu, 'Towards New Agreements on International Trade Liberalization: Methods and Examples of Measuring Non-tariff Trade Barriers', *Weltwirtschaftliches Archiv*, Band 107, Heft 2, 1971.

22.   Curzon and Curzon, *Global Assault on Non-tariff Trade Barriers*, Thames Essay No. 3 (London: Trade Policy Research Centre, 1972), p. 6. The termination of the 'grandfather clause' was also urged in the McFadzean Report, *op. cit.*, and has been taken up in the European Community's initial bargaining position for the Tokyo Round negotiations (see 'Overall Approach to the Coming Multilateral Negotiations in GATT', Document I/135 e/73 [COMMER 42], Commission of the European Community, Brussels).

23.   Tumlir, *Proposals for Emergency Protection against Sharp Increases in Imports*, Guest Paper No. 1 (London: Trade Policy Research Centre, 1973).

24.   Bellagio Memorandum, *op. cit.*

25.   For a review of East-West business, see Executive Secretary of the Economic Commission for Europe, *Analytical Report on Industrial Cooperation among EEC Countries* (Geneva: United Nations, 1973).

26.   See, for example, the Report of the Commission on International Development, *Partners in Development*, Pearson Report (New York and London: Praeger, for the International Bank for Reconstruction and Development, 1969), and *Development Cooperation*, Martin Report (Paris: OECD Secretariat, 1973).

27.   David Jones, *Europe's Chosen Few* (London: Overseas Development Institute, 1973), for an account of the policy and practice of the European Community's aid programme.

28.   Germany is going to take steps in this direction. Following changes in the Entwicklungshilfe-Steuergesetz, the more labour-intensive German investments in developing countries will enjoy higher incentives than the more capital-intensive ones. In this connection, see Jamuna P. Agarwal, *Zur Novellierung des Entwicklungshilfe-Steuergestezes* (Kiel: Institut fur Weltwirtschaft an der Universität Kiel, 1973).

29.   It was understandable in the weeks following the precipitation of the oil crisis that governments should focus on the impact on inflation and on the level of economic activity of the increase in petroleum

prices. But they have continued for some while after to maintain this focus. While the point was sometimes made that the surplus funds of the oil-producing countries should be directed into productive investments, the implications were not spelt out. In this last connection, see W. M. Corden and Peter Oppenheimer, *Basic Implications of the Rise in Oil Prices*, Staff Paper No. 6 (London: Trade Policy Research Centre, 1974).

8 Concluding Remarks

In conclusion it could be useful to recapitulate the main lines of our report so that the significance of its recommendations, as well as its limitations, can be made more explicit. We began our work with a broad appraisal of the economic realities of our time, each of us endeavouring to clarify the prospects for the economic development of the European Community, having regard first and foremost for what is attainable in contemporary circumstances.

The pursuit of economic and social objectives by national governments cannot be divorced from the process of economic integration in the European Community as a whole. The creation of a customs union, then a common market and eventually an economic union is bound to affect the conduct of national policies. And the reverse is also true. The goal of economic union poses for the Community, as part of a rapidly integrating world economy, problems of a much more difficult nature than anything produced by customs unions in the last century. For the reasons given in Chapter 2, it is unrealistic to expect national governments to renounce their freedom of action with respect to exchange-rate policy, at least until conditions prevail that make it possible for economic policies to be effectively coordinated. Indeed, the functioning of a customs union could be seriously handicapped, and in the long term seriously compromised, by imbalances and distortions if it does not set about fostering conditions for closer economic integration — including monetary union.

Recognition of the interdependence of national and Community policies, and of the consequent need to broach pragmatically the problems that arise between then, has not deterred us from a rigorous critical assessment of the

numerous and grave failures in European economic cooperation that have been plain for all the world to see. Strong
criticisms have been made of the approach hitherto adopted
in pursuit of monetary union, in the conduct of the common
agricultural policy and in external economic relations.

With the European Community in difficulty, we have
agreed on a number of proposals, conceived in our view in
more realistic terms, that could serve to facilitate increased
economic cooperation between member countries on the
problems that have been exacerbated by inflation,
commodity shortages and the oil crisis. The proposals could
also open new possibilities for national policies, rendering
them more coherent and more consistent with one another;
and conferring on them a greater degree of continuity, within
certain limits. In formulating these proposals we have sought
to avoid political undercurrents. Our intention has been to
propose nothing that could not be substantiated in economic
terms.

In this perspective, one of the central points in the report
is represented by Chapter 2, which argues in essence that
even if monetary union is necessary to the European Community's customs union it has so far been pursued in the
wrong way. 'If monetary union were pushed through prematurely', we conclude, 'without being reinforced by complementary policies and without complementary powers and
common institutions to give effect to those policies, the
result might well be needless unemployment and waste of
resources and the breakdown of the union.' Because of the
importance attached to the liberalization of capital movements and the narrowing of margins of fluctuation between
national currencies, the approach to date would amount to
the progressive dismantling of instruments of national
economic policies, leading — in the absence of Community
instruments — to a state of economic anarchy and a weakening of the public authorities that would have to cope with the
backward regions and low-income groups that would be the
first to be hurt.

Beginning with these observations, and with the reserva-
tions on the control of capital movements that experience
seems to justify, we have accordingly preferred to urge a
more limited — but, we believe, more effective — course

towards monetary union. This course would include the institution of an exchange-equalization account (sufficient to withstand large capital flows) to support exchange rates without fixing them; and it would include the issuing of a parallel European currency, the europa, to be used initially as a reserve currency by central banks and later, when circumstances permit, as an intervention currency by a common monetary authority. These proposals are not aimed at squaring a circle. Their function would be to protect the customs union of the European Community against external shocks — such as those that have been the result of international monetary turmoil — until the coordination of national economic policies has progressed far enough for a full monetary union to be possible.

The key to achieving such a degree of coordination perhaps lies in fiscal policy, as the means of influencing the distribution, and the formation, of the national incomes of member countries. Emphasis must be placed on the qualitative, as well as the quantitative, aspect of public expenditure; that is, on its orientation. To promote the general conditions necessary for a monetary union, a serious effort has to be made to coordinate social and economic policies at a national level in order to achieve a common orientation on development. In this respect, our attention has not been aimed at achieving uniformity in rates of taxation et cetera; rather it has focused on the development of a common budget, on a larger and larger scale, as the main means of overcoming disparities in fiscal charges and public services in the various regions of the European Community. To this end we propose the consolidation in a common budget of all funds administered by the Community. The institutional implications would require working out, but they should present no serious difficulties, once matters of principle have been decided.

Turning to specific policies, it was not by chance that we concentrated next, in Chapter 3, on regional policy. For it is necessary to ensure that the formation of a monetary union does not result in excessive intra-Community migration that would accentuate regional imbalances, thereby generating political tensions which, in turn, might jeopardize the objectives of monetary union. Our analysis is based on the way economic, social and even ecological unrest can interact in areas of high industrial and population density and in areas where the population is declining. We were also conscious of the role played by regional imbalances in stoking the fires of inflation. In formulating proposals, our chief concern has been to ensure that regional policies produce self-sustained growth in backward areas, based on economically sound activities capable of surviving in open international competition once the additional costs, inherent in their location, have been overcome.

In order to enable political attention to be drawn to the interests of backward regions, and to promote the coordination of national economic policies, we have proposed the establishment of a chamber of regions. What might also be underlined is our proposal for a Community tax on land values or increases in land values which could help to redistribute income from the agglomeration centres where land values rise fast to the backward areas which are in need of capital.

As with regional policy, our objective in considering agricultural policy has been to achieve a more efficient allocation of resources, in the context of an economy open the international trade. In this framework, the further movement of labour from the land is seen as a necessary condition for increasing productivity in the sector, but having regard for the economic development of the region. The shift in labour from one activity to another should not be allowed to worsen regional imbalances. Appropriate structural, and educational, policies are required to rationalize agricultural production with industrial development. Moreover, the Community should adopt a policy of direct income support for low-income farmers which would avoid distortions in the allocation of resources, the generation of high-cost surpluses and the disruption of international markets and yet, at the same time, ensure reasonable security of supplies. It is from such a standpoint that we are highly critical of the protectionist nature of the European Community's common agricultural policy. Instead, we propose a shift away from the system of farm support through the price mechanism to one based on direct income payments, with security of supplies assured by means of stock-piling policies coordinated by international agreement.

The same concern for the avoidance of waste of resources and human capabilities, with the possibility of old protectionist habits being consolidated at Community level, inspires our proposals for a common industrial policy. The need to establish a concerted approach to adjustment assistance — both in terms of company conversion and sectoral adaptation — is spelled out as part of a programme for the progressive removal of tariff and non-tariff barriers to international trade. It is in order to maintain the benefits of free trade that our report calls for a more severe anti-trust policy at Community level. We generally endorse the Commission's proposals which seek an extension of its powers in respect of mergers to ensure that they are in the interest of the economy as a whole.

While putting in perspective many of the criticisms of multinational enterprises, we have noted that some aspects of their operations, particularly in respect of tax treatment, call for a greater degree of policy coordination among governments. For the internationalization of industrial production has not been accompanied by an internationalization of government regulation. This disproportion in itself justifies concern, over and above economic considerations, and can be overcome by reinforcing the coordination of relevant policies at Community level. Our proposals on the removal of obstacles to the formation of European-based enterprises and on technological collaboration, aimed at escaping the paralysing limitations imposed by the principle of 'fair return', are meant as a pragmatic response to that concern.

The importance given in the chapter on social policy to ecological problems and to the problems inherent in labour migration is a further reflection of an approach that assesses difficulties in a structural dimension rather than make any concessions to a 'subsidization' outlook. Throughout the report we stress the inter-relationships between regional, agricultural, industrial, social and environmental policies. These are evident in the urban problems of industrial concentrations and in the social tensions that develop where immigrant workers are employed in concentrated numbers. In this last respect, labour from abroad is usually engaged in activities which local workers refuse to accept and, almost for that reason alone, tend to be isolated from the social life of the host country. Under these conditions, the free movement of labour in the European Community is emptied of its progressive content, for the absence of job vacancies in the areas from which immigrant workers comes means that they are not exercising a free choice.

For these reasons the report urges a closer coordination of employment policies at Community level with the provision of a similar quality of social services among member countries. We do emphasize, though, that social services should not affect adversely the propensity of beneficiaries to work. This could all too easily occur, particularly in backward areas, if unemployment benefits come close to earnings in low-paid jobs.

Given the general philosophy which runs through our discussion of domestic policies, it was natural that we should conclude with a chapter on international economic policy, which is seen as a further means of promoting the social and economic objectives of the European Community. Regard for the social and economic aspirations of other countries, and not least those of the Third World, caused us to stress at the outset the responsibility which the Community, by virtue of its size and prosperity, has come to share with the United States and Japan for the international economic order. For it is to the multilateral system of trade and payments, to principles and rules embodied in the GATT and IMF, that smaller and weaker countries must look for their interests to be protected. In formulating our proposals we have accordingly been impressed by the need for the European Community to adopt more constructive means of pursuing economic integration than by discrimination against the rest of the world.

But the open world economy we urge will not be achieved by paying lip service to grand ideals. It will only be achieved through leadership which, in any language, means offering concessions in advance of others. By taking initiatives in international economic relations the European Community could find a distinct identity between the United States and the Soviet Union.

Similarly, the European Community will only break out of the malaise, which has gripped its internal affairs since the mid-1960s, by the exercise of leadership on the part of member governments to develop the Community's functions. The Community cannot survive on pretence and propaganda. Concrete initiatives are required. And this means that political thought and initiative must reflect a closer acquaintance with the forces of economic integration on both a regional and a global plane. Economists can advise on the policies that might contribute to the development of a 'European model', as we have sought to do in this report, but the whole endeavour depends on a high order of statesmanship.

Institute für Weltwirtschaft

The Institut für Weltwirtschaft, at the University of Kiel, is an independent centre for research on problems in international economic relations. It is directed by Professor Herbert Giersch and the editor-in-chief is Hubertus Müller-Groeling.

The institute publishes a quarterly journal, the *Weltwirtschaftliches Archiv*, and a bi-annual review entitled *Die Weltwirtschaft*. Occasional papers appear as either *Kieler Diskussionsbeiträge* or *Kieler Arbeitspapiere*.

Major research projects are published as *Kieler Studien*. Among the titles published most recently have been:

Radanev Banerji, *Exports of Manufactures from India: An Appraisal of the Emerging Pattern* (1974), 314 pp.

James Riedel, *The Industrialization of Hong Kong* (1974), 160 pp.

Jürgen B. Donges, Bernd Stecher und Frank Wolter, *Industrial Development Policies for Indonesia* (1974), 178 pp.

Lotte Müller-Ohlsen, *Importsubstitution und Exportdiversifizierung im Industrialisierungsprozess Mexikos: Strategien, Ergebnisse, Perspektiven* (1974), 272 pp.

Klaus-Werner Schatz, *Wachstum und Strukturwandel der westdeutschen Wirtschaft im internationalen Verbund: Analysen und Prognosen* (1974), 266 pp.

Frank Wolter, *Strukturelle Anpassungsprobleme der westdeutschen Stahlindustrie: Zur Standortfrage der Stahlindustrie in hochindustrialisierten Ländern* (1974), 182 pp.

Heinz-Michael Stahl, *Regionalpolitische Implikationen einer EWG-Währungsunion* (1974), 238 pp.

Jürgen B. Donges, Gerhard Fels und Axel Neu *et al.*, *Protektion und Branchenstruktur der Westdeutschen Wirtschaft* (1973), 393 pp.

Dirk van der Werf, *Die Wirtschaft der Bundesrepublik Deutschland in fünfzehn Gleichungen* (1972), 132 pp.

Wolf Schäfer, *Der Euro-Dollarmarkt* (1971), 92 pp.

Jamuna Prasad Agarwal, *Das Zahlungsbilanzproblem im Rahmen der indischen Wirtschaftsentwicklung* (1970), 127 pp.

Wolfgang Kasper, *Zur Frage grösserer Wechselkursflexibilitat: Fazit aus der Diskussion und ein Beispiel zur Illustration* (1970), 159 pp.

Hugo Heeckt, *Der Wandel von Nachfrage und Angebot auf dem Weltschiffbaumarkt* (1970), 126 pp.

Eckard Grohn, *Spektralanalytische Untersuchungen zum zyklischen Wachstum der Industrieproduktion in der Bundesrepublik Deutschland 1950-1967* (1970), 176 pp.

Moreover, the papers and proceedings of the symposia held at the institute are published in mostly bilingual form:

The International Division of Labour: Problems and Perspectives, Herbert Giersch (ed.) (1974), 556 pp.

Möglichkeiten und Grenzen einer Verbesserung des Ost-West-Handels und der Ost-West-Kooperation, Herbert Giersch (ed.) (1974), 143 pp.

Fiscal Policy and Demand Management — Fiskalpolitik und Globalsteuerung, Herbert Giersch (ed.) (1973), 262 pp.

Demand Management — Globalsteuerung, Herbert Giersch (ed.) (1972), 255 pp.

Integration through Monetary Union? — Integration durch Währungsunion?, Herbert Giersch (ed.) (1971), 178 pp.

All the above titles are published for the institute by J. C. B. Mohr (Paul Siebeck) in Tubingen.

Index